P E

and

RUTH ANN'S

Journey

THROUGH 59 YEARS

Wonderful Memories of Our 59 Years Together

PETER BUNGUM

"So beautifully written. I could feel your passion.
It is wonderful to have such beautiful memories" (Elsie N.).

NEWMAN SPRINGS PUBLISHING
320 Broad Street
Red Bank, NJ 07701

First originally published by Newman Springs Publishing 2021

ISBN 978-1-63692-512-7 (Paperback)
ISBN 978-1-63692-513-4 (Digital)

Printed in the United States of America

To my son, Brad, and daughter, Carron, and my three grandchildren: Wesley, Ellyn, and Alexandra

INTRODUCTION

My name is Pete Bungum—the author of this book. You are about to read the story of my marriage to Ruth Ann; we made it to fifty-nine and a half years. It all started when, at age fifteen, we held hands at the outdoor theater. After several years of dating and engagement, we got married in 1960. We were only nineteen and twenty. For fifty-seven years, we had a wonderful marriage. The last two were not good as cancer and other medical problems invaded Ruth Ann's body. The end came on January 9, 2020, when she lost her battle to cancer.

By March, I was so lonely for her I decided to share, on Facebook, the story of our life together. I thought it would help my loneliness if I wrote about it. I started my daily posts on March 18 and completed my story on June 15, 2020. The number of readers increased as the word spread that my posts were not only interesting but fascinating and definitely worth reading about love and devotion between myself and Ruth Ann. I had readers from twenty states and two foreign countries, plus a merchant marine stationed in the Indian Ocean and Persian Gulf.

What I did was describe our life in each year from 1956 to 2020. Readers told me every day, they looked forward to my next post.

Below are a few of the comments I received after I ended my story on June 15. I received over forty comments.

- "I'm glad you shared your journey. It gives people of our vintage a lot to think about and be grateful for" (Bernie P.).
- "You're a great storyteller. Thanks for sharing" (Dee I.).
- "Pete, you and Ruth Ann were so blessed to have so many wonderful memories. Keep on writing. We look forward to your next project" (Pat S.).
- "Loved reading all your memories. You two were the best. You were blessed to have such a great life together" (Michelle T.).
- "So very touching. Enjoyed your whole journey thoroughly" (Jeff N.).
- "This has been such a beautiful story and tribute. What a fabulous life you had together" (Rhonda K.).
- "So glad I could share my journey with you. You are a great writer and story-teller" (Dave E.).

My hope is that many of you will have a chance to read my story. ENJOY!

Taken in 2010

1957—Photo taken on a band trip

PeteandRuth Ann Bungum
March 4, 2020 • Wednesday

I am lonely. Ruth Ann, my wife for 59 years died on January 9 after a lengthy battle with cancer.

Comments

Rhenee Grabau Sending my hugs Uncle Pete.

Pat Cooley Hugs to you also ♡. We're gonna try & make it down to see u this spring!

Deb Rickels Pete, we didn't know Ruth Ann had passed. We are so sorry and sad to hear this. I always enjoyed spending time with her when we were in the same company over the years. Sending hugs and love to you.

Jan Siebels Always thinking of you Pete! ♡ 😊 🙏

John Smaby ♡

Susan Koppenhaver Thinking of you, Pete!

Linda Blattie Smaby Love to you. I am sure it is so lonely.

Steinar Bungum Peter...we send you our deepest greetings from Norway and the deserted Bungum farm.

ShynWoan Wong-Bungum 🙁 🙏

Dee Ihlenfeldt Stay busy, more volunteering. That sure helped me!! And socializing with friends!! 🤗

Richard Stout Let's meet for coffee...or a beer. Soon.

Bonnie Walderbach Your partner in crime will be back to be with you in a couple of days! Bob and you are quite a pair! 😂 ♡ Enjoy your vacation!

Phil Bungum Heart Uncle Pete

David L. Eaton We are here for you, Pete

Majbritt Rindom Thinking of you Pete ♡

Shelley Bungum DeBernardi I can only imagine. Sending my love…

Ann Caswell Xoxo. Lots of love to you!

Inge Bungum Thinking of you Pete!

Janice Blattie Was so good to see you again this weekend. Come anytime.

PeteandRuth Ann Bungum
March 19, 2020

About 2–3 weeks ago I made the statement that I was lonely after losing my wife in January. So, I decided to do something about it and get out of town.

On Thursday the 5th of March I packed my suitcase and headed north. At 5pm I parked in Jerry Narveson's driveway in Chatfield, Minnesota. Jerry and I were friends and classmates from seventh grade through graduation. We played baseball, basketball and football together and we were good. When we were juniors and seniors, we were conference champions twice in baseball and once in football and once in basketball. In basketball I was a guard and Jerry was a forward—in football he was running back, and I was quarterback—and in baseball he was a 3-year starting pitcher and I had the privilege of being his catcher for all 3 years.

Our sophomore year we were 1–7. But in our junior year we were 7–2 and got beat in extra innings by Austin by a score of 3–2. Austin got to go to the state tournament, and we didn't.

That afternoon we had beaten the big and mighty Rochester Rockets by a score of 6–5.

On that Rochester team were 3 division one football players. T. R. Moore played for Iowa State—T. Y. Moore played for the Hawkeyes and in recent years was the defensive coach for the NFL Indianapolis Colts—and Roger Hagberg played for the Minnesota Gophers and The AFL Oakland Raiders.

Our senior year we went 7–2 and were district champs again. Jerry had a fantastic year. He had 2 no-hitters, 2 one-hitters, 2 two-hitters, and 2 three-hitters. The sad news is that Austin beat us again for the state tournament. Jerry had these words about our 14–4 record. "Not bad for a bunch of small-town kids. We were blessed with good teammates and it didn't hurt to have the pitcher and catcher living two blocks apart who had thrown a lot of baseballs in the Bungum backyard for five years."

Jerry's wife is Elsie—she was Ruth Ann's best friend. In fact, it was Jerry and Elsie who arranged the two of us going on our first date in June 1956.

When we would get together over the last 60 years Ruth Ann and Elsie would say they should wear boots because the shit would be getting pretty deep when Jerry and I started talking about how good we were in high school. Regardless what our wives thought we were pretty darn good.

I helped Jerry diminish his quantity of Busch Lights on my first night of reducing my loneliness. I was off to a good start.

Comments

Rhenee Grabau ♡ ♡ ♡

Rhenee Grabau What a great story! Love you Uncle Pete

Kathi Kop Mr. Bungum, I remember catching quite a few footballs Brad was chucking down the street. With you right there telling him how to improve. I don't know if I helped or was just some girl in the way, but I had a pretty good time. As I recall our team was a decent one.

Brad Bungum Kathi Kop, I'm still bummed you never taught me how to golf…that's one thing in the sports world Dad was never able to help me improve on… ;-)

Martin Frasher Fascinating story!

Stephen Zimmerman Great story Pete. You are still pretty damn good!

Becky Helgerson It was so good that you could stop in Waterloo for a visit last week! ♡ ♡

Kimberly Bungum Love you Uncle Pete. Your welcome here in Cali anytime ♡

Phil Bungum Uncle Pete!!

Pat Cooley Great memories! R u still on the road...come to Eau Claire 🤗

Chris Trogstad Great stories, Pete. I didn't have the privilege of growing up in Chatfield but Terry Trogstad my Dad's stories about Chatfield always have that same home town pride that your stories had just now. Please keep sharing. Reminds me so much of the great days visiting Lester & Eldora (Grandpa and Grandma!), Aunt Mert, Betty & Tilford's farm with the deadly 3-wheeler and awesome minibike, and everyone else. Thank you for sharing.

Pat Cooley Chris Trogstad luv it!

Brad Bungum Chris Trogstad, I'm trying to remember Betty & Tilford? Not sure I ever got that experience? Tho' I did see Kevin Meyer at Mom's funeral, and we shared some stories about him teaching me how to drive a moto-cross bike...amazing I still have all my limbs...

Kathy Schutt I was so very sorry to hear about Ruth Ann! I hope your doing well. Sounds like you've had a great trip. Good for you!!

Bret Lewison Gotta say, PeteandRuth Ann Bungum, this story sound eerily familiar. Just change Pete & Jerry to Brad Bungum & Bret and It's pretty much the same storyline. While we've only been getting together for 40 years since our days as Raiders, I'm sure Lene & Lorene (not to mention Alex, Nisse, Jack & Sam) would 100% agree on the need for boots & propensity for lots of beers disappearing. I have a sneaking suspicion that the need for boots is directly proportional to the number of beers. But just like you & Jerry, I gotta say, "We were good" (and we've been getting better for the last 40 years). Take care #1 Hawk.

Brad Bungum You nailed it Bret Lewison ;-)

Tim Bungum Pete: Great stories! I have heard the one about beating Rochester, but you omitted your favorite part. The part about the Rochester guys saying, "Let's get this game over quickly so the Chatfield guys can get back and to their chores." I'm sure that they said that! Oh, I may be incorrect, but I think that TY Moore was an offensive coach and worked closely with Peyton Manning. Keep telling the stories Pete, they are always good to hear

Brad Bungum Tim Bungum, I was thinking the same thing—how could Dad PeteandRuth Ann Bungum, leave that part out!?!? I'm quite sure it was a true story…that one's hard to make up…

Aaron Thomas Good for you Pete, always thankful for good news

Elsie Narveson What great memories. It was great to have you stop in to and catch up. Do that again sometime

Craig Serbousek Sorry for your tremendous loss Mr. Bungum. I appreciate your visits to my Grandma. You don't know how much I wish I could be a part of that. Please take care of yourself.

Rusty L. Russell Now that, is a great story!!!

Richard Stout Pete, I know you as a friend…but didn't know you were quarterback and catcher. What a great story you wove. Interesting details…and it explains much about the successes you've experienced in life. Thanks for seeking out old friends.

Brad Bungum One more good story about Dad PeteandRuth Ann Bungum from the past couple days… So I'm checking in on him once a day or so, and Teresa Engelbart is doing so at least that many times—Class of '80 friends always help each other, especially when their daughters are best friends and we get plenty of doctorly advice from both of them these days ;-). The other day, I asked Dad if BTN had shut down since there was nothing to broadcast, so he turned it on while we were talking, and of course they were still on, just showing Big Ten Classics. At that point, there was a basketball game on… Ohio St-Illinois from some point in the past…suddenly he said, "I'm just watching these guards, and I think they're a bit quicker than I was on the '58 team in Chatfield." I don't know how he remembers all these details noted above, but at least he's honest about his BB skills…and Bungums have never been known for their quickness :-)

Richard Stout Except in wit…

Brad Bungum Good point, Mr. Richard Stout

Bernie Paulson Sorry I missed you when I stopped by. I'm sure there are some stories we could share.

Pat McQuaid Schoon Pete, Thanks for sharing your great memories—and we are so glad you're enjoying your trip north. You will always have our love and support!

Deb Rickels Have a great visit

PeteandRuth Ann Bungum

Thanks to all of you who commented on my first post. Nephew Tim in Las Vegas and son Brad in Denmark mentioned that I left out a good story about our 6–5 victory over Rochester—so here it is. When you read this you might sense a lot of arrogance and maybe a whole bunch of ignorance.

When we were taking infield, I could hear the Rochester kids talking in their dugout—What I heard was "Let's get this over with in a hurry so the Chatfield boys can get home in time to do their chores and milk their cows." I also heard another kid say, "Where is Chatfield anyway?"

It so happens Chatfield is 18 miles south of Rochester on Highway 52. After the game they probably went home and got a map to find out. If they didn't, they should have. Also, after the game the two teams had to shower in the same room. Most of the Rochester boys were pretty quiet but TR and TY did come and talk to Jerry and congratulate him.

I want to say one more thing about Jerry. He was a superb athlete and a great hitter in baseball. That day he had a 2-run homer against Rochester and a 2-run homer against Austin which tied the game and got it into extra innings.

After the game the Austin coach came in our locker room and congratulated Jerry and jokingly said, "I'll get your dad a job at Hormel Packing." After high school he played two years of basketball at Rochester junior college. Then he had a career at IBM.

In 1957 Chatfield had 1,800 people and Rochester was around 25 to 30,000—so it was a big deal to beat Rochester. We had 52 in our class and they had at least 5–600.

One more thing—we had American Legion baseball in the summer. One month after they beat us 3–2 we went to Austin and we beat them 4–0. Sweet revenge but no state tournament.

Comments

Tim Bungum Pete: As a Rochester kid I must confess that my junior year we lost to Kasson-Mantorville in the district baseball tournament. Don't remember the score but the game was played in Winona. I'm sure those KM Komets have enjoyed that memory similar to how you have recalled your victory over Rochester. Do you remember any of the players from the Austin teams that you played? They were strong up through the 1970s but have tailed off since.

> **PeteandRuth Ann Bungum** The only one I therefore remember was Manley Osborn; he went to Luther and played baseball there. He was good

Darrel Stufflebeam I'm going to stop by the next time I'm in town to discuss how I incorporated Mr. Bungum teaching strategies. The 2020 election might come up as well.

Andrea Bungum Uncle Pete, I love hearing these stories—keep sharing!

Shelley Bungum DeBernardi Love your stories too. Tim just called to see if I'm reading them. He is really enjoying them. Take care Uncle Pete ♡

Brad Bungum Tim Bungum and Shelley Bungum DeBernardi, I think Dad told me he also was able to see Aunt Verleen on his road trip north??

Tim Bungum Yes, she told me. She was really happy to see him!

Kimberly Bungum I love your stories

Brad Bungum Dad PeteandRuth Ann Bungum, didn't Jerry have a few MLB teams looking at him? Maybe tell that story next...? I know they weren't knocking on your door... 😂 😂

Phil Bungum ;~]

Kirk Ketelsen Great history! I love this Pete!

> **PeteandRuth Ann Bungum** Kirk Ketelsen thanks kirk

Elsie Narveson Austin had a catcher named terry brown. He went on to catch for Minnesota. They had a centerfielder clayton reid, he signed with the Philles right out of high school. Jerry

Brad Bungum Thanks Jerry! I'm wondering if Tim Bungum saw this since he's the one who asked?

Tim Bungum Thanks Jerry! Those names do not ring a bell… Do you recall their coach? It might have been a guy named Dick Seltz who was coaching there in the mid-1970s when I played against Austin. I'm pretty sure that he won at least one state championship at Austin.

Tim Bungum It looks like Seltz would have been there. He did a lot of winning! https://www.postbulletin.com/…/article_c6ae8937-d66d… POSTBULLETIN.COM

Richard 'Dick' Nibbe Seltz—Austin Richard 'Dick' Nibbe Seltz—Austin

Brad Bungum maybe dad knows? PeteandRuth Ann Bungum??

> **PeteandRuth Ann Bungum** yes it was Dick Seltz—I remember him telling Jerry he'd get his dad a job at Hormel when he came in the locker room to congratulate Jerry

> **Brad Bungum** PeteandRuth Ann Bungum thanks dad… Tim Bungum did you see this?

Tim Bungum Thanks Pete and Jerry!

PeteandRuth Ann Bungum
March 20, 2020

Day 1: Thursday, March 5, 2020

I stayed overnight on Thursday 5 March 2020—in the morning of the 6th I went to coffee with Jerry and two of his brothers and his brother in-law. I said goodbye but before I headed north, I drove by the house I lived in from seventh grade to graduation. It looked the same, but it is a BnB now. When I lived there from 1952 to 1958 it was a nursing home.

Then I followed the route I took delivering the Minneapolis Tribune newspaper from 6:15 to 7:00 every morning. There have been many changes since 1956—many of houses are gone that I delivered to.

Now a story about Sid Hartman and our baseball team. Sid was the sportswriter for the Tribune. Sid must have heard about Jerry and our baseball team, so he called our school and talked to our coach Savre. When the article ran it was mainly about Jerry. But coach was kind enough to mention there were other good players on the team and he mentioned me as one of them. So I got my name in one of Sid's columns sometime in May of 1958 (or maybe June). I don't know if that is researchable—I tried to find it once but had no luck. If any of you readers find it let me know.

I have so many good memories of my teenage years in Chatfield. But I'm going to save those for later.

Tomorrow I'm going to write about Day 2 of my 9-day stress and loneliness reduction trip.

Comments

Richard Stout Uf-dah.

Angie Andersen Russell I really like reading your stories Pete!

John Spilde I enjoyed reading your stories. The years have gone by too fast!

> **PeteandRuth Ann Bungum** What a surprise to see your name pop up. I agree time has really flown by since you were in my class. Thanks for your comment. Please fill me in what you've done all your life. Tell me The Who-what-when-where-why of your life.

John Spilde After graduation from UNI in 1976, I found a job at the Glenwood State Hospital/School as an Activities Specialist. (By the way, my claim to Fame is that I was in the first class to graduate in the dome ☺) I worked in Glenwood for three years, until I accepted a job as a Recreation Therapist at Jennie Edmundson Hospital. I worked mostly on the Psychiatric Care Unit, from 1979–2005. THEN, my position was "eliminated" after 25 years 7 months. I guess they called it an economic short fall and Bush diverting money to the "war" vs. health care. I worked in three nursing homes during the next 15 years. Also, after my divorce in 1990, I became a single parent for my two kids, Bethany and Alan. I also worked at the Super Saver grocery store part time. I decided to take SS money in January and work part time delivering flowers and pharmacy prescriptions. I don't know if you were told the story how my dad was working in a body shop in Decorah for someone else. In 1959 he took a chance and left the family weekdays to start a body shop in a town called "Anamosa." I remember he lived above the shop that summer. I did not appreciate that until later years when Dad had me go up in the attic in the summer to get things. "Hotter than Hell" up there!! (By the way our family moved to Anamosa in 1959, when I was 1/2 way through kindergarten.)

John Spilde My parents had a great retirement and had a mobile home in Port Isabel, Tx. For 28 years. They lived in North Liberty 1/2 the year. They moved to Marion about 7 years ago in senior housing. My older sister, Nadine retired from being an RN. Muriel retired from teaching at the Prairie Middle School. And Randy retired from the Army as a Lt. Col. He worked for a Global Positioning Co in CA after Military retirement. (works at a golf course part time now?) That's some family news! Sincerely, John

PeteandRuth Ann Bungum Thanks John. I was closely acquainted with your parents—we all went to Saint Paul Lutheran church. I'm sure you remember. Have many good memories of them.

By the way—I went to Luther, graduated in 1962—then got a teaching job in Anamosa. I taught 3 years, left for two and came back in 1967—been here ever since. We had two kids, Brad and Carron—they graduated in 1980 and 1981. Couple of questions: I worked with a Bob Spilde at Super Valu store in Decorah. Did you know him? And is he still alive? Didn't you used to mow my terrible lawn? And how much did I pay you?

John Spilde First, my brother, Randy, mowed your lawn. Yes, Bob Spilde is my cousin. As kids when we were visiting in Decorah, we enjoyed hearing Bob do commercials on the radio. His niece, Debbie Brandt, originally from Cresco, lives in Bellevue, Nebraska now. Anyway, she works at American National Bank in Council Bluffs, where I bank. She recognized the Spilde name a few years ago on a drive through. I got her all her uncle's address. Send me your address, perhaps, more securely, a text at my phone number: 402-813-2070 or email: spildejs@cox.net. Yes, I your family from church and the Norwegian group. I remembered Brad, but I forgot your daughter's name until you mentioned it!

John Spilde A small world story: A few years ago my girlfriend and I were celebrating Thanksgiving at her brother's in-laws home. A man and his wife, from Des Moines were also there. He was Paul Lewison's brother. I met a lady in a nursing home in Papillion, Ann Swanson, who was related to the George Swanson family in Anamosa.

John Spilde Back to the Bob Spilde story. His parents Leonard and Florence had several kids and I did not get to know my older cousins very well! There were so many of us at the few reunions we had, and it was hard to get to know everyone, and perhaps, I was shy then also. My aunt Grace, the great family organizer, arranged reunions. The last one was at the Decorah Fair Grounds. No small event!! LOL!!

John Spilde I must tell you one more story: My uncle, Myron, and my dad were buying cemetery plots at Cedar Memorial a number of years ago. Myron told how the funeral director was trying to sell my dad a plot near, is it 3rd. Street? it is it 3rd. Ave. Anyway, my dad said that street had lots of traffic and was too loud. I guess they laughed, as usually people do not care about noise level when they are buried!! My dad had a good sense of humor, as I am sure you know. Probably, a "trick" by my dad so we would laugh as visit his grave site!! (I guess I already mentioned that he died January 12, 2018. A month before his Feb. 20 th. M. Birthday). Mom and Dad just moved to Garnett Place assisted living in CR. My dad had a few falls, fluid on the lungs, and the right side of his heart was failing. He went from Veteran's Hosp. In Iowa City to a nursing home rehab. in CR. He died in his sleep. My dad got amazing care at Veteran's Hosp. over the years Pete!!!!!!!! He volunteered there for over 24 plus years. At around age 94–95, he had heart valve surgery to keep him going (At Univ. Hosp). About 30 years ago Dad had bladder cancer and they did a research treatment that worked. The treatment was called to the biggest town near them when they in Texas (Brownsville), as they had not heard of such a treatment!

John Spilde Being a social studies teacher you probably would have been amazed at the stories Mom and Dad would tell about. It was the wild/Wild West! Many border stories, places where the Mexican people got to the USA for a better life. They showed us where a car, etc. could be pulled across the Rio Grande river by a small boat, pulled by ropes. Many bribes, shootings, etc.

John Spilde Pastor Behrends and his wife ended up in Blair, Nebraska. I ran into them a few times over the years. He even was a sub pastor at Emanuel Lutheran in Council Bluffs on one occasion. Pastor died and his wife is in a nursing home near Blair. I used to send them a

Christmas card until her son-in-law suggested one a nice letter that I not sent a card anymore. as she had Alzheimer's and did not remember me. Did I say one more story? I lied! LOL

John Spilde Another small world story: A few years ago my girl-friend and I were celebrating Thanksgiving at her brother's in-laws home in Pappilion

John Spilde I worked at the Millard Samaritan Nursing Home, in the activities dept. from 2005–2010. I met a nurse, named Dick Hochinson, originally from Oelwein, Iowa. (He was on the golf team years ago.) Anyway, we befriended each other and had fun teasing Big Red fans!! I even bought USC tee shirts when NU played football against them. The next small world story goes like this: I had a second cousin who drowned in Decorah. On the way to Decorah I stopped in Oelwein and bought a newspaper. A few months later, Dick was visiting his parents, who retired to Ankeny. A neighbor lady brought Dick's parents some tomatoes and she saw the paper Dick was also sharing with his parents. Dick told the lady about me and to make a long story a little shorter, the neighbor lady was my cousin, Shirley, originally from Decorah.

John Spilde In February Randy and I visited my Mom and we took my mom and Muriel's son Dan to Anamosa for a tour. We ate at the old T&D store, now a restaurant run by Dirk Downing. Had a good meal and visit from Dirk. That's all my stories! Take care and stay well! John Spilde

Brad Bungum Dad PeteandRuth Ann Bungum, be sure to read all of John Spilde John's stories here!

PeteandRuth Ann Bungum
March 22

Day 2: Friday, March 6, 2020

After Chatfield I drove to Rochester. My next visit was going to be Verleen, my sister-in-law who had been married to brother Jim for 65+ years. I found her address in the address book I had brought along—she was in an assisted living location on second avenue. I asked the nurse on duty if I could visit Verleen Bungum and at first she said no because she had been sick with no visitors but then she said, "Just wait a minute. I'll call the nurse and see if the doctor has cleared her for visitors." She gave me a smile and said, "You can go— the doctor gave her the okay yesterday."

I went down the hall, pounded on her door, she opened it and she was very surprised to see me. I had not seen her since Jim's funeral in 2016 (I think). We sat down and a 79-year-old me and an 85-year-old Verleen tried to communicate. Our main problem was hearing. I noticed right away she had hearing aids and the 85 years of her life had done some damage to her hearing. I'm not that far along on the bad hearing route so I could hear her okay. She'd put her hearing aids in, and they kept falling out. I'd ask her if she heard what I just said and most of the time she did not so I would repeat it louder and we would do better.

As I was visiting, I was thinking that getting older is when people start repeating things and can't remember what they had just said 5 minutes ago. She did say 5–6 times that getting old is not much fun and I agreed with her every time. After all we had both lost our spouses in our late seventies or early eighties, we both were losing our hearing, we were both finding it harder to walk, we were both struggling to remember things and/or finding the right words to use at the right time, etc. She is no longer in her home and I'm fortunate to be in mine. But I have to keep in mind I am six years younger and when 85 years comes for me who knows where I will be.

I stayed about an hour, we gave each other a big hug and said goodbye. I'm so glad I stopped, and she was so grateful I took the time to include her in my jaunt. I think we both hoped we would be able to see each other again before the pearly gates do.

Just a word about Jim. He was good athlete and played football, basketball and baseball for Mantorville and Dodge Center high schools. And guess what, like his brother Pete, he was a quarterback in football, guard in basketball and catcher in baseball. The main difference between the two of us was he had a dark complexion and black hair. I was the opposite with a light complexion and red hair. In 1947 the Mantorville little league team won the Dodge County Little League championship. Jim was the catcher and Chuck was second base. I think our dad was one of the two coaches.

There were 9 kids in our family. Mark had brown hair; Betty, Jim, and John had black hair; and Paul, Don, Jan, Chuck and I had red hair. The only thing I can figure out is the Vikings went to places like Italy and Spain and took a whole bunch of black-haired women back to Norway. I'm beginning to think that we Bungums may not be the pure-bred Norskies we think we are.

The rest of my Day 2 was driving to Bloomington to begin my two day stay with sister Jan and husband Don.

Comments

Phil Bungum Thanks Uncle Pete Happy Trails

Kimberly Bungum I love reading these, I can picture it in my mind. Sending love to you all

Bob Hines Thanks, Pete. Keep up the good work!

Pat Cooley Love hearing your stories ♡

Ann Caswell I love. Your commentary. So good to hear about my family. Love you.

Tim Bungum Thanks Pete! I think that you are right about us not being 100% Norski. Some in my family have had their DNA checked and we somehow had a "dot" on the Iberian Peninsula. My original thought was "No way!" At that time I had a colleague from Portugal. He said that everyone knows that the Portuguese sailed around Africa to Hong Kong, but fewer are aware that they had also sailed North, past Norway to the Arctic Circle. 2) I think it was Wade who mentioned that there was a fish processing plant in Fromfjord and some years, in the 1800s I think, they were short of workers and invited men from Portugal to come up and help can the fish. That arrangement could also had occurred in other places in Norway. I'm sure that there are more possibilities, but my $ would be in #2.

PeteandRuth Ann Bungum
March 24

Day 3: Saturday, March 7, 2020

On Friday, I drove the 2 hours to Bloomington (Minnesota) to spend Friday and Saturday nights with sister Jan and husband Don Blattie. I spent a pleasant Friday night visiting with them. We talked about growing up in Mantorville and Dodge Center Minnesota, dating, getting married etc. Jan was 7 years older than me—graduating in 1951—1958 for me. She got married young just like me—we were both 19. Don was 3 years older than her and they started dating in high school also.

I have a couple of good stories to tell about them. We lived in Mantorville at the time and I was 8 years old. Jan was babysitting with me and John and Mark. Don came to visit Jan. So they took a blanket and went to the back yard to sunbathe and have a little privacy. I took it upon myself to visit them and generally be a nuisance and ruin their sweet talk.

Finally, Don got sick of me, reached in his pocket and pulled out a 50-cent piece and tells me to take Mark and John down to Erdman's grocery store and get some candy and pop. I was pretty excited because I had never had that much money given to me. I was used to nickels and dimes. It took me until I was a teenager and dating myself to figure out why he gave me so much money.

My second story was when I was 11 and we lived in Dodge Center at the county poor farm—we had moved there in 1949 when dad gave up the county treasurers job. They took this job in order to make more money as their kids were getting to adulthood. His 3,600 dollars a year as county treasurer wasn't cutting it.

Anyway, my story goes like this. Jan was washing dishes and I saw the daily mail laying on the table and I saw a letter addressed to Jan and it was from Don who was in the Air Force in Mississippi. So I took it and opened it and started reading it out loud. Well, there was lots of sweet talk in the letter and Jan told me to shut up, but I kept reading and she started chasing me around the kitchen table. I finally quit and gave her the letter and ran upstairs. The best apart about it was Mom was laughing—which was good because she did not have a lot to laugh about fixing food 3 times a day for 30–40 patients.

Tomorrow on Day 4 I'll write about visiting brother Don and brother Mark.

Comments

Kimberly Bungum I love this

Julie Leinen Fall This is nice

Cathy Aldrich I am following your adventures

John Bungum II That's great. I love the family stories!

Pat McQuaid Schoon We are absolutely loving your stories—keep them coming!!!!!

Phil Bungum !!!!

Ann Caswell Thanks for the stories. They are great.

Stephen Zimmerman I love reading your stories, Pete. Please write more!

Linda Blattie Smaby Priceless!

PeteandRuth Ann Bungum
March 25

Day 4: Sunday, March 8, 2020

I'll digress a bit here... On Saturday (Day 3) I continued my tour to try to relieve my loneliness after losing Ruth Ann to cancer on January 9. However, on this Sunday, I left sister Jan and drove to St. Peter to spend a couple days with brother John and his wife Lorna.

On Day 3/Saturday, sister Jan and I drove to Lindstrom to visit brother Don—he was number 3 kid in our litter of 10 Bungum kids. Lindstrom is about a 40–50-minute drive north of Saint Paul. We went to Don's apartment—he is living alone while Joan, his wife, is in a nursing home at another location. She is there because her body has been invaded by arthritis. Don graduated from Mantorville high school in 1949—so that makes him 9 years older than me. In 1951 Joan graduated from Claremont, a town 12 miles northwest. They started dating in 1952 and got married on June 6, 1954. They have 3 kids—David, Jane and Phil.

I have some special memories of both of them—I'll do Joan first. My favorite memory of Joan is while growing up she was always so nice to me. She always asked about school and how I was doing. She was genuinely interested, and she listened to what I said. She really liked kids.

Another great memory was her laugh. When she laughed you could hear her a mile away—and you still can. When we visited her at the nursing home, she showed me a photo in the Claremont annual from 1951 of her jumping in her cheerleading outfit. It was a high jump for a 4-foot 11-inch girl—she commented that she didn't think she could do that now—and she let out a good laugh. Arthritis has not stopped her from laughing. And one other good memory is she was the family geneologist—in 2003 she researched the Bungum family and came up with a fantastic genealogy book for everyone in the family. I still have my copy and refer to it frequently.

Brother Don and I have always been close. When I was in third grade in Mantorville and he was a senior I would always ask him for a nickel and he would always give me one and then I would stop at dad's office and get another nickel and I would stop at Erdman's store and get my favorite pop which was Orange Crush.

But my best memory and the one I'm most grateful for is this one. It was April of 1962 and I was applying for my first teaching job. Ruth Ann and I drove to western Iowa and I interviewed at a school district called Charter-Ute. The job was to teach 7th, 8th and 9th grade social studies plus coach football, basketball and track for all three grades. The pay would be $4,200 per year. I was offered the job. Thank God I didn't sign anything.

When we got back to Decorah, I called Don, who was the principal in Ceylon, MN. I told him about the job offer and he emphatically told me to forget it. He said I would go nuts trying to do all that in my first year of teaching. The next day I called the superintendent and told him I was not accepting the job.

Now you know why I'm forever grateful to Don. I would have gone crazy. The good news is the next week I got a call from the principal at Anamosa junior high and he hired me. This job was one preparation for 7th grade social studies and no coaching—the pay was $4,600.

So I say, "Thank you, brother Don, for your lifesaving advice."

That afternoon we drove to Hudson, Wisconsin and visited brother Mark and wife Margie and Don's daughter Jane, my niece. Tomorrow I'll write about that visit.

Comments

Pat McQuaid Schoon Keep on with your adventures Pete, we're enjoying them right along with you!!!

PeteandRuth Ann Bungum Pat McQuaid Schoon thanks pat

Kimberly Bungum Keep sharing. And hugs and kisses to all of you ♡

    PeteandRuth Ann Bungum Kimberly Bungum thanks kim

Elsie Narveson Sounds like you had a great trip

Richard Stout Wow. Your family has wonderful stories. The way you tell them lets us forget about stuff for a while and picture life in long ago rural Minnesota. (Pete, did anyone in your family take advantage of the wonderful fishing...or the outdoor opportunities of such a beautiful state?)

Phil Bungum Yep, lots.

Herbert Stufflebeam I'm so sorry for loss! We can do a little A N A D if you want? I often think of you and your wonderful family!

Brad Bungum Herb Herbert Stufflebeam, that's a great idea! I wonder if Dad PeteandRuth Ann Bungum could name all the new countries the world has added since he retired 20 years ago?? Might be a good challenge for him ;-)

Phil Bungum ;~]

Phyllis Michels What a wonderful way to pass the time and commune with loved ones from the past! I have a dear friend who shared her life every day when she lost her dear husband. She wrote online every day. I think it was 😊 good for her, and us her friends.

Maline Bungum Thanks for sharing these stories, Uncle Pete. :)

PeteandRuth Ann Bungum
March 26

Day 5: Monday, March 9, 2020

A bit more about brother Mark, and our Saturday visit with him in Hudson. As mentioned, on Saturday the 7th, Jan and I left Lindstrom and followed brother Don to Hudson, Wisconsin to visit brother Mark and niece Jane.

Mark was Number 10 kid in Mom and Dad's litter of 10. He was born on April 1, 1946. Karen, the ninth kid died on her first day of life in May of 1944. Mark nearly died but the doctors managed to save him. But Mark was left with handicaps which he had to face the rest of his life. One of those was a hearing impairment and another was not having good balance. Because of those he was never able to participate in sports like his older brothers. I am grateful he was able to deal with his short shortcomings and did well in life. He spent most of his life doing electrical work and installing computers.

Unfortunately, Mark was diagnosed with pancreatic cancer last fall. He was taking chemo treatments for many months. When I talked to him in early February, he told me he had lost his hair and eyebrows and his hearing was gone. The main reason I wanted to see him was to say goodbye before he passed. I fully expected him to be on his death bed when I went in the house. Now the good news.

I went in the house and here was Mark sitting in his recliner—and his hair was growing back on the back of his head. The chemo must be working. He said he was now on radiation five days a week and taking a highpowered pill each day. I couldn't believe it, but I was so happy for him.

Anyway, wife Margie and Mark wanted to go to Perkins for lunch—it is their favorite. Niece Jane and husband Lou and daughter joined us, and we had a great visit.

My hope is that this miracle continues. Mark is six years younger—he deserves many more years. It was really a great day to see Mark doing so well. I say a Prayer for him every morning.

Jan and I drove back to Bloomington and I spent Sunday night with them. The next morning, I headed for St. Peter and brother John's place.

Comments

Elsie Narveson That's great news on Mark

Phil Bungum Uncle Mark is a genius with engines, wood, metal, electric, any trade his hands and eye are the most skillful. And he's very kind. And NOBODY has a grip like his.

Tammy Feist Sletten It has been so much fun reading about your road trip each day! I am learning so much more about your family. You continue to be in my prayers during this super hard transition. And now with all that is going on, continue to stay safe!

Ann Caswell Wonderful news praise The Lord!

PeteandRuth Ann Bungum
March 27

*Day 6: Tuesday, March 10, 2020

Today I left brother John and Lorna in St. Peter after breakfast, and drove to Cresco, Iowa to visit our old friends from Anamosa, Bob and Grace Story.

*Before getting into that (see another "Day 6" below), a bit more about sister Jan and her life...

Jan and I drove back to Bloomington—it had been a good day—especially the way Mark looked. That night we talked more about our lives in the 1950s. Jan had the most interesting things to say about her life in the 1950s so that is what I will write about.

In 1952 she went to Barksdale Air Force base to join husband Don. It was located in Bossier City, a suburb of Shreveport, Louisiana. It was in the Deep South. Jan got a job at Sears as secretary to the manager of the personnel department.

One day a black man came in and wanted to see the manager. Jan went to the manager's door and told him that "Mr. Rogers is here to see you." After he left she was called in and the boss told her, "You never call a black man or woman Mr. or Mrs. You have to remember you are in the South now and we have certain rules for them."

Jan was stunned. She couldn't believe that white people could treat other people like that. Jan said she had only seen 2–3 black people in her entire life. Then she went on to tell about the other kinds of discrimination she observed:

— Blacks had to sit in the back of the bus.
— They had to walk of 3–4 flights of stairs to see a movie.
— They couldn't drink from public fountains.
— They couldn't eat at most restaurants.
— They couldn't use any of the public rest rooms downtown.
— On Saturday night when most people went to town, the blacks had to walk in the gutter while the whites got to walk on the sidewalk.

One good thing is the base hospital was not segregated—this is where their daughter Linda was born.

Jan said, "I must say, my heart was broken many times while living there."

It's not too hard to figure out why Rosa Parks refused to move on the bus—it started the civil rights movement.

Comments

Pat McQuaid Schoon Thanks to your sister for keeping "Oral History" alive and thanks to you, Pete, for writing about it!!!!!

PeteandRuth Ann Bungum
March 28

Recap of Day 4–5. March 8 and 9—Sunday and Monday of my loneliness mitigation tour.

A bit more about the past few days (Days 4–5)…

On Sunday the 8th I left Don and Jan and headed for Saint Peter to visit brother John and wife Lorna.

On the way I stopped in Lesuer to get gas. Across the street was a historical marker—I went across the street and discovered it was the birthplace of Charles Mayo—the father of Charles and William Mayo—the founders of the Mayo Clinic in Rochester.

It was not open so all I could see was a house built in the 1850s, and a sign explaining some information about the Mayo family. It caught my attention because I grew up 20 miles from this world-famous clinic plus Ruth Ann worked there after high school from 1958–1960.

Then to Saint Peter about 3 pm. We went to Lesuer to visit their son, John junior, and his daughter—Linea—she is a seventh grader. She entertained us with some keyboard tunes. I guess she has a boyfriend named Ezekiel—they broke up but now they are together again, and everything is peachy. That night we went out to eat at Whiskey River.

On Monday Lorna and I went to Mystic Lake, a casino on the south side of Minneapolis. All the casinos in Minnesota are owned by the Indians. I understand that the profits are divided among all the members of that particular tribe. I made 10.00 dollars playing my video poker—that is the only game I play at a casino. My thinking is that slots are pure luck while video poker requires some thinking and gives you more chances to win or at least break even.

On Monday night we drove to Mankato to a Mexican restaurant and met their daughter Bethany, her husband Jesse and their six-year-son Jaxson. We had a very pleasant evening and the food was excellent.

Brother John is two years younger. I was born on November 20, 1940 and he was born on December 17, 1942.

I was number 7 kid and he was number 8. As a result, we played a lot of ball—especially football and baseball. Plus, we spent many hours playing ball in our backyard. John was a good athlete—in football he got to start at left guard as a sophomore—so he got to protect his older brother when I was a senior and the quarterback.

As adults we have spent a lot of time together—we have taken some trips together—San Francisco, Phoenix, twice to Mexico and several Hawkeye bowl games. Plus, he and son Brad and I took a 17-day trip to 10 major league baseball stadiums in 2013. We saw games in Milwaukee, Chicago, Cincinnati, Cleveland, New York Yankees, New York Mets, Baltimore, Philadelphia, Pittsburgh and Kansas City.

And we were the best man in our weddings.

The next day—Tuesday—I packed my bag and headed for Cresco, Iowa

Comments

Myrna Wesselman William Worral Mayo built that house and had his office in the upstairs before moving his family to Rochester.

PeteandRuth Ann Bungum Myrna Wesselman thank you Myrna. Do we know each other? I don't recognize your name.

Tim Bungum So interesting Pete! Say, years ago I read a book on Rochester and if my memory serves me correctly the Mayos had moved from Indiana to practice medicine in Lesuer. At that time all the Minnesota soldiers going to the Civil War needed a physical before shipping out. The Mayos were called to Rochester to help with the physicals, and they stayed.

Pat McQuaid Schoon Keep on going Pete! We're enjoying your stories! Everyone should take the time to travel and reminisce like you are doing!! 😄

> **PeteandRuth Ann Bungum** Thanks for your comments—glad to see you enjoying them. I intend to continue—it helps me cope—it isn't easy.

Elsie Narveson You really covered a lot of ground

Myrna Wesselman I graduated with you and Ruth Ann. The name was Baker.

Thomas Hatcher Enjoying your journeys. Assuming there will be an amusing story soon about an all-you-can-eat Lutefisk restaurant during your travels. 😆

Brad Bungum That's a good one, Tom Thomas Hatcher!! Dad, PeteandRuth Ann Bungum, you left out the lutefisk stops along the way!

Phil Bungum ;~]

PeteandRuth Ann Bungum
March 29

Day 6: Tuesday, March 10, 2020. My loneliness mitigation tour takes me to Cresco, Iowa.

I left John and Lorna's in mid-morning and headed south and east for Cresco. I stopped in Austin, Minn. to go through the Hormel Spam Museum. Sister Jan had told me it was a must see—she was right. It was on Main Street and easy to find. It was so interesting that I spent two hours. The most interesting was the role spam played in feeding our troops in WWII, and also Russian troops. It showed how spam is sold world-wide today.

They also told us the six simple ingredients that are used in making spam—there is pork of course plus salt, water, potato starch and two others I can't remember. Hormel also has many other foods they produce. I found it interesting to read about the history of the George A. Hormel Corporation started in 1891. They even have a place where you can stand and measure your height in spam cans. I'm going to go back someday and go through it again.

Then I made it to Cresco about 4pm. I easily found Bob and Grace Story's house. Bob and Grace were good friends of ours when they lived in Anamosa—they moved to Cresco in 1974 when Bob decided to work with a different attorney. We had many good times from 1967 to 1974. Ruth Ann and I were also sponsors for their daughter, Krista in 1969. She now teaches second grade in Cresco. She came over and had dinner with us.

Grace fixed a wonderful meal—we talked about some of the fun times we had in Anamosa—Ruth Ann's losing battle with cancer—their health and my health—our kids—and on and on.

They were so happy I stopped to visit them, and I was so happy I did—it was an enjoyable 20 hours.

I left about noon on Wednesday but not until Grace gave me a bag of snacks. My next stop was Waterloo.

Comments

Linda Blattie Smaby Love reliving your visits Pete!

Phil Bungum ;~]

Ann Caswell What a wonderful trip. I love your commentary.

Brad Bungum Keep 'em coming Pops!!

Pat McQuaid Schoon Pete, we were glad to get an update on Bob & Grace Story! Keep up your reporting!! 😊

Renee Frankfurt-Dooley Bob used to be my folks' attorney... I think.

Grace Story Was so very good to have you come for a visit!!!

> **PeteandRuth Ann Bungum** Thanks for the comment. I truly enjoyed seeing you and Bob and Krista also. I'm glad I stopped. Let's keep in touch. Pete

PeteandRuth Ann Bungum
March 30

Day 7: Wednesday, March 11. Pete's loneliness mitigation tour.

I left Cresco about noon and headed south to the casino in Waterloo. I wanted to visit Ruth Ann's two cousins, Ron Syverud and Becky. Their father was Truman Syverud who was a brother of Myrtle, Ruth Ann's mother.

I rented a room and called Ron and asked him to come and have something to eat with me. He readily agreed. Then I asked him to call his sister Becky and husband Jerry Helgerson. They also agreed so I had supper lined up and now I was free to go and play video poker.

We met at 6pm at the bar and grill and had good conversation and the food was wonderful. Ron stayed until 11pm and did some gambling—I don't know if he won or lost. I did make 50 dollars by hitting four of a kind twice.

It was so different going to bed in a hotel without Ruth Ann. We had stayed at many hotels in our 59 years of marriage—so this was a first. I will have to say I liked the old way much better—it was fun to do a lot of snuggling. Unfortunately, those days were long gone.

A couple more things about my Waterloo visit. Before I got to the casino, I went through the famous Grout Museum in Waterloo. It tells the history of Waterloo and it is superbly done. I spent close to two hours there. If you like museums this a place for you.

Now a word about Jerry. Both Jerry and Ron were in Vietnam in the Army in the 1960s. When the lottery was instituted in 1968, I would guess most every young man in the US was watching/listening to hear when their birthday would be pulled from that big jar. The sooner your birthday was called the better your chances of being drafted.

So, the lower your number you were almost guaranteed to be drafted. I bring this up because Jerry was on a date with Becky and they had the radio on when the lottery started—and the first birthday called was in November (I think) and guess what—it was Jerry's birthday. His future for two years was pretty much settled right there.

Yes, he was drafted in Blackhawk County and went to Vietnam. When he got home, he and Becky got married. They had two kids—a boy and a girl.

I taught with a lot of guys who were that age and everyone of them can remember their draft number.

The next day I was heading to Des Moines

Comments

Rhenee Grabau Love this. ♡

Becky Helgerson We loved visiting with you! Jerry can say he won the lottery, not quite the jackpot he wanted though! Love reading about your travels. Take care and stay safe! 😊 😋 👍

Pat Cooley Becky Helgerson at the casino? What did he win?!

Becky Helgerson Pat Cooley The draft lottery. Not at the casino. 😊

PeteandRuth Ann Bungum
March 31

Day 8–9: March 12–13. Pete's last post on his nine-day loneliness mitigation tour.

I left Waterloo heading for Des Moines to see Carson and Connie Ode. They had been friends of ours since the 1960s. I could write a book about our relationship over the years, but I'm going to concentrate about one of my favorite stories from the 1970s. So here goes.

We met Carson at Luther College in 1960 and we met Connie in 1965 when she and Carson came to our home in Rochester for a party. Carson was an artist and a graphic designer—Connie was a medical technologist. They had met in Minneapolis and were married in January of 1966.

After stints in Owatonna and California they ending-up settling in Des Moines in 1969 when Carson was hired to work for the Meredith Corporation—that is when we rekindled our friendship. Now here is my favorite story.

In 1975 the four of us played Cupid and arranged a marriage. My brother John was a 35-year-old bachelor teaching economics at Platteville University in Wisconsin. Connie's sister Lorna was recently divorced and had moved to Des Moines from Chicago.

Carson, Connie, Ruth Ann and I talked that maybe we could get John and Lorna together for a date and maybe some sparks would fly. Ruth Ann was really anxious to get John married off because she was afraid that when he got old, he would come and live with us. So, we invited them to go to a Luther-Simpson football game in Indianola, Iowa.

The sparks didn't fly on our first effort, so we tried again the next year using the same tactic—we invited them to another football game. This time the sparks did fly. In August of 1977 John and Lorna were married and the four of us stood up for them. I was best man for John and Connie was maid of honor for Lorna. So our friendship became more than just a friendship. Now we were connected by family.

Ruth Ann was relieved. She thought John had the potential to be another Uncle Lewis. Lewis was my dad's bachelor brother and he did come and live us when I was in high school. Plus, John's middle name is, you guessed it, LEWIS.

Anyway, I had another great visit with C and C. Ruth Ann and I were so grateful to have friends like Carson and Connie.

I drove to home to Anamosa on Friday.

This ends my 9-day loneliness mitigation tour. I got to see everybody I had on my list.

Did it help? Yes, I didn't spend every day just thinking about my loneliness. And it gave me something to do every day. So, I'm going to continue to write—but it will be different topics.

Comments

Kimberly Bungum Love all of it!!

Pat Cooley Luv it!

Pat McQuaid Schoon I'm glad it helped you, Pete, and along the way it gave us a lot of enjoyment!!!! So keep on writing!!!

Elsie Narveson You did a great job recounting your trip. We are happy for you. Jerry says there is still a bush *(sic: Busch Light)* in the refrigerator

Phil Bungum ;~]

PeteandRuth Ann Bungum
April 2

I took yesterday off and debated what I wanted to write about next. I concluded I wanted to write about being grateful. In 2009 I wrote a 365-day gratitude journal.

WHY? Because from 2005 to 2008 we had suffered through five surgeries and I thought we were the 20th century version of Job in the Old Testament.

By November of 2008 we were healthy again and I was grateful we had survived. I felt we still had a lot to be grateful for so I decided I would express my gratitude for our survival in a journal for the 365 days of 2009.

I did it. By December 31, 2009, I had identified 365 people, things and experiences that I was grateful for and had enhanced my life in some way.

It was the best thing I had ever done in my entire life. When January 1, 2010 arrived, I felt like a new person.

Expressing gratitude for 365 days did this for me:

— It made me a more positive person.
— Made me appreciate all kinds of people and many of the little things in life.
— Made me appreciate what I have and not be jealous what others have.
— Helped me cope better and handle stress.
— Made me be a more optimistic person.
— Helped me look at each day as a gift.
— It convinced me that a major part (of) health is being grateful for what you have and being grateful to and for the people who have made everything possible.

So my posts will be about expressing gratitude.

Comments

Carlene Vavricek I love this Pete! ♡ We all have something to be grateful for in life. I look forward to reading your future posts on gratitude.

Elsie Narveson Sounds like a good plan

Linda Blattie Smaby Thinking mom and dad have it. Would love to read it!

Bob Hines Glad to hear it, Pete! Your journal is still one of the best things I have ever read. The copy you gave me is really special and brings back fond memories.

    PeteandRuth Ann Bungum Thanks Bob.

Phyllis Michels Good for you! A helpful activity for these quarantined days!

PeteandRuth Ann Bungum
Friday, April 3, 2020

I'm grateful to be living in 2020 instead of 1918–19, when the Spanish Flu devastated the world. I've been doing some research on the plague of the 1300s—called the Black Death—and the Spanish flu in 1918–1919.

They were pandemics just like we are experiencing now. The Black Death is too depressing to write about—the Spanish flu is also but I'll say a few words about it.

There are many similarities to what we are going through now. People were to wear masks and schools and businesses closed. There was no vaccine then and we don't have one in 2020. It attacked the lungs after people came down with a fever and a cough. It attacked the elderly—they were the most likely to pass away.

My hope is that we have learned something from history. I believe we have a better chance of getting through this pandemic in 2020 than 100 years ago. My hope is a vaccine will be discovered and I also hope some of our leaders will do some research and learn something about previous pandemics.

I was not planning on having this as my first post. Tomorrow I will get back to my original plan.

You, Bret Lewison, Yrsa Thom Chris and 10 others

PeteandRuth Ann Bungum
April 4, 2020

Pete's favorite memories from 63 years with Ruth Ann.

From here on in I'm going to be posting about my favorite memories from 1956–2019. You guessed it, those are the years Ruth Ann and I were an item. The item covered our ages from 15–79—that's a grand total of 63 years. Here goes number one.

On April 4, 2009, I posted, "I'm grateful for April 4, 1940."

I'm grateful for this day because that is the day my wife of 59 years, Ruth Ann Rain, was born in the bedroom of her parent's farmhouse. The farm is located 27 miles south of Rochester, about 25 miles north of the Iowa border.

Ruth Ann was the third child of Cyrus and Myrtle Rain—the first two were boys and the fourth was a boy so that made Ruth Ann the only girl. The older boys, Bud and Maurice, said she was the spoiled one—which she vehemently disagrees with. Anyway, we met in seventh grade, started dating in 1956 and have been together ever since. We spent our lives as a couple—it only ended on January 9, 2020, when she passed away—cancer ended our 63 year of togetherness.

This was a sad day but I'm so grateful I had Ruth Ann for my wife, my lover and my best friend for over 63 years.

Comments

Kathy Schutt That's so beautiful!

Carron Sue Bungum I thought about Mom and cried all day. I miss her so much.

Kathy Schutt It's such a beautiful love story of them two. You'll never hear this kind of story these days.

Laurie Emery You are a lucky man. She was a beautiful woman with a beautiful soul. You are an incredible man with a beautiful soul.

Thank you for sharing your memories of Ruth Ann with us. I will look forward to the next memory.

Sharon Wykle Twedt You both were very lucky. Great pair...loved you both...

PeteandRuth Ann Bungum thanks Sharon i

Brad Bungum *to* **PeteandRuth Ann Bungum** I won't over-due it here but can't help posting that Mom would have been 80 years old today, 4 April. That's a BIG DAY! We all know she's up there celebrating with her 2 brothers, her 4 bro-/sis-in-laws, parents/in-laws, a bunch of friends, Barney, Hayden and too many others to even remember. They're probably all sitting in a casino that pays out every time, planning where to go for Happy Hour that offers free Busch Light, and don't have a worry in the world about stay-at-home, social distancing, the economy, or when this mess will calm down. Go Hawks Mom! Happy 80th. We miss you.

Comments

Mark Blattie Hats off to a great lady Brad Bungum!

Rhonda Koppenhaver Happy Birthday in heaven to your mom. Thinking of you, your dad & Carron today.

Kandace Reinhardt Happy birthday to Ruthie up there in heaven

Bonnie Walderbach

Julie Leinen Fall Happy Birthday Ruth!

PeteandRuth Ann Bungum

Sunday: April 5, 2020. Another good story about Peter and Ruth Ann's life together.

I mentioned yesterday that Ruth Ann was born on April 4, 1940. I also mentioned we did not start dating until age 15. So that is where I will pick up on this good story about the two of us.

Our first date was June 27, 1956. It happened because Ruth Ann had told her friend Elsie Tollefson to tell Jerry Narveson, my best friend, that he should tell me that Ruth Ann liked me and wanted to go with me. The message he was to tell me was that she liked me and was having a picnic at her farm and wanted me to come.

He delivered the message and I agreed. I also told him I would drive. I asked dad if I could have the car to go to a picnic out in the country to a farm—he wanted to know who and where—he agreed. So, to the picnic we went.

When she told her dad that Pete Bungum was invited, he wanted to know if I was a brother of Pastor Paul Bungum. Paul had been a substitute preacher at their church, so her Dad knew him and liked him. That helped get me a stamp of approval.

We had our hot dogs, beans and potato salad and then it was time to get in my Dad's 1955 red and white Plymouth station wagon. It had bench seats in those days, so I got in the driver's seat. Ruth Ann gets in the front seat and slides right up next to me. I liked that.

We went to the outdoor theater in Rochester. About half through the movie my right hand and her left hand found each other, and we held hands the rest of the movie. That was first time we had ever touched each other. But that would soon change.

My next post will be about the month of July.

The next week we went to the outdoor theater again and things did change.

Comments

Kathy Schutt It just amazed me how you have such a great memory of every detail, Names and dates… I couldn't tell you anything from 30 years ago much less from the 1940s. Looking forward to the rest of the story. Thank you Pete!

Elsie Narveson I never get tired of your love story

Richard Stout A cliffhanger!

PeteandRuth Ann Bungum

These are photos of me at age 15 when we started dating.

However, the one in upper left is age 13 at bible camp. We were flirting a little—a foretaste of the future.

Pete's 10th grade photo

Comments

Carron Sue Bungum I LOVE these pictures of you and Mom!!!!! You were a handsome dude and Mom was so beautiful!!!!!! 😊

Angie Andersen Russell Great pictures! I see a lot of Brad in these pictures!

Galen Harms Beautiful picture! Pete Galen and Judy

Steve Boyer I love these Pete!!—Diane

    PeteandRuth Ann Bungum Thanks Steve—more coming.

Rhenee Grabau Brad is your mini me. Wow

Sharon Wykle Twedt Love the pictures…

Brad Bungum I guess in the '54 photo your growth spurt hadn't kicked in yet, Dad PeteandRuth Ann Bungum 😄

Mark Blattie Brad Bungum Ha! Uncle Pete has never been a big guy…

PeteandRuth Ann Bungum

Tuesday, April 7, 2020.

Good memories of Pete and Ruth Ann.

On my last post I said we had held hands at the outdoor theater. I'm grateful for bench seats in 1955 Plymouth's.

If It had been bucket-seats the hand holding probably would not have happened. Anyway, I don't remember anything about the movie or the ride home to her farmhouse. I know when I got home that night, I wanted things to continue and was hoping she felt the same way.

And they did—we started seeing each other frequently in the next weeks. In fact, Ruth Ann wrote in her diary on July 26, "Pete and I have seen each other 13 times since July 1." We either went to the outdoor theater or went on band trips and sat together on the bus, went on picnics with friends, etc. I'll have to confess that we did more than hold hands. We discovered our lips were attracted to each other.

On July 26 we were parked in the driveway of her Uncle Lester in Chatfield. That's where I popped this question, "Would you like to go steady with me?" She said yes. I told her I had a ring for her. It was a ring I had won at the Fillmore County fair. I think I won it by throwing darts at balloons. It had a flat top and I had my initials engraved on it the night I won it. I guarantee you it was a cheapie. It turned her finger purplish-green so she ended up wearing it on a chain around her neck. Things got better in the ring department as the next year I gave her my class ring—no more purple-green finger.

What do Pete and Ruth Ann have in common with Fidel Castro? The answer is July 26. Castro started his revolution to take over Cuba on July 26, 1953. In 1956 Pete and Ruth Ann started going steady on July 26. And for better or for worse Castro and Cuba stayed together until death and so did Pete and Ruth Ann.

We started going steady in July before our junior year. We spent a lot of time together by going to movies, school dances, being in band together, going on band trips, to the Prom. Neither one of us wanted to break up and date others. We had told each other how much we loved the other. I think we both felt, even at our young age, that we would spend our lives together.

Comments

Carron Sue Bungum Leave it to you to throw in a history lesson as well!!!

PeteandRuth Ann Bungum

Wednesday, April 8, 2020. Good memories of Pete and Ruth Ann.

I'm grateful we got to spend our senior year (1957–58) together. Ruth Ann and I continued to go steady.

Remember, she now wore my class ring and didn't have to worry about a discolored finger from the carnival ring. We got to know each other better and were really pretty serious even though we were only 17 years old. We even fantasized about what kind of house we would build someday, how many kids we would have, etc.

Ruth Ann's future plans were changed in February 1958, when her father, Cyrus, died at age 52. He lost a six-year battle to cancer. Ruth Ann had applied and been accepted at Gale Institute in Minneapolis. She would be trained to be flight attendant on major airlines. However, upon the death of her father she didn't feel she should be that far away from her Mom and she felt also that she could no longer afford to go, with her dad no longer farming. She decided not to attend Gale and instead applied at the Mayo Clinic to make use of her excellent secretarial skills and become a medical secretary. She, of course, was accepted and began work at Mayo Clinic in June of 1958.

If she had gone to Gale and became a flight attendant, I don't know what would have happened to our relationship. My feeling is we wouldn't have made it—and I wouldn't be writing this right now. With her flying the friendly skies and me looking at four years of college and having no money it would have been tough to make a go of it. It would have been tough to even see each other as she didn't drive, and I had no license for six months. Plus, I had no car.

As I look back at our lives, I sometimes think providence played a role in our ending up together as life-long partners. If her dad had died eight or ten months later, she would have been out of Gale and "flying the friendly skies all over the United States and/or the world." It would have been hard for her to marry a poverty-stricken college student and live in an upstairs apartment in Decorah, Iowa—and with no air conditioning. I'm grateful it didn't turn out that way. We have been partners since June 1956. I'm glad it turned out just the way it did.

Comments

Rhenee Grabau I never knew this. Wow.

Brad Bungum I didn't know it either, Cuz... :-)

PeteandRuth Ann Bungum

Thursday, April 9, 2020. More good memories of Pete and Ruth Ann.

We graduated in June 1958. Ruth Ann started at the Mayo Clinic right away. I was headed to Luther college in Decorah, Iowa in August to begin my four-year journey to become a teacher.

It was 70 miles to Rochester so we would be able to see each other on weekends. I was able to hitch-hike many times from September to December. Then at Christmas I did a big thing in our young love affair—I gave Ruth Ann an engagement ring.

I bought it at Cortland Jewelry in Rochester for $100 dollars. We were pretty darn young to be doing this kind of thing. I had just turned eighteen in November and she was eighteen in April, but I did it anyway. I had gotten my license back in December and could drive a car again. Dad let me have the car on December 23rd—I drove to Rochester and picked her up. I drove to her farm and parked on the road she used to walk to school. I told her I had a special Christmas gift for her. She opened it and had a big smile. She was happy to accept the diamond. I think she felt it was time to get engaged—after all we had been going steady for two and a half years. And we had talked about getting married someday anyway. And this was another step and we both felt comfortable doing it, despite our young age.

How did I pay for the diamond? Here is the story. I had bought it at Cortland Jewelry in Rochester. I paid $10 dollars down and they agreed I could send them $10 dollars a month for the next nine months. I had no checking account, so I had to send cash through the mail. Each time I got paid from K&S Super Valu I would set aside, in an envelope in my desk, a couple dollars plus coins. Each month I would send the dollars I had saved to Cortland Jewelry and sometimes I had to put in a few coins to make it to $10. Thinking back, it is amazing that all those payments made it. A postal employee could have pocketed those envelopes, especially the ones with coins. Also, Cortland's could just as easily have told me they didn't get my payment that month. Neither of those things happened in 1959. I would hate to try the same thing in 2020.

Comments

Angie Andersen Russell Great story Pete!

Terry Trogstad Thanks for the trip down memory lane Pete! Very enjoyable reading all your posts. This latest post triggered a memory of mine about Ruth Ann. I think you both graduated the same year Uncle Cy passed and that's when Ruth Ann and her best friend Elsie (Tollefson) Narveson moved to the big city of Rochester because, as your post said, she went to work at the Mayo Clinic…never knew about her desires to be an airline stewardess! Anyway, this is where one of my lasting memories with Ruth Ann starts.

She and Elsie got an apartment together and, for reasons still unknown, they invited me to spend a weekend with them in the big city… Well, this little ol boy from Chatfield jumped at the chance to spend time with 2 babes in their new digs. Little did I know what lay in store!

Friday night was the first nite there and they wanted to go see a movie, so I said GREAT! They picked a sappy love story with many tear-jerker scenes and I spent most of the time passing Kleenex tissues to one or the other. I don't remember the name, but the main song was "Love and Marriage go together like a Horse and Carriage!"… jeezzz. Sung by one of the old crooners, Frank Sinatra, Dean Martin, Perry Como etc.

Well, after surviving the Friday nite sob along, I anxiously waited to see what Saturday held in store.

At 7:30 am, I would find out… A day of SHOPPING!!! Joy joy joy! I was instructed to be ready to head out at 8:45 as stores opened at 9 and Ruth Ann and Elsie wanted to be first in line! So, how bad can it be doing a little shopping…not bad except we didn't just do a little shopping! It was POWER Shopping. I had to run around 18 mph just to keep those 2 in sight. Any speed less than that I'd have to find my own way back to their apartment. I thought about taking up Track after this little shopping trip!

Oh, I forgot to mention that they didn't shop in stores next to each other. Nooo, each store was a good 10–15 blocks away from the last one. I slept good that nite. The next day I headed back to the safety of my house in Chatfield.

I think I was invited back but I told Ruth Ann that I had to help dad re-roof the house or re-pave the driveway!!! I've never forgotten this weekend which happened over 60 years ago!

PeteandRuth Ann Bungum good story Terry. Did they buy you anything?

Terry Trogstad PeteandRuth Ann Bungum they should have got me some new shoes as I wore mine out!

Sharon Wykle Twedt You both were so young…

Elsie Narveson Oh I am suure we did. Sorry about how we entertained you!

PeteandRuth Ann Bungum

Friday, April 10, 2020. Another post about Ruth Ann and Pete and their journey to a life of togetherness.

We had gotten engaged in December of 1958. For the next year and a half, we were together as often as possible. I had bought a car in August of 1959 so it was easier to see each other when I could drive my 1951 Chevy the 70 miles from Decorah to Rochester—which was just about every weekend. I was a sophomore at Luther, and she was still working at the Mayo Clinic. During this time, we made plans to get married in June of 1960. We set the date to tie the knot on June 18.

I'm grateful for June 18, 1960. It was a beautiful day—the sun was shining, and the temperature was a perfect 78 degrees. I was pretty nervous that day.

It was because at 8 pm that night I was going to get married to Ruth Ann, who had been the love of my life for four years. We were young—I was 19 and she was 20, but we decided we were ready for the next step.

To make a long story short—we made it—we made it until January 9, 2020. That's over 59 years of marriage plus four more for a total of over 63. I'm grateful we weathered the tough times without heading to a divorce attorney—and yes, we had some tough times.

As a result of sticking it out we rewarded ourselves with a very financially secure retirement. We had 20 years of wonderful retirement in which we traveled to Europe 15 times plus Hawaii, Jamaica, Dominican Republic, Bahamas, the east and west coasts of Mexico, 48 of the 50 states, and Hawkeye bowl games in Pasadena, Miami, Orlando, Tampa Bay, and numerous Hawkeye games at Kinnick Stadium in Iowa City.

Now a word about our honeymoon's first night. After the ceremony we drove to Rochester and got a hotel room about 11pm. We checked in and the first thing I said to Ruth Ann was, "I'm hungry and I need a bite to eat."

There was a restaurant next door, so we went to satisfy my hunger. Without too much thought, I ordered a hamburger with onions, coleslaw, baked beans and a soda. Ruth Ann gave me a look of astonishment as I proceeded to chomp away. I'm guessing she was thinking, "What is this guy thinking? Is his stomach more important than what we will be doing in the hours ahead?"

Anyway, the good news is the onions and beans did not spoil our first night together as husband and wife. Ruth Ann loved to tell that story many times. It was always good for a laugh. It was another good memory we shared in our years together.

Comments

Deb Rickels Such a good life the two of you had. ♡

Terry Trogstad Sounds like you might have had a ROOTIN TOOTIN honeymoon night!

Rhonda Koppenhaver You really need to write a book. ☺ I am enjoying your story of your life with your beautiful wife.

PeteandRuth Ann Bungum

Saturday, April 11, 2020. Another story about Pete and Ruth Ann.

This one is about our weeklong honeymoon and our first home in Decorah, Iowa. The years are 1960 to 1962.

First, I want to say a few words about the wedding. Paul, my Lutheran brother minister, performed the ceremony. He was the oldest kid in our litter of ten. But he had said something to me when I was eight years old. What he said was, "Pete, do you think you'll ever amount to anything?" I never forgot that and was hoping when he performed the ceremony that I wouldn't disappoint him someday.

Anyway, the reception was held in the basement of the church. The church ladies prepared and served the food and there was no dance. When we were taking photos brother John asked me if he could have the keys to my car because he had forgotten something. I was stupid enough to believe him so when Ruth Ann and I came out of the church and walked through the rice shower and went to our car the front seat was full of hay. Then we drove the two miles to town pulling a bunch of tin cans—we went in the house and Ruth Ann changed clothes and we were on our way to Rochester to find a hotel. Our 59-year marriage was entering day one. We would be together for about the next 21,800 days.

Despite the onions and beans, we had a wonderful first night as husband and wife (but no details). In the morning we loaded our luggage in our 1951 Chevy. But I had forgotten our car had soap written messages all over it. I noticed quite a few people watching us—they all had big smiles. After all, in big letters was JUST MARRIED. I imagine the main thing going through their minds was "We know what you two did most of the night." Anyway, I stopped at a car wash and got rid of the soapy messages. Then we drove north heading for the North Shore Drive on Lake Superior. Why we decided to go there—I don't remember.

We didn't have much money to pay for a honeymoon trip. But thanks to Dad and Mom they made it possible. Dad had pulled me aside the morning of the wedding and handed me a $100 bill. He said Mom and I want you to have a honeymoon trip. This will help you have one—so enjoy. We made a list of our first three days of our expenses—see the photo.

We made it north of Duluth and found a motel—it only cost $7.50. The Rochester one was $9.00. The next day we crossed into Canada and found a hotel in Fort William—cost was $7.50. We stayed there for two nights. We tried to swim but the water was too cold. Ruth Ann did some sun tanning.

Wednesday we drove back to Minnesota and saw Paul Bunyan and Babe the Blue Ox. We stayed in Brainard Thursday night and drove to sister Jan's home in Saint Paul on Friday. Saturday we stopped in Chatfield and Fountain to see our parents. My sister Betty was in Chatfield—she made a comment I have never forgotten. She said, "Now the fun is over and the work begins." She was right. On Monday we had to go to work. On Sunday we drove to our future home in Decorah—it was an upstairs apartment a block from downtown. This would be our home for the next two years. We had lots of memories from those two years.

Comments

Phil Bungum Thanks, Blessed Easter

PeteandRuth Ann Bungum

Ruth Ann sitting on the beach in bathing suit

You, Rhenee Grabau, Dean Rickels and 5 others

PeteandRuth Ann Bungum

Pete's family in 1977

Comments

Linda Blattie Smaby Love this Pete!

Brad Bungum This was John & Lorna's wedding, right Dad PeteandRuth Ann Bungum?

> **PeteandRuth Ann Bungum** Yes it was in 1977 in Des Moines

Mark Blattie 2 observations, both meant with humor:
1—Norwegian mob family
2—When was the last time you saw so many Norwegians smile?

> **PeteandRuth Ann Bungum** Good observation Mark Blattie

Phil Bungum Maybe they told an Ole and Lena joke.

Mark Blattie Great picture.

Kimberly Bungum I love this picture ♡

Shelley Bungum DeBernardi ♡

Richard Stout Love the photo. The gal in green is flipping the photographer. She's got spunk.

Mark Blattie Richard Stout that would be my mother, Brads aunt, yes she has a little spunk but I am certain she wasn't intentionally giving the finger:)

Brad Bungum Richard Stout, Mark Blattie is right—she has spunk. She also used to play with her rings and while doing so, she flipped people off. Janice Blattie probably still does this... 😂 😂 😂

Rhenee Grabau I remember seeing your mom. ♡

Nathan Wohlfeil Biggest smile i've ever seen on Gramps! That's quite the crew.

Phyllis Michels Nice family group! 🧑‍🤝‍🧑

PeteandRuth Ann Bungum

April 12, 2020. Pete and Ruth Ann's story of 63 years of love and marriage.

I'm grateful for the wonderful memories of our two years in Decorah.

The honeymoon was over so now it was time to go to work. We drove to Decorah on Sunday afternoon—we unloaded our possessions and our wedding gifts and carried them up the twelve steps to our apartment. We were home.

On Monday we had to go to work. Ruth Ann had been hired in May to be the secretary for Mr. Kalsow, the college treasurer. The pay was $1.00 an hour. I had a job working for the maintenance department at Luther—I spent most of the summer mowing grass and painting the bleachers at the football field. My pay was also $1.00 an hour. We were making $2.00 an hour so that was more than enough to pay our bills. Our rent was $45.00 a month, and we would split the fuel bill three ways. There were two renters downstairs so I would get the fuel bill and collect their share every month. So, $80.00 a week between her dollar an hour and my dollar an hour was plenty—we even had enough for movies and whatever else we wanted to do for fun. Actually, $80.00 a week was a pretty good salary in 1960.

Another memory was this apartment had to be the hottest place on earth. It was terrible—our first investment that summer was to buy a 30" by 30" fan. As newlyweds—the fan was a lifesaver.

Our apartment became the hang-out for Paul Twedt and Terry Sorom for the next two years. I had lived with those two guys my sophomore year. Friday night became party night. One of the great memories is when Ruth Ann had too much wine one night.

Here is the story—and it was told many times over the years. I had to give blood on Saturday and I couldn't drink anything. So, Paul and Terry decided it was time I got to see what alcohol can do to a person. Ruth Ann and the two of them had seen me have too much alcohol on numerous occasions and now it was time for me to see Ruth Ann have too much. So they got a jug of Thunderbird wine for her and she drank most it. It worked—I had never seen her get tipsy. Then she goes and gets a roll of toilet paper and strings it all over the apartment—every room. Their plan worked—I spent most of Saturday morning cleaning toilet paper. Paul and Terry laughed their butts off. Their mission was accomplished. I don't think I ever saw her have that much again.

So over the years she would tell the story about me eating onion and beans and I would tell the story about her getting tipsy and spreading toilet paper.

You, Rhenee Grabau, Laurie Emery and 8 others

PeteandRuth Ann Bungum
12 April 2020

Ruth Ann standing on
beach in bathing suit

3 guys drinking beer

Comments

Phil Bungum ;~]

PeteandRuth Ann Bungum

Monday, April 13, 2020. More stories about Pete and Ruth Ann's two year stay in Decorah, 1960–1962.

A lot of things happened in 1961–1962 that were completely different from anything I had ever experienced. The biggest change was being married and living with Ruth Ann instead of two guys. The biggest change was I gained fifteen pounds—going from 150 to 165 pounds. I was now eating three meals a day, getting enough sleep and my body was getting used to a healthier daily routine. I wasn't carousing at Carolan's Bar like I had done the year before.

The other big change was I made the Dean's list with two As and three Bs. Another thing was I had an emergency appendectomy in March. The night before I had had severe stomach pains—Ruth Ann had called Doctor Hagen and had him come to our apartment. He asked me what my problem was and I told him I might have eaten some spoiled corn.

He asked me if I had pain before I ate.

I said I had some. His comment was a classic—I've never forgotten them. "Even a damn dog knows enough not to eat when he's not feeling well."

Good bedside manners, eh? Anyway, I had surgery the next day. When I came out of surgery, I guess I was screaming at him—threatening to do him bodily harm. Dr. Hagen told Ruth Ann that was pretty typical of patients coming out of ether and if she thought I was bad she should hear what some priests/ministers say when they come out of ether. The next day he told Ruth Ann it was a good thing he did surgery when he did because my appendix was about ready to burst.

In March of 1961 Ruth Ann had a big surprise for me—she said, "I think we're going to be parents—my period is late." She was right and it was a surprise. Dr. Bullard confirmed it and gave her a birthdate of late October. This was not part of the plan as far as getting my degree and getting a teaching job. But things worked out and our son (Bradley Peter) was born on November 2, 1961.

The other major event in 1961 happened on October 16. I had finished my school bus route and was walking back to our apartment. Ruth Ann and brother John were walking up to meet me. I was wondering why and then John spoke, "Some bad news today, Dad was killed at the sawmill in Chatfield."

I think my heart dropped to my feet and felt I like I had goose bumps all over me. My mind was racing over a whole lot of thoughts. My main one was how was Mom going to handle this. What I did next was walk back to the bus garage to tell my boss. Then we drove to Chatfield to be with the rest of the family. On the drive our Chevrolet did not sound right—it died when I pulled into the driveway. The family made arrangements to have visitation on Thursday night and the funeral service on Friday. I did not handle the funeral service well. Before the service I started gagging and couldn't stop. Brother Don helped settle me down. Dad was buried at West Saint Olaf Lutheran Church near Hayfield, Minnesota—this is where Dad was baptized, confirmed and married.

My final thoughts about Dad's passing. First, during the entire four days Ruth Ann handled the situation in a very strong way. Here she was, eight and a half months pregnant—people were worried about her going into labor from the stress. But she was too strong a person to let that happen. Her Dad had died four years before when she was a senior in high school. He was 52 when he died from cancer. She had been through it and knew how I was feeling. She was a pillar of strength for me.

I will finish this tomorrow.

Comments

Elsie Narveson You were so lucky to have Ruth Ann with you.

John Spilde I recognize that Dr Hagen name as he delivered me into the world on October 25, 1954. As a side note, my mom was packed in ice in September so I would not arrive early! A new hospital was later built and the old hospital was made into a nursing home, sooo,

I could end up in the same building as I was born in some day! ☺.
Sincerely, John

James Albrecht ENJOYING YOUR MEMORIES. KEEP THEM COMING.

Richard Stout What a life you led in your early teens. So much
drama…so many changes. I knew Er knew these stories. Thanks for
sharing, Pete.

PeteandRuth Ann Bungum

Tuesday, April 14, 2020. Final stories about Pete and Ruth Ann's stay in Decorah in 1961–1962.

The day before the funeral brother Don came with me to look for another car. My 1951 Chevy died when we got to Chatfield. We went to Gunderson Motors in Fountain and found the most favorite car we've ever owned.

It was a 1956 Buick Special, hardtop convertible, with a pink bottom and a white top. We bought it for $800 and the payments were $36 a month for thirty months. Making those payments wasn't going to be easy but in ten months I would be teaching and making big money! I thought when I started teaching, I'd have no problem paying our bills. What a wake-up call I got in ten months. We loved that car—it was such a smooth and comfortable ride and was definitely a big step up from a '51 Chevy.

I have a few final thoughts about Dad's death. When he died three of us boys were in college. Brother Chuck was at the University of Minnesota Dental School, John was a sophomore at Luther and I was a senior. I was wondering if we would be able to continue. But Mom talked to all three of us and assured us we could continue—she would continue to operate the nursing home and help us just as she and Dad had done.

Now I want to explain why I'm so grateful I went to Luther College.

First: When we got back to Decorah, I called my history professor at home on Sunday night because I had missed a big test on Friday. I told professor Leland I had had a tough time the last week. I told him my Dad was killed, my wife was eight and a half months pregnant and my car had died. But I was calling to ask him when I could make up the test. He listened and said something I have never forgotten. He said, "Pete, forget about that damn test—you have enough things on your mind without worrying about making up my history test. I'll give you a B, which is what you usually get." I gave him a heartfelt thank you—he was right. I did have enough on my mind and he knew that was one less thing for me to worry about and this would make me feel a little better.

Now the second reason I'm grateful I went to Luther: I went back to class on Monday and on Wednesday brother John and I got a notice we were to have a meeting with Doctor Ylvisaker, the President of Luther. We were to meet in his office the next afternoon at 2pm. The secretary escorted us into his office. First, he expressed his sympathy and asked if we would have any problem staying in school. He explained he had heard our father was killed from a friend. He then assured us we could continue at Luther if we could no longer afford to go. He said if that was the case, he would see to it that Luther would enable us to continue no matter what. Luther would help us financially so that we could graduate. We told him our mother had assured us we could continue at Luther—she would still be able to help us. We thanked him for his concern about our situation. This is a good example of why Luther College is such a wonderful place. To show such care and concern about two of their students is something you probably wouldn't see at a big university.

Here is one more example of Luther's caring for their people.

It was at the visitation on Thursday night. Many people came that night but the biggest surprise was when the Luther's treasurer, Mr. Kalsow and George Bachelder, the Financial Aid Director, came to the funeral home to express their sympathy to me and Ruth Ann and my family. Those were the two guys Ruth Ann worked for. This is just another example of what great people make up Luther College.

Now the next big thing to happen to Ruth Ann and me. Only seventeen days after Dad's death the biggest thing of all happened that would change our life forever. On November 1st, 1961, Ruth Ann told me she wasn't feeling well. She thought she had the flu, so she called Doctor Bullard. He told her that she didn't have the flu, but she was going to have a baby and that he would see her soon. At 4am she awakened me—she was having labor pains about five minutes apart. Being a rookie at this my first thought was I better start reading about home delivery. We went to the hospital about 6am. It was probably a little early, but Ruth Ann remembers me insisting we go—she finally consented. I don't think I would have been much good at home delivery—I don't think she felt I would be either. The next eleven hours involved her walking the halls and me rubbing her back. As the hours passed and the labor pains increased, she insisted more and more that I keep rubbing her lower back. She was taken into the delivery room around 4 pm. Doctor Bullard allowed me in the delivery room, but I would have to stand by her head. He was afraid I wouldn't be able to handle things from the other end. At 5:18 pm the baby emerged, and Doctor Bullard acted fast because the cord was wrapped around the baby's neck. He snipped that and we had a crying baby. It was a boy—I was happy. We went back to the room—the baby was brought to the new parents—we both got to hold him. I left about 9 pm—I went to the apartment and called the grandmas. Then I called brother John in his dorm and invited him to meet me at The Barb Restaurant to have a beer and a hamburger.

The next day we decided on a name. We had settled on two names—they were Gregory Norman or Bradley Peter.

We leaned toward Gregory at first because it would be the same initials as my Dad—G. N. Bungum. But the more we looked we decided he looked more like a Bradley than a Gregory. So Bradley Peter it was.

Two weeks after Brad's birth we got a call from the "Hatchet and Backslap Babysitting Agency." The two babysitters were Paul Twedt (Hatchet) and Terry Sorom (Backslap) my two roommates from our sophomore year.

They were looking for jobs and they said they would babysit the next Saturday so Ruth Ann and I could go a Luther basketball game. They showed up on time with a case of baby food as a gift for Brad. They had to change Brad's diaper during the night, and they had Brad laying on his back when Brad suddenly had to pee. He lets go with a powerful stream that hits Backslap right in the face. That was it—they went out of business that night.

Tomorrow—I graduate from Luther and get my first teaching job.

You, Laurie Emery, Angie Andersen Russell and 13 others

Comments

Deb Rickels Really enjoying your life story

Richard Stout Wow! Mark Twain did his early writing as serial chapters in magazines. These chapters could certainly entertain and enlighten folks who don't even know you.

PeteandRuth Ann Bungum

Wednesday, April 15, 2020. Pete and Ruth Ann leave Decorah in 1962.

I'm grateful I went to Luther.

I'm grateful for Dale Hackett.

After having a life-changing year in 1961 we headed for Anamosa, Iowa, in August 1962.

I had completed my two stints of student teaching and was ready to begin my teaching career. I had majored in history and political science. Even as a kid I was always interested in those fields and wanted to teach them. Luther's education department provided us with a list of vacancies. I started sending out letters and interviewed at four different schools.

The first was in Eau Claire, Wisconsin, the second was in a small town near Saint Cloud and the third was in western Iowa. The first two were NO but the third was a job offer. The job entailed teaching social studies to seventh, eighth and ninth graders. Plus, coaching football, basketball and track for all three grades. The pay was $4,200 a year. He offered me the job—thank God I turned it down thanks to my brother Don. He told me to forget it—he said I'd go nuts.

As I look back on my life I sometimes feel that God intervened. I say that because the next week I hit pay dirt when I got a phone call on the last Monday of April 1962. The call was from Dale Hackett, Principal of grades K-8 in Anamosa, Iowa. He asked if I could come for an interview at 2 PM. I said YES. Ruth Ann and I got a friend to care for Brad—then we headed the 120 miles south in our Buick Special.

Principal Dale was easy to talk to. He explained that Anamosa was consolidating with the two neighboring towns of Morley and Martelle. Therefore, Anamosa would be doubling the size of each grade from 60 to 120. They needed a person to teach five sections of 7th grade social studies and there would be no coaching. He said he wanted to hire me, but he had to get the superintendent's approval first. We met the superintendent and he told Dale to go ahead and offer me a contract. He asked if my wife was along and told me to go out and invite her in. I went to the car and told Ruth Ann, excitedly, that I had a job and Dale wants to meet you. We went in and Dale drew up the contract—I happily signed. My pay was to be $4,600 a year which was pretty normal for a beginning teacher in a small Midwest town in 1962. What a relief to have a teaching job. We had a happy ride home.

I need to praise Luther College once again. During the interview he admitted he called me because I was the only Luther student to apply and Luther had a great reputation for turning out good teachers. Sometimes I think the good Lord watches over you and keeps you from getting into situations where you don't belong. I think that happened this time because those other three jobs would not have been a good fit for me.

We went to Anamosa in July to look for an apartment. We rented an upstairs apartment in Martelle for $50 a month. It was above the post office—it had plenty of room, but it also had 12-foot ceilings. We stayed until Christmas and we moved because the fuel bill was killing our budget. We had to move.

Tomorrow I'll elaborate on the difficulty of trying to live on $310 a month.

You, Jan Miller and Sharon Bungum Shupe

Comments

Brad Bungum PeteandRuth Ann Bungum, Dad, you should link in the Luther College FB page to your stories… I'll see if I can help you with that. They should add you to their marketing and admissions team!! :-)

PeteandRuth Ann Bungum

Thursday, April 16, 2020. Memories of Pete and Ruth Ann in Martelle—1962 to 1964.

Some good and some not so good.

I got my first paycheck of $309 on September 18th. When we paid our first month's bills, we realized we wouldn't be living a life of luxury. Our rent was $50 ($259 left), car payment was $36 ($223 left), food was about $80 ($140 left), plus all the utility bills—electricity, garbage, phone, water, and fuel oil.

Wow, reality was setting in fast. By November we were getting our first fuel oil bills for that big apartment. The first one was $40, and it wasn't even cold yet. Ruth Ann and I talked it over and decided we couldn't afford to spend the winter in that apartment. We found an older house two blocks away that had a fuel oil space heater. Our thought was we wouldn't have to heat the upstairs so it would be a lot cheaper to heat three rooms with eight-foot ceilings. The rent was also $50. We moved at Christmas vacation with the help of teacher colleagues.

Now for a fun story—Brad becomes famous. The day before vacation the junior high had a Christmas program. We took 13-month old Brad to the concert—he had learned to talk quite well. He was close to being potty trained by that time but that night, to be safe, we put diapers on him. Immediately after the chorus finished singing "Silent Night" there was dead silence. Brad had been telling Ruth Ann in a quiet voice that he had to go potty.

She told him to go in his diaper. During the dead silence he screamed as loud as he possibly could, "I HAVE TO GO POTTY." The entire auditorium erupted in uncontrollable laughter, including the seventh and eighth graders in the chorus. In front of everyone Ruth Ann carried Brad to the doorway and had the principal take him to the restroom. People who were at that program still talk about it fifty to sixty years later and they know the exact words. So, Brad became famous at the tender age of thirteen months.

We spent Christmas vacation in Minnesota and then returned to our new home. Ruth Ann was by now four months pregnant with kid number two. We soon realized our new residence was not very warm especially for a pregnant woman and a thirteen-month boy. Our space heater was not putting out much heat. One night I put a thermometer on the kitchen floor, and it read 47 degrees in the morning. I told our lady janitor at school about it and she said she would have her husband take a look. He came and cleaned the filter—that helped, and it did produce more heat but still not enough to be comfortable. Ruth Ann had to have a heavy sweatshirt on and she put Brad in warm clothes.

Another story about that house happened the next year (1964) at Christmas vacation. We had returned from Minnesota, went in our house—it was cold with no heat at all. The space heater was dead and would not light. I went down to the cellar and I found out why the space heater wasn't working. The tank, which held 100 gallons of fuel oil, was supported by four steel legs. One of them had broken. The tank had partially tipped and had broken the nozzle off the front of the tank. The result was about 75 gallons of fuel oil had soaked into the cracks in the old concrete floor.

Ruth Ann asked, "What should we do?" I told her I have no choice but to walk up to the landlord and talk to him. He lived a blocked away. I explained to him what happened. He was not the least bit sympathetic. He insinuated it should be my responsibility to fix it. I told him it was his house, his fuel tank, his cracked basement floor. I told him I had no money to fix it and wouldn't do it even if I did. I told him I make $310 a month and can barely afford to feed my family. He was surprised at that and thought teachers were making a lot more money than that. Then he made one of the most all-time stupid statements I ever heard in my lifetime.

He said, and these are his exact words, "If you had never gone to Minnesota for Christmas this wouldn't have happened." I couldn't believe it. I asked him if what he was saying was that if we had stayed home and I stayed in the basement watching the fuel tank that would have prevented it from breaking. My thoughts were "How could a human think like that?" I got up and was ready to leave when I told him, "It is your responsibility as the landlord to repair the tank and pay for the refill." Then I said, "I have a wife at home, a two-year-old and an eight-month-old and they don't have any heat tonight." I left and slammed the door. The next day he fixed the tank and paid for the refill.

Tomorrow I'm going to write about Ruth Ann's pregnancy with Carron.

You, Bret Lewison, Rhenee Grabau and 5 others

Comments

Bret Lewison PeteandRuth Ann Bungum, I recall Bradley (Brad Bungum) yelling, "I have to go potty" a number of times when we roomed together our freshman year at Luther. I always had thought that he'd just had too much to drink. Now it all makes sense.

Brad Bungum Good one Hound, Bret Lewison... :-)

Tim Bungum Pete: I swear that I remember visiting Martelle. Did you live about one block east and one block south of "downtown"?

Bret Lewison Tim Bungum I think that describes an area covering close to 50% of Martelle depending on what you count as "downtown," so there's a pretty good chance you're right.

Brad Bungum Tim Bungum is correct in the location...

> **PeteandRuth Ann Bungum** Tim we lived three houses north of the school and one block west and about one block south of Main Street. The house had curved windows on the upstairs. You couldn't have been very old when you were there. I don't remember you being there

Carlene Vavricek Pete, do you remember your address when you lived in Martelle? Just curious since I've probably driven by it 100 times over the years.

PeteandRuth Ann Bungum No I don't remember the address but I can describe the location. We lived about three houses north of the school—it had curved windows on the upstairs—I think they are still there.

Tim Bungum I have looked on line too. Has the school been torn down? I looked at place at 212 South street that has kind of a turret.

PeteandRuth Ann Bungum no the school is still there—it is now a warehouse for a construction firm

PeteandRuth Ann Bungum

Friday, April 17, 2020.

I am grateful for April 24, 1963.

Ruth Ann told me in September she thought she was pregnant. The doctor told her she definitely was pregnant and gave her a delivery date of late April.

Ruth Ann had a tough pregnancy with Carron. The baby kept flipping and Doctor Randolph thought she might be a breach baby. In the early morning of April 24, 1963, Ruth Ann was not feeling well. She called the doctor at his home. He was gone but his wife took the call and said, "I think you're ready to have a baby and you should go to the hospital right now." She should've known because she had had eight kids.

I called my principal to line up a sub. We made it to the hospital by 9:30 and twelve hours later we had a baby girl. Doctor Randolph would not let me in the delivery room. The baby entered this world at 9:30 PM. I got to see our baby at 10:00. I couldn't believe the massive amount of black hair she had. Brad was born blonde and nearly bald and our new baby was the opposite. We were happy it was a girl because now we had one of each and that would be it for us in the child-producing department.

When I went to bed that night I wrestled with a name. We had considered Kathryn Jolene and Stephanie Malone. But I thought it would nice to have another Karen Bungum, in honor of my sister who died in 1944.

However, I had one change. I wanted to spell it "Carron" instead of "Karen" and pronounce it Car-on rather than Care-en. The next day after school I took Myrtle (Ruth Ann's mom) and Brad to see the new baby. Ruth Ann took her mom to the nursery to see her new granddaughter and asked her to pick which of the three babies was ours. She picked the other two and couldn't believe that little black-haired baby was her granddaughter. Ruth Ann and I discussed the name situation—she thought Carron Sue was a good idea. So

Carron, when you read this you can blame your Dad for your rather unique name.

Carron's first six months were rough. She could not keep her formula down and would throw up frequently. The milk coming up and out was like water coming out of a hose. She would cry a lot, night and day. She was obviously in pain and it was hard on us as parents. We would take turns getting up at night to try to settle her down. Ruth Ann felt she had colic. But the doctor disagreed—he told Ruth Ann that if Carron was getting enough to eat, she wouldn't be vomiting and crying all the time. We switched doctors at that point, she was six months old. The new doctor told Ruth Ann babies could have colic until they were a year or more old. He gave Ruth Ann a liquid medicine and told her to put one drop in each bottle of formula. It was a miracle—it settled her stomach down and she quit vomiting and started sleeping all night.

It was sad to think what Carron had gone through when it could have been prevented. It was a big relief for the two of us also—now we could get some sleep.

You, Angie Andersen Russell, Carron Sue Bungum and 17 others

Jan Siebels Carron Bungum! You have a birthday soon!

PeteandRuth Ann Bungum

Saturday, April 18, 2020. More memories about Pete and Ruth Ann's journey through 59 years of marriage.

After Carron's birth we decided we did not want any more kids. In 1960 a birth control pill had been developed for women—it became part of Ruth Ann's life for the next 25 years.

In 1963 I signed another contract to teach in Anamosa. The salary would be $4,693—that was a whopping raise of $93 dollars for the year, not per month. It amounted to $7.75 a month.

Ruth Ann decided to get a job in Cedar Rapids—she was hired by the Bjornson Insurance Agency for $1.75 an hour. She did it for eight months and then quit. By the time we paid the babysitter and paid for the gas we netted one dollar a week. It was not worth it. She started doing babysitting to bring in some extra dollars.

When Carron was born Brad was almost 18 months. He was starting to talk a lot but there were a couple of words/phrases he had trouble with. When he wanted Mom or Dad to fix something he could not simply say, "Fix it." He came up with ti-ka-ti-ka-it-ka—we finally figured out that he wanted something fixed. Another one was he could not say his sister's name. So his name for her was "Hang Sue."

On November 22, 1963, my principal, Ted Hungerford, came in my room and whispered in my ear, "President Kennedy has been shot and killed in Dallas, Texas." Ruth Ann heard the news at the insurance office where she was working. I was stunned and spent the rest of the afternoon talking to my students. On Sunday I was watching TV and saw Jack Ruby shoot Lee Harvey Oswald.

1964 was a pretty good year. I thought I was doing a better job of teaching. Ruth Ann was bringing in some spending money. I got a summer job selling World Book encyclopedias and did well. I trained for a week and then we were on our own. The week of training was great. We had to memorize the sales pitch but the most important thing we had to learn was how to overcome excuses and objections. We learned about four or five comebacks for every excuse the customer could come up with as a reason not to buy. Typical excuses would be that they couldn't afford it, or they wouldn't use them, and they'll just gather dust, or they would buy them next year, or their kids could use the encyclopedias at school, etc.

After three days of training I knew the sales pitch well enough and made my first call. I called on the banker in Martelle and believe it or not I made my first sale—I made $60.00. The next day I was pretty proud to report to the class that I had made a sale. I was the first one in the class of eight to do so. We actually had five products to sell—the encyclopedias, Childcraft books for kids, an atlas, a dictionary and a learning machine. That summer I sold thirteen sets of encyclopedias, seven Childcrafts, two dictionaries and two learning machines. I made $650 which was equal to two months of teacher pay. My most memorable day was when I made $105. I was ecstatic, I had never made $100 in a day and it was a great feeling.

The rest of 1964 was pretty uneventful for us. I taught my third year and Ruth Ann continued babysitting so we had some spending money for fun. A few things happened that I'll mention.

Our wonderful Buick that we loved bit the dust. We were visiting some friends—they had a couple of preschoolers also. When we adults were visiting in the house Brad and their two young ones unscrewed the gas cap and all three of them were pouring sand into the gas tank. Needless to say, our Buick couldn't run anymore—sand is not a fuel. We ended up draining the gas tank and managed to drive it to Cedar Rapids at 30 miles per hour. We pulled into Zimmerman Ford and bought a new Ford Falcon.

In December we left Martelle and moved to Anamosa where we found a small house. We decided to move because we thought we could save money on heating costs and it would be more appealing to live in a town of 4,500 instead of 450.

1965 is a year of big change for Pete and Ruth Ann.

You, Erland Christensen, Yrsa Thom Chris and 13 others

Comments

Jill Darrow Keep the stories coming. And Brad Bungum, make sure you are printing them for you and Carron!

Tammy Feist Sletten Hey Mr. PeteandRuth Ann Bungum and Brad Bungum, I might of hit or ran over a few things, but I always knew to put gas in the tank. (I'm blocking out that little detail about being a preschooler) 😃

Rhonda Koppenhaver I am truly enjoying these stories. Keep them coming but especially the ones about Brad. We have a class reunion coming. They will give us something to talk about. Lol. Just kidding Brad.

Phil Bungum ;~]

Pat McQuaid Schoon We look forward to your stories, Pete—keep them coming!!!

PeteandRuth Ann Bungum

Sunday, April 19, 2020. The 59-year journey continues for Pete and Ruth Ann in 1965–1966.

I'm grateful for these two years.

The school year (1965) went smoothly from January to May. I really liked teaching and was improving every year. I don't think I would have ever left teaching if I had gotten paid more. I was 24 years old and had heard a lot of teachers in their 30s and 40s saying they wished they had tried something else. I decided that if I was ever going to try something different now was the time to do it. The longer I waited the harder it was going to be. I didn't want to be one of those teachers complaining in later years that I wish I had done something else.

So that is what I did. I interviewed at 3M in Minneapolis, the Mayo Clinic in Rochester and at Sears in downtown Chicago. Sears hired me. I was assigned to Rochester. I would be a manager trainee in the men's clothing department and my salary would be $6,000 a year. The money sounded good as I had already signed my contract in Anamosa to teach my fourth year for $5,300. I accepted the Sears offer—I resigned and we moved to Rochester in early July. I started on July 28, 1965.

The first thing I learned was how to run the cash register. The second thing I learned was how to measure a suit. That included measuring inseams and pin them, how to take in the waist and seat and pin them, how to pin the cuff length and how to pin the suit coat if it needed adjusting. I enjoyed selling but many other things about Sears I didn't like.

For example, I was to work Monday, Thursday and Friday from 12:30 to 9:30 and Saturday from 8:30 to 5:30—Tuesday was my day off. I soon found out what corporate America was all about. The first month I took my day off. Then I was called into the head office and told the following. I was told that I better start showing up on my day off or I would have a short career at Sears. I was to work at least four hours on my day off to show that I was dedicated, or I would never move up the corporate ladder. And if any union organizers came in, we were to lie and tell them we worked 40 hours a week.

The second thing that upset me was missing a golf outing for all five of us trainees. I didn't go—the next day I was called into the head office—he asked me why I didn't go golfing. I told him we had a party for Ruth Ann's mother on her 60th birthday. His exact words to me were "Don't let your family interfere with your career." I knew right then that I had no future with Sears. I was thinking that teaching school wasn't so bad after all. I was going to go to back to teaching school even if I made less money.

I worked at Sears until the end of February. I enrolled at Winona State College to begin working on my Masters degree—it was forty miles away but I arranged to find a ride with other guys going there. Ruth Ann went back to work at the Mayo Clinic—we found daycare for Brad and Carron. I managed to get the spring quarter in plus summer school. Then I contacted Luther College and told them to send me job offerings for teaching positions. We wanted to move away from Rochester—and go back to Iowa. I found an opening in Dubuque—I applied and got the job for 1966–67. We moved in August. I taught there for one year.

Then something happened that changed our life forever. Some of my old colleagues from Anamosa called me and said they were having a party and we should come. Anamosa was only 45 miles from Dubuque. At the party was an old colleague, Lyle Wilharm, who was now principal. About midnight he took me aside and asked me if I wanted to come back to Anamosa and get my old job back. The guy who took my place was leaving and I could have my old job if I wanted it. I took Ruth Ann into another room and told her what Lyle had said. She was in total agreement. I told Lyle we would definitely like to come back. He said the contract would be in the mail tomorrow—just sign it and get it back to me by next Tuesday. I did and it was going to be our home for the rest of our lives. So, the rest of my posts about our journey through our 59 years will be from Anamosa.

Some reflections on 1965–1967.

Am I glad I left teaching and tried corporate America? The answer is a resounding YES. I did what a lot of people would like to do and that is to try something different in their life, especially at a young age which wouldn't mess up an entire career. I got it out of my mind that life was greener on the other side of the fence. Secondly, it is rewarding and easier on your health if you have a job you like even if it means making less money. Third, I came to the realization that I could make a bigger difference in the world teaching kids than selling underwear and suits. So back to Anamosa we went for the second time. Over the next 33 years I would teach and Ruth Ann would work at the Reformatory for three years, church secretary for eight years and as a Deputy Treasurer in the Jones County courthouse for twenty-one years.

I'm grateful for we tried something different at a young age. I'm also grateful we went to that party in Anamosa in April of 1967.

Brad Bungum **Love**

PeteandRuth Ann Bungum

Monday, April 20, 2020.

I'm grateful we moved back to Anamosa in 1967.

Our two years away from Anamosa was a great learning experience for me. Teaching in a school the size of Dubuque was not my cup of tea. Having 33 kids in all five classes was too many. There were 12 sections in each grade for a total of 1,200. That was the result of the baby boomers coming through the schools at that time because of the millions of GIs who had come home after WWII. By March I had decided I was going to leave Dubuque and go to a smaller school. Then that party in Anamosa fulfilled my desire. I was in the right place at the right time.

I also learned that corporate America was not my cup of tea either. So things couldn't have worked out any better.

But I'm glad I had those two years to get my life and Ruth Ann's life straightened out so we could settle down and be in one place longer than 2–3 years. And we did settle down and stayed in Anamosa for the next 53 years. Ruth Ann was my partner all the way until January 9, 2020.

In May we went to Anamosa to find a place to live. This would be our ninth place to live in our seven years of marriage—and it would be our home for the next twenty years. We found a house we liked. It was 24' x 24', with three floors, three bedrooms, a full bathroom on top floor, kitchen and living room on the main floor and family room and a utility room in the basement. It was perfect for our family and the price was right. Kay and Neal Dougherty sold it to us for $13,750 on a contract for deed with a monthly payment of $90. We had to pay $500 down and could move in by August 15th. We moved in August 18th, 1967. It would be our home until October, 1987.

School started on August 28th. I was introduced as "We now have the return of the Prodigal Son, Pete Bungum." It brought a good laugh.

I was anxious to get started. I had several things to look forward to. My classes sizes would be down to 25–27 students and I would have only one preparation instead of three and most important I was happy to be back in Anamosa, Iowa.

Brad was five years old and was ready to start kindergarten. The first two days Ruth Ann walked him to school, only a half-block from our house. The third day he went by himself. Brad didn't cry but his mother did. It was one of those life-changing events for parents, especially for mothers.

For the next 13 years he would be at Anamosa schools and no longer Momma's little boy. His teacher was Miss Chapman. He liked her, liked school and was off to a good start in his school career. In 1967 Ruth Ann turned 27 on April 4, I was 27 on November 20, Carron was 4 on April 24 and Brad was six on November 2.

One thing I forgot to mention about Carron's birth was I had to pay for my sub. In May I got a letter from the school telling me that I hadn't paid my sub. It said I owed her $12. I had no idea I was supposed to pay. So, I sent her the $12. Now my take home pay went from $309 to $297. No wonder teachers wanted to form a union.

Dean Rickels, Bob Hines and 7 others

PeteandRuth Ann Bungum
April 20

This is Ruth Ann's urn. A fellow church member, Barry Anderson, made it for us. It is on the coffee table. We can watch TV together now.

You, Erland Christensen, Angie Andersen Russell and 33 others

Comments

Kandace Reinhardt I'm sure Ruthie is there watching TV with you ♡

Phil Bungum Hug hug

Deb Rickels Hugs

PeteandRuth Ann Bungum

Tuesday, April 21, 2020. Pete and Ruth's journey through life.

This story is about our life in 1968. There were many memorable things taking place this year.

Carron started kindergarten. Yes, Ruth Ann walked her the first two days. On the third day Carron went on her own and you guessed it—her mother cried. Her baby daughter was gone from home to be gone during the day for the next 13 years. She had Miss Chapman also. Carron liked school and did well. I have a good story to tell about her next year in first grade. I'll share that tomorrow.

Brother John came home from Vietnam. He had spent a year in Vietnam in the Army Security Agency. He was located near the DMZ in a mile square base protected by Marines. He did not see combat but was mortared several times. When they were mortared during the night, he had to leave the barracks in a hurry and go man a machine gun to defend the base against a possible attack. It never happened, thank God. He was discharged a little early so he could come home and go to the University of Iowa to get his Master's in economics. I'm grateful he came home unharmed.

Iowa City was only a half-hour drive from Anamosa. He came to visit often and Ruth Ann told me several times that she hoped he didn't turn out to be an Uncle Lewie because she wasn't going to take care of him when he got old.

In the summer I went back to Winona State College to finish my master's degree. I took my final exam and passed. It was a four-hour ordeal where I was given five questions, I had to pick three of the five and pass two of the three, which I did. I was grateful I now had my Masters. It helped me make a lot more money over the next 31 years.

We signed Brad up for a T-ball team. His athletic career had begun—he was really pretty good.

After my master's was over, we were ready for a vacation. So, we went to Denver to see my sister Betty and husband Bill. They showed us a great time. We visited Pike's Peak, Red Rock, Central City,

Colorado Springs and went camping in Estes Park. We headed home after a week. We had $20 left to make it from Estes Park to Anamosa.

The plan was to drive straight through. We almost didn't make it—because when we stopped to get gas in Nebraska a lady tried to cheat me. The gas was $5, I gave her my last $20. She hands me $1.00 and $5.00 bills with the $5.00 bill on top. Thank God I looked at it and caught her. I told her I needed a ten-dollar bill and not a one. She didn't even apologize—she knew what she was trying to do. If I hadn't spotted her deception, we would have had only $6.00 for gas and food for the last 400 miles. We made it to Anamosa by 2 AM.

A couple of newsworthy events in 1968 were Nixon and Humphrey running for president, Martin Luther King and Bobby Kennedy getting killed and Carron and Diane Norton making history on our street.

Before school started a funny thing happened with Carron and her friend, Diane Norton. Our neighbor down the street had his sidewalk decorated with some naughty words. The Betty and Bing Norton family lived around the corner from us. They had a five-year-old daughter named Diane and we had Carron, who was also five. They had become best friends. One day they ran in the back door and told Ruth Ann that "if a man comes up here and tells you we wrote on his sidewalk, don't believe him." They had chalk dust all over their hands and some mighty guilty looks on their faces. Ruth Ann walked the girls down to the neighbor to see the damages. They had written "shit" on every section of the concrete. Ruth Ann marched the girls up to Diane's house and the two mothers had a talk. They gave each girl a scrub brush, a bucket filled with water and detergent and put them to work erasing the many "shits" from the sidewalk.

Ruth Ann asked them how they knew what to write. Diane knew how to spell it and Carron knew how to write it, so they got the job done. That was really good coordination of using each other's skills and talents to accomplish a task. Carron and Diane remained friends through school and into adulthood. I'm grateful for good/funny memories like this one.

You, Angie Andersen Russell, Tim Bungum and 13 others

Comments

Steve Boyer The first of many of our adventures throughout the years! Many happy memories!!—Diane

Bret Lewison I'm impressed, not only with the coordinated spelling & writing effort of two kindergartners (not something Brad and I could have pulled off in any legible form for quite a few more years), but the proactive damage control attempt shows some pretty advanced thinking. For better or worse, a couple of high functioning 5-year olds.

PeteandRuth Ann Bungum

Wednesday, April 22, 2020. Pete and Ruth Ann's journey through 59 years.

I'm going to start today's post with a memory from 1966. I forgot this story about Brad. Yesterday I wrote about Carron and her naughty word on our neighbor's sidewalk. Today I will write about Brad's potty mouth at age four.

We were living in an upstairs apartment in Rochester at the time. Brad was playing outside with his cousin Tim, who was eight years old. They must have had a disagreement because all of the sudden, we heard Brad yell as loud as he could, "Tim, you fucker."

Brad's grandma was with us and she heard it too. Her reaction was one of shock just like it was for us. At first, we thought we heard wrong but almost immediately he yelled it again. I told Brad to come inside and Ruth Ann and I took him in the bedroom and asked him where he heard that word. He said the neighbor boy used it all the time. We didn't yell but calmly told him it was a naughty word and he should never use it again. To be honest, I don't think we ever heard him use it again.

I'm up to 1969 in our journey through 59 years of marriage. I ended up working as a painter for over a month. Paul Lewison, a teacher colleague, asked me if I wanted to help him and two other teachers (Bob Algoe and Doug Albertson) paint the nine buildings on a farm. I agreed. We got paid $3 an hour. When done I made $550.

We used that money to take a vacation to Arizona. We had seen advertisements from Gulf American Land Corporation. For $150 (for each of us) they would fly us to Tucson for a three-night, four-day stay if we would listen to a sales pitch about buying a lot in the desert. We decided to do it. Our friends, Bob and Grace Story, agreed to watch Brad and Carron. We flew out of Des Moines and landed in Tucson. Gulf American showed us a great time by taking us on bus tours of the major attractions in Tucson. Their employees were so friendly and helpful.

That ended on day three. Day three was sales pitch day. They took us on a bus tour to a look-out in the desert where the lots were. They kept us a mile away from the city they were supposedly building. We could see buildings but couldn't tell if they were real or not. They told us we couldn't get any closer because the road wasn't finished. We went back to their office and as we walked into the sales room the sales reps were lined waiting for their assigned prey. We were assigned to a man.

The first thing he did was show us video of their future city. Then the CEO talked to the entire group. He assured us it would be a great investment—it was a "can't miss deal." Then the sales pitch began. We noticed right away the previous friendliness was gone. He was intimidating and downright nasty. We said NO. They wanted $1,300 for a small lot and $2,500 for a big lot. He got sick of us saying NO so he gets up and sends a woman to try and get us to change our mind—we still said NO. She left and sent over a third person— we still said NO. Thank God we said NO.

In a couple of years Gulf American was sued for fraud and it went bankrupt. The people who bought ended up with a worthless piece of Arizona sand. Other than the sales pitch the trip was a great time.

We traded our Ford Falcon for a 1969 Plymouth Fury III. It was a hardtop with a red body, white top and white wall tires. It had an automatic transmission and air conditioning. And it would move, and I drove it that way. I got picked up for speeding twice in the next three years.

The biggest change in 1969 happened to Ruth Ann. She applied for a job at the State Reformatory. She was hired and was to be the secretary for the Reformatory doctor. The hospital was inside the walls, so she had to be escorted everyday by a guard while walking to the hospital. She was not allowed to wear slacks, so she had a few catcalls while walking.

Ruth Ann had to be at work by 7am, so that meant I had to get the kids ready for school. Taking care of breakfast was no problem but doing something with Carron's hair was a problem. My fingers were not made to do anything with a seven-year-old's hair. Often times I made a pigtail higher on one side than the other. Carron and I have had some good laughs when we talk about it now.

We made the kids watch Neal Armstrong walking on the moon even if they didn't want to.

Brother John got a job teaching economics at the University of Wisconsin in Platteville. Ruth Ann was happy and relieved that John probably wouldn't be an Uncle Lewie after all.

Brad Bungum A few comments Pops. You're getting into territory now where I remember most of it—makes it even more fun and interesting! Cousin Tim Bungum was only 4 years older than me, but I'm sure that didn't lessen the impact of my trash mouth on Gramma, or you. Tim was probably used to it by that time :-)

Brad Bungum Had you bought that AZ land back in the '60s, you probably could have retired at 50 instead of 60...where was it located? I for sure remember you trying to do Carron Sue Bungum Carron's hair during those days when mom was off to work early... some days she was cross-eyed, with one pigtail being tighter than the other...you did your best :-)

Mark Blattie Mom washed my mouth out with soap and pepper one time after I swore, in retrospect, I am convinced that the punishment backfired:)

Terry Trogstad I remember that boxy Falcon and the snazzy Plymouth! It made me buy a Plymouth convertible myself.

Rhenee Grabau Uncle Pete, I do remember you telling my parents about Carron's naughty word on the sidewalk. If I remember correctly it was "shit." And I can't believe that Brad ever swore! 😄

Brad Bungum LOL cuz Rhenee Grabau!! Yes, it was "shit" that Carron and Dianne wrote (see yesterday's post). As for me, I've more than made up for Carron Carron Sue Bungum over the years... I think Dad's losing some of his memory when it comes to my mouth :-). Or maybe it's only that I swear when it comes to the Hawks playing poorly, or politics, and he gives me a free pass on those two categories LOL!

PeteandRuth Ann Bungum

Thursday, April 23, 2020. Pete and Ruth Ann's journey through 59 years of married life—today's post is their life in 1970.

Ruth Ann had a full-time job at the Reformatory. In the early 1970s penal philosophy was to get well-behaved inmates into the community as much as possible. Ruth Ann and I tried to do our part.

She worked with inmates at the prison hospital. She got to know the inmates as human beings and not as hardcore criminals. We had two inmates come to our home for Sunday dinner on two occasions. Of course, a guard escorted them and ate with us. The inmates were Tom and Robert. Tom was in for arson—Robert was in for armed robbery.

Tom was a pathetic human being and had had a tough life. He had been adopted as a young child and when his adoptive parents realized his limited intelligence, they rejected him to the point of abuse. Ruth Ann read, in his psychological history, that as a teenager he started burning garages and would masturbate as they burned. He never burned a house or hurt anyone. Tom was white, 21 years old, had a slight build, an unattractive pimply face, a low-level IQ and was a bed wetter. He didn't have a lot going for him, but he did have a good sense of humor. Tom was perfect prey for the hardcore inmates for harassment and sexual exploitation, so he was given protection 24/7 by having a cell in the hospital and working there.

Ruth Ann was nice to Tom. She worked with him every day and would not talk down to him and would joke with him. She would tell him about her kids and family and tried to make him feel like he was a worthwhile human being. She was probably one of the few decent women Tom had ever met. I think Tom looked at Ruth Ann like the mother he never had. When Tom came to our house, he was fun to talk to and joke with. Tom was released in 1973 and worked for a local farmer as a hired man. Carl, the farmer, had been a guard and knew Tom and was willing to give him a second chance to go straight. The sad news is Tom started stealing from Carl and forging checks. Carl told us later that he felt the only place Tom could function was in a protected setting like the Reformatory. We don't know what happened to Tom.

Robert, age 20, the other inmate to come to our house, was an African American from Des Moines. He told Ruth Ann he got into alcohol and drugs as a teenager and that's what did him in. One night, while high on drugs, he committed armed robbery. He told her he didn't remember the crime because he was so high. He obviously had not been an angel because he owned a pistol. He did tell Ruth Ann he was no angel. Robert had a good personality, a good sense of humor, a nice smile and was easy to talk to. He had a lot more going for him than Tom.

The last thing we heard about him was that he was released, went back to Des Moines and did the same thing—he went back to the Reformatory to rejoin Tom. So much for Ruth Ann's efforts to rehabilitate!!

Another inmate we met at a Reformatory J. C. Banquet was Darrell. He sat with us at the banquet and started telling us about his background. He told us he used to run "white lightning" in North Carolina—he did it for ten years. The more we laughed the wilder his stories got. Ruth Ann had read his psychological report. He had been diagnosed as a habitual liar. One day Ruth Ann and a guard kept track of his stories and when they added up the years, he would be 124 years old.

He was also a quick-change artist. One day, using play money, Darrell showed her how to do it. She was so confused by his fast actions that he ripped her out of her money in less than a minute. Darrell was released on work release to go to Mason City. His orders were no drinking, be on time every day for work and no leaving Mason City. He worked the first week but on his first Friday night he started drinking and went to Minnesota to continue his drunken binge. He didn't show up for work until the next Thursday—he got fired. His parole officer revoked his work release and sent him back to the Reformatory. Darrell complained he hadn't been treated fairly. He said, "All I did was go out and have a few beers." What a guy!!

Ruth Ann knew America's most famous serial killer. John Wayne Gacy, who killed 33 boys in Chicago, was at the Reformatory in 1970 and 1971. He had committed a crime in Waterloo, that's what got him sent to Anamosa. Gacy was the head inmate chef and a model inmate. He served Ruth Ann her food every day when she ate in the prison dining room. When released he moved to Chicago and his killings began in 1978.

We had a special wedding in 1970. After 12 years of being a widow, Ruth Ann's mother (Myrtle) remarried. She married the local plumbing and heating guy in Fountain. His name was Ed Meyer. He had lost his wife to cancer in 1967. We don't know if Myrtle planned it or not but in 1969 she called Ed to fix a plumbing problem. Ed came and something more than plumbing repair took place—they were dating shortly thereafter. Myrtle was 57 and Ed was 59. They would have 21 years together. Good for them.

In 1970 another event took place that became part of my life. We had a demonstration at school about YOGA. I was so impressed I bought their booklet. I've been doing yoga stretching exercises and breathing exercises ever since. I do yoga every day.

One more memory from 1970 is about Carron. She was in first grade. She loved school and she would imitate the teacher. We would hear her pretend she was the teacher. She would say, "Now students, what is 2 and 2? [And in a loud voice she would continue) And Johnny, if you don't shut your mouth, I'll kick you out of here." I guess Johnny was a real pain. It was absolutely hilarious to listen to her. Ruth Ann and I would laugh our butts off. I'm grateful for good memories—we had a lot in 1970.

Carron Sue Bungum, Yrsa Thom Chris and 15 others

Comments

Rhenee Grabau I so love this. Uncle Pete, how do you remember all of these details? And bless Ruthann's heart for spending time listening to those men.

PeteandRuth Ann Bungum Rhenee Grabau Thanks Rhenee. I remember many but I wrote about many of these events in my autobiography that I wrote from 2003 to 2006 plus looking at old photo albums.

Elsie Narveson You did have a variety of memories. Some tragic and some happy and fun

Richard Stout I love your stories.

Pat McQuaid Schoon It's especially interesting to hear about your and Ruth's interactions with the people who crossed your paths throughout the years. You've probably got some priceless stories about your students, too???

Carlene Vavricek Love reading your memories Pete!

Pat Cooley So fun reading all your memories...luv it!

PeteandRuth Ann Bungum

Friday, April 24, 2020. Pete and Ruth Ann's journey through 59 years.

The year is 1971.

This was good year for us. We had more money than ever before, so it was time to take a big vacation. We planned a three-week vacation to the west coast. Our goal was to visit my two roommates from Luther College.

Since Ruth Ann was working at the Reformatory, we could afford to do things we had never done before. In early July we headed for Huntington Beach, California to see Paul Twedt.

Our first stop was Kansas City. We went to a Kansas City Royals baseball game. The next day we went to Oklahoma City. We cooled off in the pool that night. It had been a hot drive to Oklahoma City. The most frequent words I heard from the kids was "Max high, Dad." That meant the air conditioning. The next day we stayed in Gallup, New Mexico. The fourth day we entered Arizona and had a great time. We toured the Painted Desert in the morning and the Grand Canyon in the afternoon.

I had a problem. When looking over the canyon I got so woozy I had to leave and go back to the car. I thought I was going to pass out. That night we stayed in Kingman, Arizona. The next day we drove to Needles and stopped to get gas. Thank God the attendant found a leak in the radiator hose and replaced it. We were ready to cross the Mojave Desert and I don't like to think what would have happened to us if he hadn't found it. Sometimes I think the good Lord looks over us. We made it to Los Angeles and with Ruth Ann as my navigator we drove to Twedt's house by late afternoon.

We spent a week with Twedts. Paul and Sharon had a list of activities for us. In the next week we went to Disneyland, spent a day in Tijuana (we bought Brad a guitar), a day at the beach and numerous get-togethers with their friends. The highlight was when Paul, Sharon, Ruth Ann and I took a three-day trip to Las Vegas.

Their friends took care of Brad and Carron. We had a ball in Vegas. We visited Hoover Dam, did some gambling, saw Engelbart Humperdinck at the Riviera and saw another show at the Palomino nightclub. The most exciting thing for Sharon and Ruth Ann was seeing Engelbart.

Then we returned to Twedts—the next day we went to the beach. It was a beautiful California day. I should have known better, but I spent six hours on the beach with no protection for my skin. Since I am a light skinned Norwegian, I was asking for big trouble. That evening I ate dinner, feeling okay. Then I went to bed and woke up at 1 AM. I was sick, very sick. I had chills and was vomiting. I was getting sore rapidly. I was up most of the night and by morning I was so sore from sunburn I could hardly sit, walk or have clothes on. I was pretty much disabled that day.

The next day we left and headed north to Oregon. It had been a wonderful week of fun and reminiscing and we hated to leave but we had stayed long enough. Paul and Sharon had been great hosts, but it was time to drive to Portland and see Terry and Suzanne Sorom. Terry was a Doctor and the Twedts were both teachers.

The day we left Twedts I was still so sore I could hardly get in the driver's seat without extreme pain. Once I got in, I was okay to drive. We drove north on Highway 1, the coastal highway, to San Jose and stayed. The next day we toured San Francisco seeing Fisherman's Wharf, driving down Lombard Street (the most crooked street in the world) and taking a boat tour around Alcatraz Prison. Ruth Ann sent her inmate friends a postcard saying, "Wish you were here." She heard later they got a kick out of it. In the afternoon we crossed the Golden Gate Bridge and headed for Ukiah. We took our time and saw the giant redwoods, including the one big enough to drive through. We stayed in Crescent City, 25 miles from the Oregon border.

We made it to Portland in mid-afternoon. Terry and Suzanne were ready for us. Over the next three days they showed us a good time. We had a picnic on Mount Hood and watched people ski in mid-July, toured a museum, and dined at a fancy Japanese restaurant. I attended a Saturday morning class with Terry and went with him when he visited his patients at a veteran's hospital. Terry had to go to class on Monday, so we decided to leave and start traveling east and have a leisurely trip home.

We got on I-84 which runs parallel to the Columbia River. We drove five miles out of our way to go to Washington so the kids could say they had been in the state of Washington. That night we stayed at a Holiday Inn in Boise, Idaho. My main memory of Boise is laying on the bed and the kids peeling sheets of skin from my sunburned body.

The next day we made it to Yellowstone National Park. We saw all the highlights of Yellowstone including "Old Faithful." The next day we made it to South Dakota. We saw Mount Rushmore, the Black Hills, the Badlands and the Wall Drugstore. Then it was home to Anamosa. It was a fantastic vacation. We made the kids keep a diary—they didn't like it, but we made them. It was fun to read their entries—they were pretty short.

Ruth Ann and I had set a goal of trying to get to all 48 continental states by the time they graduated. We did make it to 40 of the 48.

In September Brad and Carron did something that was to add much joy and many good memories for all four of us. One afternoon after school Brad came in the kitchen carrying a puppy and Carron was carrying a kitten. They said the neighbors were moving and were going to kill them. They pleaded with us to keep them—we gave in pretty easily.

We named the kitty Midnight because he was all black. We named the puppy Barney because Ruth Ann thought he looked like Barney Google. Barney would be part of our family for the next 12 years. Midnight didn't last very long—he ran away.

Erland Christensen, Andrea Bungum and 16 others

Comments

Thomas Hatcher Enjoyed the story. Quite the trip! I remember staying in Gallup, New Mexico as well on our family California trip in

1980. And counting dead jackrabbits on the pavement on the way to Kingman AZ.

Cecilia Hatcher Thomas Hatcher you forgot to mention the two flat tires on the way home!

Richard Stout That West Coast trip was full of all the best places. You saw it all. I've spent many a day in Kingman. My brother lived there for 45 years. His wife, my sister-in-law turns 70 today…still living in Kingman. Pete, what were you thinking…all those hours in the California sun when you were designed for Scandinavia?

PeteandRuth Ann Bungum Obviously I wasn't thinking

Brad Bungum PeteandRuth Ann Bungum and Richard Stout, I definitely remember the hotel stay in Boise and peeling all the burnt skin off… Dad was feeling fine by then, but it came off in sheets… don't think I've experienced anything like it since. Those were also the days before sunscreen or concern about the effects of sun in the body. But it's true, he wasn't thinking. That's obvious. And neither were any of the other adults. 😄 Not sure why the three of us didn't get fried?

Richard Stout Brad Bungum

Jill Darrow Great journey!

Phil Bungum ;~]

Grace Story That was so much fun. A great memory!!!

PeteandRuth Ann Bungum

Saturday, April 25, 2020. Pete and Ruth Ann's journey through 59 years. Today I will describe our journey in 1972.

In January of 1972, I was chosen by the Anamosa Jaycees as Outstanding Educator of the Year. Jim Fields, my principal, recommended me and I was chosen over the high school and elementary nominees. He must have said some kind words about me. Ruth Ann and I went to the Jaycee Banquet and I was honored with a flattering introduction and a plaque. I was very honored to be recognized and I'm grateful for that good memory.

In June Ruth Ann left her job at the Reformatory. By this time, she had switched from the doctor's secretary to become secretary to the Deputy Warden, but it was still inside the walls. The Deputy Warden's job was to be in charge of security. So she became well acquainted with discipline problems and how they were handled.

One of her jobs (with no extra pay) was to inspect wives and girlfriends when they came to visit their husband or boyfriend. On numerous occasions she was called at home in the evening or on weekends to examine the women. She and another lady had the woman strip. They were to examine all the female cavities and look for drugs or contraband of any kind. She told me her examination of the vagina and anus was not exactly thorough, but she looked to see if anything was visible. It was not a fun job. She came to feel she was being taken advantage of, plus she came to feel concerned about her own safety while working inside the walls. She had been told that if there was ever a riot by the inmates, they would attack the Deputies Office first. Those two things helped her decide to quit and do something a little less stressful.

In July we took a three-day trip to Chicago with Jim and Marilyn Heitland and their two kids, Lisa and John. The highlight was seeing a Chicago White Sox game. It was a first time the four kids had been in Chicago.

In August I started my painting career. I painted our neighbors house. When done I decided this was something I could do in the summer. That is what happened—I painted for the next 32 years. It was a great summer job and I made good money during all those years.

That summer Carron started playing softball and Brad was in his second year of Little League baseball. We also purchased a Wurlitzer piano for Carron in June and Brad had one year of guitar lessons under his belt. Roger Seaton gave him lessons. I tried to learn some songs from Carron on the piano. I kind of learned "I Left My Heart in San Francisco." Carron tells me to this day that I about drove her nuts as I played it so often. Brad tried to give me a lesson or two on his guitar, but my fingers wouldn't do what he told me to do. So much for my music career. Both of my teachers refused to give me any more lessons.

In September I had a new principal. His name was Walt Fortney—he came from the nearby town of Oxford Junction. Walt believed in using the paddle, especially for junior high kids. He said at the ages of twelve to fourteen that was the only thing that some of the tough kids understood. And he got the message out to the junior high kids right away. In his first four months on the job he paddled over 30 kids. The word was out you don't mess with this guy. Authority and order were restored at the junior high—and the kids liked it. Walt was firm and fair; the kids knew it and they respected him for it. And we teachers felt the same way. Walt was my principal until he retired in 1997. Unfortunately, he had a short retirement—he died of lung cancer in 2002. I really think we can improve America's schools by having strong and effective principals.

After we had lost our cat, Carron wanted another one, so we adopted Missy from our neighbor. Missy was a female. Within in a couple of months she gave birth to four kitties. Being a new mother, she was very protective of her children and would not let any humans touch them. However, it was okay for Barney, our dog, to do so. Barney must have felt he had a fatherly role to play so he would lick and cuddle the kitties. Mommy Missy would just lay there, and watch Barney take care of his four adopted kitties. When Barney wasn't licking, he would lay on the floor in front of Missy's bed. He was the big man on guard duty and took his job very seriously.

In November Dick Clark was elected to the U.S. Senate. He gained recognition by walking across the whole state of Iowa. Carron fell in love with him, met him when he was walking to Monticello from Anamosa, got his autograph and had a photo taken with him. She had his autographed photo in her room. Carron entered fourth grade in 1972. In October Mrs. Mayer, her teacher, was having a class discussion about the upcoming election. She asked who was running each office and whether they were Republican or Democrat. Carron was the only one to name each candidate and their party. Mrs. Mayer was very impressed. Ruth Ann and Pete were also.

Scott Newhard, a former student of mine from 1963 was running for the state legislature. We volunteered to help Scott in his campaign. Ruth Ann and I essentially ended up being his campaign managers. We helped Scott raise money, organize fundraisers, recruit volunteers for door-to-door drops, stuffed envelopes until 3 AM and other things that go into a campaign. In November Scott was elected and was the youngest member of the Iowa Legislature.

In December we had our first lutefisk dinner. Several of us younger Norwegians in Anamosa had discussed how much we enjoyed lutefisk and lefse when we were young. We decided to organize a dinner party and enjoy it again. Bob and Grace Story and Ruth Ann and I were in charge of the inaugural event. Bob and Grace hosted it in their family room. We made a list of guests and of course, one of the spouses had to be Norwegian or part anyway. Grace and Ruth Ann got the menu planned and then assigned each guest to bring some other Norwegian food. The four of us were in charge of getting the lutefisk ordered and Ruth Ann and Grace would prepare it and serve it. We had over a dozen Norskies at this first dinner. It was a rousing success and an Anamosa tradition was born. It would continue for 23 years.

Wes Rickels, Carlene Vavricek and 16 others

Comments

Bonnie Walderbach Bob and I enjoyed a Norwegian Dinner at your house. My first taste of Lutefisk was an experience!! Thank God a napkin was on my lap and I could secretly place it on my mouth… enough said!

> **PeteandRuth Ann Bungum** Bonnie—that hurts my feelings—you cheater you. How could you do such a thing?

> **Bonnie Walderbach** PeteandRuth Ann Bungum I told you that years ago! Just not for me!

Carson Ode 1972 was a quiet a year—Teacher of the Year, prison searches, and lutefisk. You and Ruth Ann lead a colorful life.

Richard Stout Pete, what a Journal you are sharing! 1972 is when we moved to Anamosa to begin my career. I don't know when we became friends…probably within a year or two of then.

> **PeteandRuth Ann Bungum** I think you're right. What was your wife's name and when did she die? And what from?

Jan Siebels Great to see you today!!! 👍 😊 😊 😊

Phil Bungum ;~]

John Spilde Hi! I presume my mom and dad attended this event! I especially enjoyed the lutefisk eating contest at the Nordic Festival. I always thought it was a good idea to make the contestants put the bowl on their head when they were through, so there was no cheating! I enjoyed reading the story about Diane Norton and Carron's writing "Shit" on a sidewalk. I texted Diane (we called her "Baby Diane") to make sure she was reading about your adventures. I also told her that she and Carron had to learn that word from a peer because her brother, Mike, sister, Janet, and the Spilde boys were all four too "saintly," to say "Shit." LOL!! By the way, with Betty Norton and Ruth Ann working at the courthouse, where in the nation could you go and get such great customer service??" A tribute to them both!

John Spilde Here's a small world story. Jim Fields "resigned" (I will say no more) and got a superintendent job in Hinton, Iowa (Western Iowa). Would you believe years later I dated a gal who was a teacher in Hinton, and of course knew Jim?

PeteandRuth Ann Bungum

Sunday, April 26, 2020. Pete and Ruth Ann's journey through 59 years. My post today is 1973.

In the 1970s I introduced two projects that were fun and effective. The first one was making play money that the kids could earn by getting good grades on tests and daily work, not having late assignments, doing extra credit projects, having good behavior and having good grammar. I called my money "geography money." I found a box and divided it into six compartments. Then I ran off thousands of bills and made denominations of $1, $5, $10, $20, $50 and $100 bills. That was my cash register. The kids could use their money for paying fines for bad behavior and speaking bad grammar. I started with a $1.00 fine for saying "ain't" and "don't got none."

One day a kid came to me and handed me a $50.00 bill. I asked him why, he said, "I'm paying for my next fifty *ain't*."

The most fun and educational thing we did was to invest in the stock market. I made a form that they could use to keep track of their investments. It included the name of the company, price per share, date bought, selling price, profit or loss. I taught them how to read the stock market page and every day I would post it on the bulletin board. Most liked it.

Some unintended consequences of geography money were as follows: At lunch time kids started buying and selling food. They also started playing poker. A few kids tried to counterfeit—it didn't work. I used geography money for eight years. In 1979, a mother complained to the principal that her son was so upset when he got fined for bad grammar that he couldn't sleep. The principal called me in, and he had decided I should hang it up and try again next year if I wanted to. I decided it had run its course, so I stopped. One good memory of those eight years is one kid was so excited about the stock market he talked his parents into investing in the real market.

When school started in August 1973, I decided to try something I had been thinking about for a year or so. I wanted something I could use to open class every day. It would be a year-long project and something the kids would learn from and remember. I came up with ANAD, which meant—A Nation a Day. The plan was to take one nation a day and learn its location, pronunciation, spelling and a few facts about it. With articles in the newspaper telling of the geographic ignorance of the American people, this was something I could do to help eliminate a little bit of it.

I provided each student with maps of Europe, Asia and Africa. I numbered the countries from one to 110. The first five years I did only those three continents. Then I expanded it to the whole world. By the 1990s the number of nations in the world had expanded to about 200.

One method we used was to learn what mnemonics were—they were memory helpers. One of the favorites was for Central America—the nations of Belize, Guatemala, El Salvador, Honduras, Nicaragua, Costa Rica and Panama. The mnemonic was "Bob Gives Every Human Nice Curly Perms." We had another good one for South America. It was "Cocaine Eliminates Painless Brainless People And Costs Unlimited Bucks For Stupid Guy Ventures." To figure this one out, start with Colombia, go down the west coast, come up the east coast and end with Venezuela. At the end of the year I would give a final ANAD test. If they had a perfect score they were identified as a Perfect Global Genius. If they missed 1–5 their title was Global Genius, missing 6–10 was a Global Master, if they were under 50 percent, I called them a Global Beginner. By the way, ANAD was always extra credit.

Some other events in 1973 that had an influence on our life.

The state legislature passed a Collective Bargaining Law for public employees in Iowa. Ruth Ann and I would both be very active in future years. I did help get the vote arranged for our teachers to vote to accept or reject the new law. Our teachers accepted by a vote of 80 yes and 7 no.

In February I got my first student teacher. He was Jerry Van Dyke from Cornell College. I had six more, but he was the best.

We bought a pop-up camper. We took a trip to Nashville—we camped at Opryland and went to the Grand Ole Opry. We stopped in Indianapolis to take a ride around the 500 track. A final stop in Springfield, Illinois, to see the Abe Lincoln attractions.

In late July we had our 15th class reunion in Chatfield. In the 15 years since graduation the divorces had started. Most of us had settled into our careers, were raising young kids and bought houses. It was a fun night.

In July I decided to try to recruit someone to run for school board. I heard that Pat Schoon, a woman my age, wanted to run. I talked to her and she agreed. I think she might have run anyway. She won by nine votes. Pat served four terms and was a definite asset.

And my last message about 1973 is I started my summer painting career. I did a couple houses plus a big barn. That barn is the only time in 30 years of painting where I could've been seriously injured or worse. I was about 25 feet up when the bottom slipped, and I went straight down. I hung on to the top rung—I landed hard, my shins hit the rung. I was lucky the only thing I got out of that fall was a bruise on my shins. The other thing I got was a wake-up call to be more safety conscious.

In 1973 Brad entered sixth grade and turned twelve. Carron entered fifth grade and turned ten—Ruth Ann and I turned 33.

Bret Lewison, Yrsa Thom Chris and 12 others

Comments

Jill Darrow I remember Alissa studying the nations! You were such a good teacher!

Elsie Narveson It certainly was a big year for you. **Congratulations** on all your achievements

Stephen Zimmerman I remember "Geography money" You made me your banker. It's your innovative teaching techniques that made you the Best teacher.

PeteandRuth Ann Bungum Thanks Steve—much appreciated

Martin Frasher Loved ANAD!

Brad Bungum Dad, when did you start the Current Events competitions? Must have been around this time, as I remember Valorie Martensen beating me in the finals, and I wasn't happy. I think I cried. She actually whipped my butt—it wasn't even close. I think I was over-confident…

> **PeteandRuth Ann Bungum** Brad Bungum It was in the 1970s, I don't remember the year. The next year Carron beat Tom Hatcher in the championship. She was very happy—she called Tom a walking encyclopedia. Text her about that.

Valorie Martensen Brad Bungum you, my dear, have a great memory!!! Hahaha

> **Brad Bungum** Valorie Martensen, Val, do you remember that?? I'll never forget it… ;-)

> **Valorie Martensen** Brad Bungum I didn't until you brought it up!!!! 😎—I'll buy you a beer the next time I see you. Will that make up for it???

> **Brad Bungum** It will help…

> **Valorie Martensen** Brad Bungum ok. Well it's the least I can do for making you carry around this disappointment for 40 years give or take!

Valorie Martensen Pete, I always LOVED ANAD!! What a fun way to learn! 💚

Phil Bungum I won a Friday current events in 8th grade because of Uncle Paul. The question was "What North Dakota town is named after the soft brown coal?" At the time he was in Lignite. How that got into current events I have no clue. But the whole class went silent and they all stared at me, Mr. Gorder too. They all thought I was some genius or what.

PeteandRuth Ann Bungum

Monday, April 27, 2020. Pete and Ruth Ann's journey through 59 years.

The year is 1974 in our journey. While thinking of this year a couple things come to mind.

To make a little extra money I applied for a part-time job as janitor at Anamosa City Hall. I felt a little funny completing the application for a job that involved sweeping, dusting and cleaning toilets. The application asked for my education history. I had to answer that I had a bachelor's and master's degrees in social studies education. I did it anyway and was hired by a unanimous vote of the City Council. Wow, pretty impressive!!!

The job involved cleaning the offices of City Clerk, Secretary, the office of the Chief of Police and the big room above city hall. That room was used for dance classes, karate classes, receptions, etc. I had to sweep the floor and the 45 steps that led up to it. The worst part was cleaning the public toilet. It was usually a mess with unflushed toilets, stuff on the floor and graffiti all over the walls. I asked the City Clerk to buy some paint and I would paint it. I did repaint it and it looked very nice for a couple days. Then the graffiti reappeared, and I forgot about keeping it looking decent—it was a losing proposition. Ruth Ann helped me several times. We would get up 5:30 AM and clean for an hour or more. We didn't have to do this every day, twice a week was sufficient. Sometimes we would go in on weekends. I only did this for five to six months. I was paid $2.00 an hour—working six or seven hours a week wasn't worth the effort. The City Clerk and Secretary wanted me to continue—they told me their offices had never been so clean. Their pleas fell on deaf ears.

In April I was honored again by being chosen as Anamosa Teacher of the Year. This time I was chosen by my colleagues. Our Teacher's Association decided to recognize a teacher and a volunteer aide for the year. Delores Chadwell was the volunteer selected. Delores and I were recognized at a dinner with Board members and Administrators attending. We each received a plaque. It was definitely an honor to be chosen by my colleagues. At that dinner one of the Board members came up to me and said, "You sure had a lot of guts to take that cleaning job at city hall."

The year before, Pat Schoon had run for the school board and got elected and she was a good one. I had a neighbor lady who was a retired teacher. I thought she would be a good member. So, I talked to her. Elsie Clark was her name, about running-after a couple days of thinking about it she called me and said she would run. She was elected. The board now had two women and five men. I believe women have more empathy than men when it comes to understanding people's needs and wants.

In the summer we made a big change to our house. We added a garage, a driveway, remodeled the kitchen, poured a patio and installed a sliding glass door from the dining room to the patio. It was a wonderful addition to our house. We had to borrow money to do this. We borrowed enough to pay off our balance to Neal and Kay Dougherty. The big problem was our monthly payment went from $90 to $163 a month. But we managed because Ruth Ann was now working as our church's secretary and I was painting full time in the summer. It was the best thing we ever did to our house.

The big fun thing we did in August was take Ruth Ann's Mother (Myrtle)and Stepdad (Ed) to Washington D.C. This was a biggie for them and for us. Nixon had just resigned—Gerald Ford had been sworn in as President.

As we drove into D.C. the first thing I noticed was the Watergate Hotel and the Potomac River. I excitedly told everyone what I was seeing. Ed wasn't much interested when he said, "I wish I had brought my fishing pole."

We stayed in downtown D.C. and saw all the highlights. We visited the White House, the Bureau of Printing and Engraving, Washington, Lincoln and Jefferson Memorials, Arlington Cemetery, Tomb of the Unknown Soldier, Jack and Bobby Kennedy's gravesites and Gerald Ford's house. He chose Nelson Rockefeller as his Vice-President the day after we left. We also went to the Capitol and visited their representative in his office. His name was Al Quie. Ed got to sit in his office chair. Quie was a good friend of Myrtle and Ruth

Ann's cousin (Elton Redalen) who lived in Fountain, Myrtle and Ed's hometown. So they visited about Elton.

We left D.C. and drove north to New York City. We saw the World Trade Centers and took a ferry to the Statue of Liberty. Carron, Brad, Ed and I walked the spiral stairs to the crown. What a thrill it was for us. Ed really warmed up and seemed to enjoy everything we had seen and done. We drove out of New York City and started for home. We stayed that night in Stroudsburg, PA. The next day we drove to Anamosa. What a wonderful trip. We learned so much and the kids had a lot to tell their friends. So did Ed and Myrtle and Pete and Ruth Ann.

In August Carron entered sixth grade and Brad seventh. That meant Brad was going to have his Dad for a teacher. I'm sure Brad was wondering what it was going to be like. As his father I had similar thoughts. Thank God, Brad was a good student. It certainly made things easier for both of us. I did notice one trait that Brad still has to this day. If I gave students five minutes to study, he would use it. He was one of the few kids smart enough to realize that if he used that five minutes it would be five minutes less he would have to study that night. Brad is still that way, very efficient with his time and very disciplined in his work habits. Overall, it was a good year for both of us.

Speaking of father-son, I employed Brad as an apprentice painter that summer. He was only twelve but old enough to learn a few things. He learned pretty fast. I would let him paint siding and I would work on the windows and the high parts. I only paid him $.65 an hour to start and he did not have collective bargaining rights.

He did get a raise to $.75 an hour the next summer. The moral of the story is that if you treat your employees right and give them good working conditions and good pay, they have no reason to form a union.

From September to December we were busy with a variety of activities. Brad participated in seventh grade football. He played mainly defense (BB note: it was actually mainly offense). In November and December, he wrestled. It was not his sport. He spent a lot of time on his back looking at the ceiling. He gave up wrestling after eighth grade.

Scott Newhard, our state representative, was up for re-election and we helped again. We raised money and recruited fellow teachers to pound doors. We got a lot of teachers involved who had never thought about politics before. I explained to them that with the legislature determining our fate as public school teachers we needed to contribute some time and money to help elect supportive legislators for our own welfare. Scott was easily re-elected.

At Christmas time we had a Luther College reunion. It was a fun time at our home with Carson and Connie Ode from Des Moines and Paul and Sharon Twedt from Huntington Beach, California. We had a ton of laughs talking about our Luther days, our jobs, our kids, etc. We called each other by our Luther names. I was Big Daddy and Ruth Ann was Ma. Paul was Little Son. Carson was The Prodigal Son. Terry Sorom couldn't make it from Wenatchee, WA. His name was Big Son. Ruth Ann and I were called Big Daddy and Ma because we were the only ones married at Luther. I'm grateful for so many wonderful memories from 1975.

Yrsa Thom Chris, Dean Rickels and 9 others

Brad Bungum Dad, PeteandRuth Ann Bungum, a few recollections of having your dad as a teacher in 7th grade… The first few days, maybe weeks, were not fun. The first day was the worst. I saw you in a totally different realm, and asked myself more than once, "Who is this guy?" ;-) You were tough from the get-go, and no one got away with messing around in your room. Of course, we didn't get away with much at home either, but these were my friends and classmates you were coming down on, and that wasn't comfortable to see, or hear. That took some getting used to, and it all worked out. I remember your class as a highlight. Fun, we learned a ton, and as everyone got comfortable with the rules and your way of running your classroom it was great and we all laughed a lot while doing a lot of interesting things together. Just what a learning environment should be like. I also figured out quickly that I wasn't going to get special treatment. Not even in that current events tournament where Val Valorie Martensen kicked my butt. One other thing that I recall being difficult was figuring out what to call you. I don't think we ever talked about it before 7th grade started, but those first few days were confusing… You certainly weren't "Mr. Bungum"… "Dad" felt weird in a classroom setting… Those who knew you suddenly had to call you Mr Bungum, and not Pete (like Bret Lewison and Lisa Heitland Williams)…that was also weird. I think I finally ended up calling you "Dad," but for the first few weeks I think I just raised my hand when I had something to say, without using a name :-)

Darren Hurt Brad Bungum it was always tough for my kids to know what to call me in class as well. Most of them acted kind of weird when they had me as their teacher.

> **PeteandRuth Ann Bungum** Brad Bungum thanks for your thoughts—we made it together, didn't we?

> **Brad Bungum** It worked well! For sure…

John Spilde I again enjoyed reading about your journey, "Mr. Bungum." Sincerely, John. (By the way, did anyone else know about Dr. Hagen, a few journeys ago?)

PeteandRuth Ann Bungum

Tuesday, April 28, 2020. Pete and Ruth Ann's journey through 59 years.

The year is 1975.

Ruth Ann continued her six-hour day as church secretary. Walter Behrens, our pastor for six years, had left to go to Northwood-Kensett, Iowa. We were in transition at that time with an interim pastor from Wartburg Seminary in Dubuque. Ruth Ann had been elected to the church council the year before. She made history because she was the first woman ever elected to the council since the founding of St. Paul Lutheran in 1923.

Being on the council and church secretary made her a good partner for Dick Kurtz, the council President, to run the congregation until we got another pastor. Dick relied on her a lot to keep things going as she knew the ins and outs of the church office, such as knowing how the bulletin was done, etc. The two of them made a good pair until Marvin Mueller came that fall to be our new pastor.

Carron tried sixth grade basketball—it was easy to see basketball was not her cup of tea. Then she played softball in the summer and did well. This sport was more suited to her skills. She didn't have a great arm, but she could hit. She had good hand-eye coordination and could hit line drives which was unusual for twelve-year-old girls. By ninth grade she took her hand-eye coordination skill to golf clubs. She made the golf team as a freshman and was a member all through high school.

Brad gave basketball a try that winter. He was like his Dad—not very skilled. He tried basketball in eighth, ninth and tenth grades but gave it up after that. In April he made the eighth-grade track team. He would have much success in track through his high school career. He had inherited his mother's long legs and would be a good sprinter for the next four years. By high school he was running the 4x100, 4x200 and the 4x400 plus high jumping. In the summer he played Babe Ruth baseball. He was no longer in Little League.

School started in August and now Carron had her Dad for a teacher. She was also a good student—that made life easier for both of us. She was very good at current events. One week I had a current event competition and the two finalists were Carron and Tom Hatcher. Tom was called "The Walking Encyclopedia" by some of the kids. It was nip and tuck all the way. Carron nailed the last question and Tom didn't. She was one happy young gal to have defeated Tom. If I remember correctly, no one had defeated him all year.

Another fond memory of Carron had to do with Barney, our dog. We had been to Minnesota for Christmas. When it was time to go home, we had no Barney—he had escaped. It was ironic that on the way back, south of Calmar, there was a dead dog on the side of the road. We could see it was Black and Tan—just like Barney. We all thought it could be Barney. I stopped and all four of us got out to examine the dead dog. It looked exactly like Barney and I thought it was. Carron looked at the ears and said it wasn't Barney. This dog had a slit in the ear—she said Barney did not have a slit in either ear. So that settled the discussion as to whether it was Barney or not.

Ruth Ann's mother (Myrtle) put an ad on the local radio station in Preston about a missing Black and Tan dog that answered to the name of Barney. A lady called and told her she knew where Barney was. Her neighbor had him tied up—Myrtle went to talk to the guy—he willingly gave Barney to her. Myrtle called Ruth Ann to tell her the news. Then she called Walt, my principal, and told him to tell me that Barney had been found. So, Walt comes to my room and tells me the news.

Carron happened to be in that class so I wrote her a note, *"Barney has been found."* She had one big happy smile when I gave her the note. And she still has that note.

Ruth Ann told her mom that if she and Ed could get Barney to Cresco before Saturday, our friends, Bob and Grace Story, would bring him to Anamosa. They were coming to see us that weekend. When they came on Saturday, they had Barney. I can still see Bob getting Barney out of the back seat of their car with what I swear was a log chain around his neck. It was a funny scene. Bob wasn't going

126

to be responsible for Barney escaping. Barney was happy to be home and his family was happy to have him back.

That fall Carron became a seventh-grade cheerleader—she liked that. Brad was out for football again—he became the quarterback on the eighth-grade team. He would remain the starting quarterback until he graduated in 1980.

Walt, my principal, was a real innovator. In September we had our first seventh grade camp out. We took 140 kids to Camp Wapsi Y near Central City for a two-night, three-day educational camp out. Teachers doubled up to chaperone about 30 kids per cabin. Classes ranged from canoeing, self-defense and rifle shooting. I taught a class on yoga.

In 1975 Brad and two of his buddies formed a band. Jeff Langenburg was the drummer. Darren Hurt played guitar and was the lead singer and Brad played guitar and did some singing. They practiced in our basement most of the time. They came to our seventh-grade camp-out in September for their first public appearance. After that they played at several junior high dances. The song I remember best is "Big Bad LeRoy Brown." They really were pretty darn good and fun to listen to.

A final memory from 1975 is a collective bargaining agreement Brad and I negotiated. No, it wasn't over his painting wage but over his use of the English language. Brad was in the eighth grade, had entered puberty and on occasion turned into a typical 12–14-year-old jerk. His voice was changing, his language was changing, and his personality was changing. His language was considered cool by eighth grade standards but not by his parents. He was consistently using "ain't" and "don't got none." We decided we weren't going to have him sound like an uneducated idiot. Brad and I sat down at the dining room table and negotiated an agreement about his grammar. The basic agreement was that Brad would receive $2.00 a week for his allowance but every time he used bad grammar, he would lose a dime. He did lose dimes quite often. Then Brad wanted to renegotiate the contract. He wanted some incentives built in so he could make more than $2.00 if he spoke correctly and did extra work. He was a good negotiator and we made those things part of the contract. He became motivated and started making more than $2.00 per week. The contract was working.

This was also the year Ruth Ann was going to give Brad away. She said with his different personality she couldn't stand him at times. She offered him to the grandmas for free, but they turned down the offer. She thought about putting an ad in the local paper to give him away. Ruth Ann had to stick it out as no one accepted her offer of a "free fourteen-year-old boy." I told her he would grow out of it. I had worked with that age group all my life and knew what they were like. I was right in my advice to Ruth Ann. By the time he got into ninth grade he acted differently, talked like an intelligent teenager. We discarded the contract.

Rhenee Grabau, Yrsa Thom Chris and 12 others

Thomas Hatcher Thanks for opening old wounds Pete. I've been carrying around the weight of that loss for 45 years.

> **PeteandRuth Ann Bungum** Sorry Tom—hope it hasn't affected your sleep over the years. Good to hear from you. I'll try not do it again. Keep in touch.

PeteandRuth Ann Bungum

Wednesday, April 29, 2920. Pete and Ruth Ann's journey through 59 years.

The year is 1976.

This year was one of the favorite years in our married life. We did so many fun, educational things that year. The highlight was a three-week camping trip to southeast U.S. We went through Gatlinburg, Great Smoky Mountain National Park and camped in Opryland and then South Carolina. Then we drove through Atlanta heading for Plains, Georgia.

Jimmy Carter was running for President, so we wanted to see Billy, Jimmy's beer drinking brother. We stopped at Billy's gas station. I pulled up to the pump and a teenager came out to pump gas. I told him to fill it up and Ruth Ann asked if Billy was inside. He said he was, and we should go in because Billy would be glad to see us.

All four of us went in and there was Billy drinking a 7-ounce can of Pabst Blue Ribbon. We introduced ourselves and said we would like to take some photos. I told him Ruth Ann and I told our friends in Iowa that that we were going to Plains to have a beer with Billy. He was more than happy to oblige so I bought a Pabst and Ruth Ann took a photo of us drinking the beer. I also took one of her having one with Billy. Then we took one of Carron and Brad standing beside Billy in front of his station—with the Pabst sign in the background. We also visited Plains Baptist Church where Jimmy was a Sunday school teacher and still is to this day.

We drove to Jimmy's residence but it was blocked off by Secret Service agents. However, Amy, the daughter of Jimmy and Rosalyn, was standing by an agent waiting to go someplace. She was eight. The agent said it was okay to take a photo of Brad and Carron standing with Amy, which we did.

We left Plains and went south to Andersonville, the notorious Confederate prison camp for Union POWs in the Civil War. It was sad to see and to realize how much suffering took place there in the 1860s. What a difference between reading history and actually seeing it.

Our next stop was Ocala, Florida. We stopped and camped at Jellystone. Bob and Bonnie Walderbach, our friends from Anamosa, had moved there a couple months before. They visited our campsite and invited us to their home. We had a great visit. That was the last time we saw them in Ocala, they moved back to Anamosa the next year.

Next, we went to Orlando and visited Disneyland. Then we travelled east and went through the Kennedy Space Center. Next we traveled west to Tampa-Saint Petersburg and we camped. My best memory there is the little tree lizards running around our feet. They looked like miniature alligators, but they were perfectly harmless. Ruth Ann and Carron used the camp toilet and they both came out screaming. The lizards were running over their feet while sitting on the stool. For some reason lizards and mice make women scream. The next day we were going to go to Busch Gardens but got rained out.

It was time to hit the road, so we got on Interstate 10 and headed west for New Orleans. Ruth Ann wanted to eat at the famous Brennan's Restaurant, where Jackie Kennedy would dine. We dressed up and found Brennan's. It is one block off Bourbon Street. It was quite the experience for all four of us. We had our own personal waiter. He stood by our table with a towel on his arm, taking care of our every need. Ruth Ann was our etiquette teacher by telling us which piece of silverware to use with each course. The bill was $60.00, quite a bit for our budget, but worth it for one time.

The next day we headed north. We stopped at a town where the New Orleans Saints were having summer training. When practice was over, we approached head Coach Hank Stram. He was very willing to talk to us. He told us the Saints wouldn't be very good that year because he didn't have enough good linemen. When we told him we were from Iowa his eyes lit up. He said one of the best players he ever coached was Eddie Podolak, the former Hawkeye running back. He had him when he had coached the Kansas City Chiefs. Hank posed for photos with us.

Our final stop was in Saint Louis—we saw the Cardinals. I don't remember who they played but I do remember every time Lou

Brock got on base the fans yelled, "Lou, Lou, Lou!" wanting him to steal another base, which he did.

The next day we made it home. It was nice to be home safe and sound. We were all grateful for the many good memories we now had.

The rest of the memories from 1976 will be much shorter.

We started playing golf this year. Paul Pinney, a good friend and colleague, had taken me golfing several times and I was hooked. I bought the kids and Ruth Ann a set of golf clubs. I had a friend who gave me his old clubs. Ruth Ann was never in love with golf—so she retired from golfing in 2004. She became famous for her retirement speech—I'll tell you later. All I can say at this point is it was the shortest retirement speech ever made.

In October, Jim Mayer, the editor of our local paper, wrote an article about our visit to Plains and drinking a Pabst with Billy Carter. I don't know how he found out about it; someone must have told him. Anyway, the next week we got a call from a Des Moines Register reporter wanting to come and interview us. He had read the article in our local paper about us and decided it would be a good one for the Register. He came, interviewed us, got the photo of me drinking my Pabst with Billy—the next week we made page one of section B of the Register. Carson Ode, our friend in Des Moines, couldn't believe what he was seeing. He had a good laugh as did a lot of others.

Jimmy Carter was elected president over Gerald Ford in November. I said I had voted for Carter—it made some of my colleagues unhappy that I had voted for him. One said he was going to leave the United States. A lady teacher shook her fist at me and said, "You SOB Democrats, we'll get you next time." And then I had to break up a fight between two eighth grade girls. One was upset that Ford had lost—the other was happy Carter had won. They were on the floor pulling hair, hitting each other, screaming and cussing at each other—they both had hate in their eyes. I got them separated. I told them this wasn't really necessary—somebody had to win and somebody had to lose—that's why we have elections. I was told later they were really friends. I guess they made up and walked home together.

Mark Blattie, Dean Rickels and 9 others

Comments

Mark Holub Mr. Bungum, I am really enjoying all of your daily entrees. Amazed at your memory and all of the memories you and your family created. Stay safe and healthy.

> **PeteandRuth Ann Bungum** Thanks Mark. Couple questions. Where do you live? What have you done all your life? What was your brother's name? How were you related to Rosie?

> **Mark Holub** PeteandRuth Ann Bungum I have lived in Seattle for the last 20 years. I can say that I have not done anything with my life as compared to the quite incredible life and times that you and your wife enjoyed. My brother's name is Kraig. Rosie was my Grandma, though you wouldn't have known it. Looking forward to your continued posts Mr Bungum. What a wonderful marriage you enjoyed raising two great kids. So glad that you are allowing us all to share in your memories and adventures. Seems like a long time ago that I sat in your class and walked by your house every day. You and your wife were always so kind to all of the kids in the neighborhood. You were and are loved by so many. Now, on to your next post.

Bonnie Walderbach Remember your visit!

Mark Blattie Uncle Pete, you missed a very important event in 1976, your favorite nephew graduated high school that year:)

Phil Bungum ;~]

PeteandRuth Ann Bungum

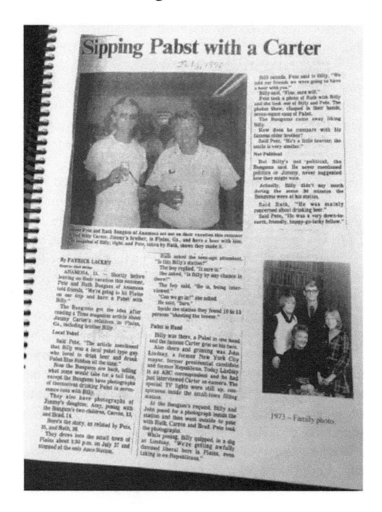

Tim Bungum, Yrsa Thom Chris and 16 others

PeteandRuth Ann Bungum

Thursday, April 30, 2020. Pete and Ruth and Ann's journey through 59 years.

The year is 1977.

Carron finished eighth grade and entered ninth. She was confirmed in October. Carron and Diane (the *shit* speller) were still best friends. They provided us with a great memory from something they did in January.

John and Lorna were visiting, and the two girls asked Ruth Ann if they could prepare a meal for all four of us. Ruth Ann said YES. They did all the cooking, serving and clean-up and the meal was wonderful. Uncle John was so impressed he wrote a letter to their home economics teacher, Marsha Ketelsen, thanking her for being such an excellent teacher. Here was his message. "I recently had the pleasure of eating an absolutely delicious meal prepared by Carron Bungum and Diane Norton. The food was superb, the service impeccable and the atmosphere sensuously romantic. I have conveyed my delight and satisfaction to the girls, and I thought it appropriate to communicate the same feeling to you, their teacher to whom they both acknowledge a great debt. My congratulations to you for providing such superior instruction. Sincerely, John L. Bungum, Professor of Economics, University of Wisconsin-Platteville."

When Marsha got the letter, she showed it to me—she was very touched. Most of what John said was true but the "atmosphere sensuously romantic" may have been a bit of a stretch. I'm grateful for good memories like this.

Brad entered tenth grade. He had a good track season and showed real talent as a sprinter. In the fall he was quarterback on the sophomore football team.

The big event of the summer was the marriage of brother John to Lorna in Des Moines. All nine of us kids were there. It was the first time we had all been together since Dad's funeral in 1961. Probably the happiest person of all was Ruth Ann because now Lorna would have to take care of John in his later years and not her. Her Uncle

Lewie nightmare no longer existed. Since we had been responsible for John and Lorna getting together, they asked us to be their attendants. Connie was maid of honor and I was best man.

We had a family photo taken with Mom and all nine of her litter. Mark was the youngest at age 30 and Paul was the oldest at 50. We all looked so healthy and happy and so much slimmer than we do today. That photo was taken 43 years ago. In those 43 years four of us have died. The five still alive in 2020 are Don at 88, Jan at 86, John at 77, Mark at 73 and me at 79.

We had to buy three different sizes of jeans for Brad in 1977. He kept growing out of them. He grew six inches and added 35 pounds in one year.

Ruth Ann started a new job after John and Lorna's wedding. She was hired to be secretary-receptionist for a realtor named Mike. Ruth Ann and Mike were not a good match. Ruth Ann got pissed off when she would make a decision and he would change it and would not tell her why. She told him to "take this job and shove it." He told her she couldn't do this because he was going on vacation. She said, "Watch me walk out the door." And she did.

Comments

Steve Boyer Hey Pete, it's the shit speller here! 😁 I can't tell you how much I enjoy reading your daily posts! Such happy and wonderful memories. ♡

Pat McQuaid Schoon I happen to have been a witness to the "Mike the Realtor" story. With a smile of satisfaction on her face, she totally ripped the rug from under his feet and left him sputtering. Absolutely the best!!!

> **PeteandRuth Ann Bungum** I remember her telling me that you were working together with Mikey. She hated that man. I'm not sure I got all the details right but what I wrote was what I remember. Was I pretty accurate in what I wrote?

> **Pat McQuaid Schoon** 👍 You were spot on!! 😜

PeteandRuth Ann Bungum

Friday, May 1, 2020. Pete and Ruth Ann's journey through 59 years.

I will write about our life in 1978.

1978 was a good year for our financial future. Ruth Ann began work on February 28, 1978, at the Jones County Treasurer's Office. It was to be her workplace for the next 21 years and four months. She retired on June 22, 1999. The pay was pretty meager to start but the plus side was that she would be paying into Social Security and IPERS (Iowa Public Employee Retirement System).

In 1998 she bought back her two and one-half years at the Reformatory, so she ended up with 24 years of credit in IPERS. So, she got to enjoy both retirement checks when she retired in 1999. They were nice to see in her bank statement every month. She got to enjoy them until she passed away on January 9, 2020. Her retirement money enabled Ruth Ann and I to have a wonderfully good life in the next twenty years. We traveled a lot, thanks to her retirement money.

It was a good year for Carron and Brad. Carron was a sophomore. She made the varsity golf team. She had a natural swing and had the potential to develop into a fine golfer with a lot of practice and dedication.

Brad was a junior. He gave up basketball and concentrated on track and football. He was a sprinter—I can assure you he got his speed from his mother. The seven Bungum boys had a lot of skills and strengths but speed was not one of them.

Brad became the starting quarterback. They had a good year with a 6–3 record. There was another quarterback named Darren but Coach Algoe decided to have Darren be a running back (BB: actually Darren played Linebacker when I took over at QB) and leave Brad as the starting quarterback.

I have a good story to tell about Darren and Brad. One night after practice Coach Bob Algoe heard a heated argument going on in the locker between Darren and Brad. He listened for a while and decided he better intervene. They were arguing about a girl (Meg) and who was going to date her. Bob went out to break up the argument. He told the two that he couldn't have two stupid people on his football team, so both of them should just leave. Bob left and started thinking, "Holy cow, what did I just say? I just lost two of my best players." Ten minutes later Brad and Darren went to Coach Algoe and said they had gotten their problem straightened out and wanted to keep playing. Algoe said he was relieved.

A couple other memories about Brad.

He was voted into National Honor Society. He was also accepted into the Sadie Street Singers, Anamosa High School's singing and dancing group. Brad had a nice voice, but his dancing needed some improvement. After one performance a fellow teacher came to me and asked if Brad had recovered from his appendectomy as he looked pretty stiff while dancing. By his senior year he improved and looked pretty darn good.

We took another vacation that summer. We asked the kids if they wanted to go east or go west and visit Paul and Sharon Twedt again—they chose west. On the way we traveled through Arkansas, Texas and Juarez in Mexico. We ate dinner at a nice restaurant in Juarez. It was a mistake because the next day while driving it hit me—and I mean really hit—it was Montezuma's Revenge. I had unbelievable pain and cramps. I had to stop and make a potty call. I also bought a couple of bottles of Pepto Bismol and started drinking it right out of the bottle. It took three days to make me feel like a human being again. We continued through New Mexico, Arizona and into California. We made it to Twedts—we stayed a couple days. We did go to the beach, but I was smart enough to wear a T-shirt this time. Twedts are such good hosts—we had a great time.

We left Twedts and headed for Las Vegas. We took the kids to a dinner show at the Riviera. We sat by a young couple from the Bronx in New York City. During the conversation it came up that I was a teacher and Brad and Carron had had their Dad for a teacher. The guy started laughing and said, "You really had your Dad for a teacher—I can't believe it. That would never go over in the Bronx, the way we treat teachers."

After dinner we saw Joan Rivers do a comedy routine and then the Mac Davis show. We went to another show at Circus-Circus. We did a little gambling—Brad stepped on the gambling floor to watch us gamble—immediately a man told him politely that he would have to step outside the entrance. The kids really liked Vegas and expressed the desire to go back someday.

The next day we left Vegas. I went to the grocery store at 7 AM to get some rolls and snacks for the day. I got in line at the cash register and there was this guy in front of me with a cart full of groceries. I unloaded my groceries with a divider between us—I didn't pay any attention to the guy ahead of me. When I got done unloading, I looked at the guy. It was Redd Foxx, the comedian and star of the TV show, *Sanford and Son*. I remember Redd's bill came to $87.00. He pulled a wad of bills from his pocket and paid cash. The manager of the store came over and talked to Redd. I heard Redd say he was doing three shows a night at the Star Dust. Then he had gambled and was on his way home for breakfast and sleep. Redd looked the same as he did on TV. When I got back to the motel, I told the kids I saw Redd—they all wished they had gone.

We left Vegas and drove through Utah and into Colorado. We stopped to see sister Betty and husband Bill in Grand Junction. They owned a restaurant and art store there. The next day we drove to Nebraska, stayed in a motel and then to Anamosa the final day. The kids were able to add Arkansas, Nevada and Utah to the number of states they had visited.

In early December Ruth Ann and I made our usual big batch of lefse. Lefse is the potato bread we Norwegians make at Christmas every year. It looks like a pie crust or pizza crust. We eat it with real butter and either white sugar or brown sugar. Some Norskies will put butter and potatoes and gravy and lutefisk on it and roll it up like a taco.

Ruth Ann decided to put an ad in our local paper to see if she could sell some and make a few bucks. She did make a sale to a very distinguished looking 60–70-year-old man. What happened in the next three weeks was such a great memory that I had to share it with people. So, I wrote the story and sent a copy to the Journal—Eureka,

Anamosa's local newspaper. The next week, James Mayer, the editor of our paper printed it in the paper. It was almost verbatim from what I wrote. It is posted on the next page.

You, Yrsa Thom Chris, Ellyn Rickels and 6 others

Comments

Bret Lewison One of the things I remember most about Ruth Ann working at the County Treasurers office is that 1979 was also the year that Iowa license plates changed from the ones with the county coded numbers on the left hand side (Jones County was 53 I remember) to ones that had the county name printed on the bottom. Anyway, because we all had to get new plates and the place you got your plates was the County Treasurer's Office (at least in Anamosa it was), if you were really nice to Ruth Ann, she would put aside a special number for you. I remember the license plate on our car was DEG 063 because my football number was 63. That's the closest thing we got to vanity plates back in those days. Couldn't tell you today what the license plate number is on my car currently. Wish I had Ruth Ann to pull a special one for me.

> **PeteandRuth Ann Bungum** Bret Lewison thanks Bret—I think she saved 000 for Hank and Karen.

> **Bret Lewison** Pretty sure the old Pinto that Brad drove had 012.

> **Brad Bungum** Bret Lewison yep, I have 012 on the shelf in my home office to this day…

> **Bret Lewison** PeteandRuth Ann Bungum I think mom & dad also had 107 (our street number) at one point. Having those numbers made you feel kind of special.

> **Bret Lewison** Brad Bungum what are the letters?

Brad Bungum Bret Lewison…it's actually in my garage, not my office…but here it is:

Son Brad-#1 Hawk fan

Mark Blattie Brad Bungum and are those the "dynasty days" you talk about?

Brad Bungum Mark Blattie, that would be those, yes.

Mark Blattie Brad Bungum we have some good athleticism in our family, both female and male.

PeteandRuth Ann Bungum

Saturday, May 2, 2020. Pete and Ruth Ann's journey through 59 years.

The year is 1979.

This year was an exciting and very enjoyable one for Ruth Ann and me. As you read this you will see why.

Carron turned sixteen, finished her sophomore year and began her junior year. In April the high school girls' bowling team qualified for the State High School bowling tournament, held in Des Moines. The team didn't place in the top three, but Carron had a super series and made the all-tournament team. She placed fourth in the state with a total of 496. Her average was 165—not bad. The winner was a girl from Lansing, she rolled a 520. Carron was a happy girl and her father and mother were very happy and very proud. The photo of the top five girls is still in the trophy case at Anamosa High School.

She made the golf team for the second year and did well. She also had some part time jobs. She was a waitress at Moon's Restaurant. She goofed one day when she was supposed to put sugar in something and instead put salt. Needless to say, it was not edible. Mrs. Moon just laughed about it and put it in the garbage and had her start over. She helped me paint that summer and then started working at Kouba's Pharmacy—she kept that job until she graduated in 1981. She went to the Prom in May. Her date was a nice young man named Scott Hanna.

Brad turned eighteen on November 2, 1979. The track team had a great year and he got to run in the state track meet. It was definitely a thrill for us to see Brad competing against the best high school track athletes in the state of Iowa. I believe he got to run in 4x200 and the 4x400. In the summer he got to play in right field on the baseball team They almost made it into the State baseball tournament. They got beat pretty badly in the sub-state final by Waterloo Central. Central was definitely the better team.

August meant the beginning of football practice. Expectations were high for a championship season, as most of the team was returning. They started off in a disappointing way. In the first game we got beat by Mt. Vernon. It was a heartbreaker. In the third quarter we were ahead 13–7. We were on their seven-yard line ready to march in for a clinching touchdown. You guessed it—we fumbled, and they recovered on the thirteen. They marched 87 yards for a touchdown to lead by 21–13. We never scored again. The guy who caused the fumble was Paul Hufford who went on to become an All-American at the University of Iowa.

In game two we played Linn-Mar, a much bigger school. They kicked our butt by 25–0. We were 0–2 in what was supposed to be a championship season. We were thankful those first two games were non-conference. In the third game we started conference play.

We finally won a game and that got the ball rolling. We won six conference games in a row—we beat Vinton, Manchester, Tipton, Marion, Monticello and Independence. We only had Maquoketa left for an undefeated conference season and the championship. It was quite a game.

We were leading 7–6 in the middle of the fourth quarter. Maquoketa marched to our 20-yard line and kicked a field to win it 9–7. On their final drive a controversial call was made. It was a fourth-down play and would have given us the ball, and the victory. The official called a Maquoketa receiver inbounds when it looked like he was out of bounds—he caught the ball for a first down. They went on to kick a field goal. Brad was so upset about the call he went into their bus after the game and asked that receiver if he was in or out of bounds. He said he was in. When the game was over 4–5 Anamosa guys were cussing and shaking their fists at the officials as they got in their car and drove away. No fights broke out, but Superintendent Poulter and I stayed by the buses to prevent any fisti-cuffs. Anyway, the final standings looked like this: Three schools tied for the championship: We beat Marion, Marion beat Maquoketa, Maquoketa beat us. We were Tri-Champions. Also, the loss kept us from going to the state football tournament. This game was played on Brad's 18th birthday. What a birthday gift!!

1979 was the end of the decade. I'll end today with some things I forgot to include in earlier posts. They all happened sometime from 1970 to 1979.

Brad had an appendectomy in January of 1979. On the Sunday of Super Bowl, friends Bret and Darren and others, tried to sneak a pizza into St. Luke's for Brad. His nurses caught them in the act—Brad received a tongue lashing and was not able to share in the pizza.

Barney, our dog, had surgery after he'd been in a fight or someone shot him with a pellet gun. The bill was $133.

Carron fell through the garage ceiling. She fell 9 feet to the concrete—no major injuries.

Another time Diane and Carron were in the garage attic and one or both took a pee and of course it leaked to the floor. The sheetrock was permanently stained.

Brad got mad at his mom and dad. He said he was going to run away. We told him to go, so he goes to the back yard, he wanders around for five minutes and then comes in the house, he said "I have to go potty."

In 1979 Ruth Ann and I turned 39—Brad was 18 and Carron was 16.

Meg Fortney, Yrsa Thom Chris and 13 others

Comments

Rhonda Koppenhaver I still remember that Maquoketa game.

Valorie Martensen Rhonda Koppenhaver me too!!!

PeteandRuth Ann Bungum

Sunday, May 3, 2020. Pete and Ruth Ann's journey through 59 years.

The year is 1980.

In 1980 we entered a new decade. It would be a life-changing decade for the two of us. It started with many changes in 1980.

Brad graduated, enrolled at Luther College, Carron became a senior and they both went to France.

Both of them took French in high school. One of the rewards of taking French was to go to France as a junior or senior. In France they stayed with a French family for five days, toured Paris for three days, two more days on tours and two days in Strasbourg. They visited all the sites we read about in books, including the Louvre, the *Mona Lisa*, Eiffel Tower, Arch of Triumph, Versailles Palace and various chateaux.

The kids were lucky to have the chance to spend Easter Sunday in Strasbourg with their cousin, David Bungum, and Colin Pinney, the son of our Anamosa friends, Paul and Karol Pinney. David and Colin were in the Army, stationed in Mannheim. David had a car, so he and Colin drove to Strasbourg to visit them. It did enter our mind that both of our kids were on the same plane and if the unimaginable should happen we would be childless. Ruth Ann and I enjoyed being alone for 14 days. It was the first time since their birth that we had that much time alone.

Since we were alone and fancy free for two weeks, we took off with the Pinney's to celebrate the 40th birthdays of Karol and Ruth Ann. Karol was 40 on April 2nd and Ruth Ann was 40 on April 4th. We went to LaCrosse, Wisconsin, to motel it for a couple of nights and visit the famous Third Street. Paul and I had threatened Karol and Ruth Ann that since they were turning 40, we were going to trade them in for two 20s. The gals told us that by the time they got done with us that weekend we would be too tired to trade them in. We didn't trade.

After returning from France Carron rejoined the golf team and the bowling team. She also directed the Cherub Choir at church for three-year-old kids through second graders and was Vice President of the Luther League. She played the piano for jazz band and continued working at the Kouba Pharmacy. And she helped me paint again.

The last five months of Brad's senior year were good ones. The track team had a phenomenal year. They qualified for several events at the Drake Relays. They also qualified in nine events for state meet in Des Moines, also held at the Drake stadium. They ended up in third place in 1-A. Brad had his best split time in his high school career in the 4x400 with a time of 50:8.

Brad graduated on May 25th (BB: actually it was May 18th, the day Mt. St. Helens exploded—Google it). It was one of the biggest classes ever—146 students. Brad received special recognition by being awarded the Citizenship Award by the Rotary Club. It was worth $100. It was sent to Luther College—we never saw it. He also helped me paint. Our biggest job was painting a church in Morley, a neighboring town. It was pretty big. I had bid it for $1,200 plus paint costs. I should have bid it for at least $1,800. After paying Brad and Carron there wasn't much left for me.

We took Brad to Decorah to begin football practice on August 20th. He wanted to try college football. The football players had to report two weeks early to begin practice. I'll admit it was emotional driving up there knowing he would be with a hundred kids he didn't know, and he wouldn't be coming back with us. When we got there, we were directed to the football dorm. They had to report to the field to have their 40-yard sprint timed. Then it was back to the dorm and time to say goodbye. It was an emotional farewell. He didn't really want us to leave. But we had to leave sometime so we finally said our goodbyes and headed home. There were some tears.

I don't think I'll ever forget the feeling I had that day saying goodbye and walking to the car to leave. We were leaving our kid in an environment where he didn't know one person, wondering if he would be able to handle college courses, would he be good enough to make the football team, etc. I'm sure he had the same feelings plus more. I also knew in a couple of weeks he would be fine.

The team had two-a-day practices for two weeks, and then classes started. Brad tried out for quarterback. He probably would have had a better chance to play college football if he had tried for defensive back. As a college quarterback he would have had to be a better passer.

Over Labor Day weekend he called home and said he wanted to quit football. Classes had started—he said football was taking up four hours of his time—practice was from 4–8 PM every day. He didn't know if he would ever play much. His heart wasn't in it. I just told him that it was best to hang it up if that is the way he felt. "Your decision is fine with me but just do one more thing—tell Coach you are quitting—tell him face-to-face." He did. A couple of other memories: I got an Afro for a hairdo. I kept it for eight years. The boy students thought it looked terrible, but the girls liked it. I liked it.

And my final memory for 1980.

One night I was grading some research projects while sitting on the living room floor. Ruth Ann was sitting at the dining room table talking to an insurance salesman who had something to do with county employees.

When he was talking, he looked at me sitting on the floor. He was making a point when he said, "Your son on the floor there would be covered." Ruth Ann informed him—"That's my husband." Carron recounted the events in the Christmas letter she wrote that year—"If mom looks different the next time you see her it's because she's had a facelift and dyed her hair. The house was evacuated for two hours until Dad's head returned to normal size." I thought the whole thing was funny but Ruth Ann, for some reason, didn't quite see it that way.

Erland Christensen, Yrsa Thom Chris and 12 others

Comments

Carlene Vavricek Pete, I forgot Colin and David visited Brad and Carron on Easter Sunday in France. I will have to ask Colin if he remembers. Very interesting.

PeteandRuth Ann Bungum

Monday, May 4, 2020. Pete and Ruth Ann's journey through 59 years.

The year is 1981.

We became empty nesters.

Carron became a senior this year. She played baritone in band, sang in the chorus and was on the golf team.

The golf team had a good year. They came in first, second or third in most of their meets. Carron's all-time best scores were a 41 (par 37) at Fawn Creek in Anamosa, and a 42 (par 36) at the Monticello course. She had a good four years as a high school golfer. And playing golf was a sport she played for many years.

Carron graduated the end of May. She also received special recognition, being chosen the outstanding French student. The award was worth some scholarship money and was sent directly to Coe College, her next home. Linda Kerton, her French teacher, chose her to receive the award. Her original goal at Coe was to major in French and English and become a teacher.

For the first time in 21 years of marriage, Ruth Ann and I, were alone.

Both of our kids were in college and now we only had Barney, our dog, for company. That dog had been part of our family for eleven years. Unfortunately, this would be his last. In November he had been hit by a car and had lost control of his plumbing system. One day he escaped, the police picked him up and took him to Dr. Wahl. He called Ruth Ann at the courthouse and told her it was time to put Barney to sleep. She told him to do it then we wouldn't have to see him die, nor would the kids. (BB: this was actually in 1982—I got a call from mom/dad on my 21st birthday while in Oslo with UWP—Barney had been put-down.)

But Barney left the four of us with a lot of memories. I'm going to share some of the most memorable.

Barney had never been fixed, so he was very active with the females. One time he escaped and found a dog in heat on the north side of town. The problem was that the dog was inside a screened-in porch. So, Barney tried to tear the front screen door down. But no luck for Barney—a city cop drove by and picked him up, takes him to our house and ties him in our backyard. It was the city attorney's house—he could have charged Barney with attempted breaking and entering plus the potential of sexual assault. He was saved from any prison time because the cop who picked him up knew Barney and liked him and tied him up in our backyard.

After another escape on a Friday night he went to the football field. The problem was he wanted to play. The JV game was on when I got a phone call from the press box at the stadium. This dog was running up and down the field—the guy who called knew me and knew the dog was Barney. I went to the field to get Barney. He was definitely the fastest player on the field and had scored several touchdowns. He finally came to me—I took him home. His football career was over.

Another time I was ready to start class when the secretary called on the intercom. "Mr. Bungum, you need to go to the first-grade room because Barney is in the room and is ready to do some learning." I walked in and Barney was sitting in the aisle by Lance Shelton, a neighbor boy. Barney knew Lance. I will say that Barney was quite attentive. His tongue was hanging out and he was ready for some learning. I took him out and released him—I thought he would go home. No luck. He went down to the river and rolled in dead fish.

Barney liked to roll in dead fish. The smell is terrible. Brad would take him to the shower to try and kill the smell. He could never completely get rid of the smell. So, Brad would put Aqua Velva after shave on him—it helped but still some smell. It would take three days to get rid of the smell.

Carron worked on main street at a drugstore. She called home one day and says Barney is peeing on all the light posts on Main Street. I went downtown to get Barney but by the time I got there he had already been picked up by the police and taken to city hall. I went in and the cops had tied him up and he was drinking a bowl of water. The city clerk had gotten it for him. She figured he must be dehydrated from watering all the posts on main street. Barney was not arrested—I got to take him home.

Barney always slept with Carron and Barney loved grandma Bungum. When she came to visit Barney was a happy camper. Grandma was a severe diabetic and had had both her legs amputated below the knee. When she came, she always slept in Carron's bed. When she went to bed, she took her prostheses off—she only took up half the bed. This is what made Barney so happy. He knew he was going to be alone in the bottom half of the bed and wouldn't have to worry about being kicked. When Grandma's bedtime came it was also Barney's bedtime. He would jump right in with Grandma, sprawl out in his half and enjoy a wonderful night of sleep.

Barney was notorious for passing gas. When we would drive back from Minnesota, he was terrible. Many times, the smell was so bad we would roll all four windows down. In the house he was just as bad.

When he would be resting on the floor and then get up and move to the other side of the room it meant he had let a real stinky and he couldn't stand the smell himself.

Barney loved garbage day. If he had escaped, he would tear into people's bags and eat just about anything. Often times he would get sick and vomit. What came out of his stomach was unbelievable. Over the years I saw twisty ties, cellophane, aluminum foil, a postage stamp, styrofoam, paper, cardboard, half a coffee filter. No wonder he got sick.

Barney was notoriously popular with the female dogs in Anamosa. He never went steady with any of them since he believed in one-night stands only. In fact, he impregnated dozens, perhaps hundreds of them in Anamosa. It is a good thing he didn't have to pay puppy support, or he would have been working 24/7 to make his payments. When I would go running in the morning, I swear every young dog I saw looked like Barney. He definitely left a permanent mark on Anamosa. Barney didn't want to go to Doggy Heaven without leaving behind many little Barneys.

I'll write more about 1981 tomorrow.

Yrsa Thom Chris, Dean Rickels and 4 others

PeteandRuth Ann Bungum

Tuesday, May 5, 2020.
Pete and Ruth Ann's journey through 59 years.

Today is 1981, Part 2.

Brad's life was changed for the rest of his life. And the life of Pete and Ruth Ann was changed also. Here is the story on how that happened.

Brad and Carron were helping me paint State Representative Andy McKean's house located eight miles south of Anamosa. Brad was dating a girl during his freshman year at Luther College in Decorah. Her name was Kathy Winter from Forest City, Iowa. She had been accepted into a group called Up with People. In July she left for Tucson, Arizona, to begin training. In early August, Kathy's mother in Forest City, called our house in Anamosa to tell Ruth Ann she knew a guy from Forest City who was delivering a Winnebago motor home to Tucson and he would be going through Des Moines. If Brad could get to Des Moines in four hours, he would have a free ride to Tucson to see Kathy.

The irony of this phone call is that Ruth Ann was walking out the door to go back to work after lunch when the phone rang. If the call had been ten seconds later Ruth Ann would not have heard the call because she would've been in the car going back to work and Brad's life may have turned out completely different. Ruth Ann called her boss and told her she would like to take the afternoon off to pick up Brad from his paint job and take him to Adventureland near Des Moines to meet a guy going to Tucson.

Grace, her boss, told Ruth Ann that her two sons and their dates were going to Adventureland that afternoon so Brad could ride with them. Ruth Ann called McKean's house, Andy answered, and said she wanted to talk to Brad. (Andy nearly missed the call as he was ready to leave when Ruth Ann called—another ten seconds and he would have missed it.) Brad got on the phone—she explained the phone calls she'd gotten and asked if he wanted to go to Tucson. Of course, he said yes. She told him she'd pick him up in 15 minutes. Then they would drive back to Anamosa, he could change clothes, pack his suitcase and join the free ride to Adventureland. He got the free ride to Adventureland, found the motor home and he was on his way to Tucson.

In Tucson Kathy talked him into interviewing for Up with People. In a couple weeks he received a letter from Up with People telling him that he had been accepted. His life would never be the same. He did the fall semester at Luther and in January flew to Tucson to begin six weeks of training. The next year would be one of most exciting and educational years of his life. He traveled over several states, western Canada and five or six countries in Europe.

Ruth Ann and I have talked many times about what would have happened if those two phone calls had been 10 seconds later. We're pretty sure Brad's life would've been very different. Call it fate or it was meant to be.

Another great memory happened at our teacher Christmas party. Colleague Bonnie Albertson asked me to come up front for a special gift. She and her poor innocent kids had made a pyramid-shaped cake made out of silly putty. It looked like a pyramid made of dog turds. And that is what it was supposed to be—a pile of shit. As I unveiled it my colleagues started singing "Climb Every Mountain" with the following lyrics:

> *We found Bungum's mountain*
> *Yes, this is it*
> *As you may have noticed*
> *It's just a pile of shit*
>
> *Yes, Peter Bungum*
> *These are your roots*
> *When you climb your mountain*
> *Be sure to wear hip boots*
>
> *This mountain is yours*
> *And it's gladly we give*
> *You can smell it every night*
> *For as long as you live*

151

Climb Bungum's mountain
Yes, this is it
Peter and his mountain
Both are full of shit

I guess Bonnie and some of my colleagues had gotten a little sick of me talking about that great mountain in Norway—Bungum Mountain. Not really, it was done with wonderful humor and brought a ton of laughs that night. In fact, the song was repeated by the same people at Brad and Inge's wedding reception in 1986. I asked Bonnie how she could force her kids to make a pile of shit. She said she had to lie to them and say they were making pretend candy. Close to child abuse, don't you think?

One other highlight for us was seeing all the Hawkeye football games. The Hawks had not had a winning season in 20 years. We were 6–2 in the Big Ten. We tied for the championship and got to go to the Rose Bowl. Paul and Karol Pinney joined us for all the games. We had a lot of good times on Hawkeye football Saturdays.

You, Yrsa Thom Chris, Bob Hines and 5 others

Comments

Elsie Narveson Talk about memories, you sure had them and so exciting

Phyllis Michels I am really looking forward to reading your story. The Fun part is that we were working together many of the you have shared. Sweet memories. Phyl. 😊

Carlene Vavricek Gary and I remember the Hawkeye Fun Wagon and a good time was had by all! Sweet memories! 😍

Richard Stout It's true. Life is lived moment to moment. Some moments count more than others. Sometimes it's a coin-flip decision you make. Sometimes you have little to do with the decision.

Sometimes, like in this retelling, it's just timing. If anyone would think back, it's true for everybody to some degree. Thanks for the stories, Pete.

PeteandRuth Ann Bungum

Wednesday, May 6, 2020. Pete and Ruth Ann's journey through 59 years.

The photo is the pile of shit Bonnie made for me at the Christmas party in 1981. I laugh every time I see it. Sorry to say Bonnie passed away a couple years ago from Parkinson's.

In January 1982, we took Brad to Rochester to catch a flight to Minneapolis so he could fly to Tucson to begin training for Up with People. His UWP experience was about to begin. Brad joined 100 other young people from all over the world, ages 18 to 26, to begin five weeks of training. They had to learn the show, including all the songs, dance routines, set-up and promotional responsibilities, community involvement activities and how to act respectfully when staying with host families.

By mid-February they were on the road staying with host families, doing community service projects and performing the show. Their fourth stop was in Anamosa. Brad would be performing before the home folks. It was a night to remember for the 1800 Anamosans who attended the show and especially for Ruth Ann and me.

Brad got to sing his first solo that night. He sang their theme song, "Up with People." He did a great job even though he had a few butterflies. Brad made the front page of the local paper the next week and was featured in a special broadcast by our local radio station. He also had a feature story about him in the Cedar Rapids Gazette the next Sunday.

We had a party for him at our house after the show. We invited many of his friends, our friends, his teachers and Carron came from Coe with several of her friends. The next day one of the girls in my class raised her hand and said, "Mr. Bungum, that son of yours is really cute." All the other girls agreed. The Anamosa show was the highlight of the year for Brad.

Before the Anamosa performance they had performed in Arizona, New Mexico and Oklahoma. The rest of the year Brad's cast would perform in Minnesota, Wisconsin, Michigan, Indiana, and the New England states. Later they would be in California, Oregon and Washington. Then they went to Canada and performed in Saskatchewan, Alberta and British Columbia. They finished up their year-long tour by going to Europe and performing in Belgium, Germany, Denmark, Sweden and Norway.

One other highlight for Brad was on Labor Day. Brad had a nerve-wrecking but fantastic experience of singing the UWP theme song in a joint concert with the Boston Esplanade Orchestra, directed by Harry Ellis Dixon. There were 125,000 people there. No wonder he was a little uptight.

When his year with UWP was over Ruth Ann and I assumed he was going back to Luther. But UWP offered him a job as an assistant stage manager and truck driver. After some pleading and consulting with his parents we relented and told him to go ahead and take the job. We knew how much he loved UWP.

In the summer we took a camping trip to follow his UWP tour. We saw shows in Michigan and Indiana. Then we traveled to Washington D.C. to see the sites. Traveling with us was Carron and her friend, Tom Hatcher. In DC we visited Senator Grassley's office. I told the receptionist to tell the Senator that I taught in Anamosa with his niece, Gwen Wiegman. When she told him, he said he would be happy to see us. He came out and we had a pleasant conversation and then we had a photo taken with him. I remember him telling us that he attended the University of Northern Iowa and took French. He said he could never understand that stuff.

One other memory from that trip is stopping at a motel in Fort Wayne, Indiana. We walked across the street to a restaurant and guess who was also eating there? Our neighbors from Anamosa were sitting four booths from us. The neighbors were Bing and Betty Norton, the parents of Carron's best friend, Diane the Shit Speller.

We visited with them and invited them to go to the UWP show with us the next day. The next day at the show, Betty along with many others, was invited on stage to participate in a dance. While she was on the stage Brad sang the UWP song. When he was done, he gave Betty a big hug. Betty said that it wasn't everyone that got a hug from the star of the show. She was really flattered. The next day the Norton's went with us to Canton, Ohio, to see the NFL Hall of Fame. I loved the place and could have spent many more hours there. I want to go back someday.

For Ruth Ann and me 1982 ranks as one of the most memorable years of our 59 years. So many wonderful memories.

Pete with pile of shit

You, Tim Bungum, Yrsa Thom Chris and 20 others

Comments

Richard Stout I remember the dinner party...lefse, kringla, and Bungum Mountain.

Brad Bungum Whatever happened to that Dad? I bet Barney eat it...

PeteandRuth Ann Bungum I have no idea

Brad Bungum probably still in the closet with my beer can collection

Phyllis Michels We really enjoyed that show! One of the cast members stayed with us.

PeteandRuth Ann Bungum

Thursday, May 7, 2020. Pete and Ruth Ann's journey through 59 years.

The year is 1983.

So how did Brad's cast get to Anamosa in February 1982? It was because a guy named Bob Walderbach arranged the whole affair. Bob was a beautician and he and his wife, Bonnie, were friends of ours.

He was active in the Anamosa Chamber of Commerce. An article (about Brad) in the Anamosa paper in October 1981, explained that Brad had joined a group called Up with People and would be traveling for a year all over the U.S., Canada and Europe. They would be putting on shows, doing community service and living with host families. Bob was very interested and told us he was going to call UWP headquarters in Tucson to see if they could come to Anamosa to put on a show. He wanted Brad's cast to come so he could perform in front of the home folks. He called, they agreed and said they would happily come in late February. The rest is history.

As a result of Bob bringing UWP to Anamosa three more boys would have the wonderful experience of a year in UWP. In the next ten years these three would join UWP: Dave George, Dan Walderbach (Bob and Bonnie's son) and Bret Lewison. Dan and Dave would both get to perform in Anamosa. Thanks to Bob—he made it happen.

We bought a vehicle in 1983 that was a wonderful experience for the next nine years. I had been painting a house in Monticello, ten miles north of Anamosa. On my way home one night I drove by a used car lot and saw something that caught my attention. It was a black and gold small bus. It had Hawkeye Fun Wagon written on both sides, a Tiger Hawk helmet on the front along with a Herky basketball player and wrestler.

I checked it over and could see through the front window it had been converted into a motor home. I talked to the dealer—he said the price was $2,700. I went home and told Ruth Ann about it—I convinced her it would be worth looking at. She went with me that night—she fell in love with it. The next day we bought it. We traded in our pop-up camper. They gave us $1,800 credit, so we bought it for $900. We had a lot of fun times going to Hawkeye games for the next nine years. Paul and Karol Pinney joined us for every game.

In July we took the Fun Wagon to a family reunion in MINNESOTA. When I met Minnesota cars many would wave. I'm not sure all waves were with the index finger.

In August we went to our 25th class reunion. When it was over, I had to drive nine miles south to Fountain where Ruth Ann's mom lived. In the first mile I realized I was being followed by a Minnesota Highway Patrolman. I made sure I wasn't speeding or weaving. A mile from Fountain there was another patrolman on the side of the road—he joined his buddy and they both followed me into town. When I turned to go to my mother-in-law's house one of the patrolmen put on his cherries and pulled me over.

He told me to get out of the car and show him my license. At this point I figured my only chance of not getting a ticket or a breath test was to explain that I was really a Minnesotan and that I was a teacher from Anamosa, Iowa, and had been to my 25th class reunion. I told him that I'd had several beers but was not inebriated and I only had three blocks to go to my mother-in-law's house. I invited him to follow me if he didn't believe me. He declined and gave me my license back. I respectfully asked him why he pulled me over. He answered: "You didn't do anything wrong, but we follow a lot of Iowa drivers to the border and they start speeding as they get closer to the border." What an answer!! I couldn't believe what happened and easily concluded I was stopped because of my Iowa plates.

When Ruth Ann went to work on Monday she ran into Larry Rohlena, an Iowa Highway Patrolman. She told Larry what had happened to us in Minnesota. He said it was ridiculous but not to push it because we wouldn't win. We didn't do anything, but the ugly memory persists.

We didn't take any big trips in 1983. We did go to Chicago for brother Mark's wedding. He was the last of the nine Bungum kids to say, "I do." He married Margie Perez. Their Lutheran minister played Cupid. He decided they would make a good couple, so he arranged for the two of them to get acquainted at his house on a Sunday afternoon. I don't know if it was love at first sight, but they hit it off—they got married in less than a year. They were no spring chickens—both in their 30s. Mark was 37. They are still married in 2020.

You, Yrsa Thom Chris, Dean Rickels and 10 others

Comments

Nicole Walderbach Duke I was only 5 but somehow remember both UWP coming to Anamosa (we had wonderful ladies stay with us) and the Fun wagon! What great memories.

Tammy Feist Sletten Hey Nicole!! I'm sure there is no way you remember me, but I remember you. I did the PR work prior to the cast coming to Anamosa. Your Dad celebrated a milestone birthday while I was there. We decorated his shop up royally to celebrate and I believe the Bungum's had a get-together at their house for your Dad's birthday? Anyway, I have a picture of you from way back in 82 at the birthday party for your Dad. Oh, and by the way Mr. PeteandRuth Ann Bungum I remember Barney all too well. He was still around in 82, unless you got a dog the following year? Virginia and I spent the better part of a morning chasing him down in the snow to get him back in the house!

> **PeteandRuth Ann Bungum** hey—I was off by one year when Barney died. It was 1982 (and not 1981) when we had him put to sleep. Was he healthy when you stayed with us?

Bonnie Walderbach Tammy Feist Sletten Remember you and Virginia. What a fun time!

Nicole Walderbach Duke Tammy Feist Sletten I do remember! It was so exciting to meet people from outside of our small town. I think it must have been my dad's 40th! Now this weekend I will celebrate my 42nd! Wow.

Tammy Feist Sletten Bonnie, Hi!!!!! And Nicole, Happy Birthday!!! 😊 I can't believe you remember me!! Yes, what a fun time I had in Anamosa with all of you!! I don't remember your brother? And Wow, he traveled with UWP! Hey, Mr. PeteandRuth Ann Bungum I am so impressed with all the details of your journey!! I don't remember Barney being sick? I do remember that we got told NOT to let him out of the house because of some of the trouble he had been in. It was NOT an easy catch to get him back in. The cold wet snow did not help, and your house was up on a hill?? I remember sliding all over the place trying to run after him. I also remember that every night he would sleep with Virginia (she was not that thrilled), and no matter what I did to try to get him to come bunk with me, he wouldn't have it.

PeteandRuth Ann Bungum

Hawkeye Fun Wagon

Alexandra Bungum, Bret Lewison and 24 others

Carlene Vavricek Gary and I were fortunate to be included in some of the Hawkeye Fun Wagon adventures over the years! Fun times! ♡

> **PeteandRuth Ann Bungum** glad you had a good time. Show this to your parents. They would like to see it.

> **Carlene Vavricek** PeteandRuth Ann Bungum I will Pete!

Bonnie Walderbach Oh what fun we had a couple of times with you guys! Go Hawks!

> **PeteandRuth Ann Bungum** I agree—wish I still had it.

> **Bonnie Walderbach** PeteandRuth Ann Bungum We took that bus to The Library (Bar) with the girls from UWP!

Brad Bungum Bonnie Walderbach, I'm sure Betsy Myers & Tina remember it well 😊 😵

Brian Sissel PeteandRuth Ann Bungum… I think my parents may have traveled on that??

> **PeteandRuth Ann Bungum** i don't remember. If they did, they would've had a good time—I can't remember ever having a bad time. Lots of beers were consumed in that Fun Wagon.

Jeffrey N Norton So 🤓

Phyllis Michels I remember that 🚌 bus! What fun!

PeteandRuth Ann Bungum

Friday, May 8, 2020. Pete and Ruth Ann's journey through 59 years.

The year is 1984.

Before I get into 1984, I want to tell how UWP promotes a show. We had a capacity crowd of 1,800 people at Brad's UWP show in February 1982.

Here is how UWP does it.

The show had been promoted for three weeks prior to the cast arriving. It was promoted by two girls who were members of the cast. Every member of the cast has to do promotions—at least twice or it could be three times like Brad did. They get training on how and what to do when they go on promotion.

In February we picked them up from the Cedar Rapids airport. The girls were Virginia Ware from Tuscumbia, Alabama, and Tammy Feist from Faith, South Dakota. They were with us the entire three weeks. The girls turned our basement into their office. And we let them use our Ford Pinto. Being Tammy was from South Dakota we let her drive because she was used to driving on snow and ice. However, one afternoon she backed out of our driveway and slid sideways into the telephone pole between the sidewalk and the street. Tammy was embarrassed but there was no damage. We all got a good laugh out of her so-called South Dakota driving skills.

Their job in those three weeks was to line up host families for 100 cast members. Then they had to let people know about the show so they would attend the February 28th performance. The girls gave speeches to Rotary, JCs, Chambers of Commerce, City Councils, Sunday morning church services, the schools, plus any other places that would spread the word. They went to all the neighboring towns in the county—Monticello, Olin, Wyoming, Martelle, Morley.

Both were good speakers, had great smiles, pleasant personalities and a good sense of humor. Virginia had a real Southern accent—lots of people liked to hear her talk. The end-result was that the girls did a wonderful job. They were the talk of the town and they sold out the show.

After the year was over Tammy went home to Faith and married John, her hometown boyfriend. They had a daughter who was born with Downs Syndrome. Through her Christmas letters we realize how fortunate their daughter was to be born to those two, loving people—Tammy and John. Tammy had great self-discipline. She was well organized and was a hard-working girl from the Midwest. Her father ran a Super Valu grocery store in Faith. A year later Tammy's parents stopped in Anamosa to see us.

Virginia went home to Alabama. She became a secretary/receptionist for her Congressman in the mid-80s. She married and had two children. In 2003 we heard the shocking news that Virginia had died of an aneurysm at the age of 40. Ruth Ann and I always remembered Virginia for her wonderful Southern accent and her smile and sense of humor. Virginia's father was a banker in Tuscumbia.

I'm grateful Ruth Ann and I had those girls for three weeks. By doing so it created many more good memories for us.

Now it's time for 1984. I have a couple favorite memories from that year.

The Hawkeyes had been winning football games for three years now so there was all kinds of Hawkeye stuff to buy. I found a pair of black panties with these words on the back, "I'm behind the Hawkeyes." I bought a pair for Ruth Ann. I went to her office and told her I had special gift for her. She opened it and told me, "You have too much time on your hands." She actually wore them many times. When she wore her white slacks, you could read the words.

In 1984 Lute Olson quit coaching the Hawkeyes and went to Arizona to coach. Brad was enrolled there. Ruth Ann told me in October she wanted to fly to Arizona to see Brad. Then she added that she was going to make some lefse and take it to Coach Lute Olson. We knew Lute was a Norwegian and had eaten lefse while growing up. Brad and I laughed it off and told her to forget it. Ruth Ann had her mind made up and wasn't going to let her husband and son tell her what to do. So, she wrote a letter to Lute and told him she was coming to Tucson at Thanksgiving to see her son and she would be happy to make him some lefse so he could enjoy the Norwegian delicacy. I'll be darned if she didn't get a personal hand-written note from Lute a week later. He said following the game he would meet us outside the locker room.

I had to eat crow, especially when I told her I would like to go also. She wrote to Lute again asking if she could get one more ticket—"My husband has decided to come." A couple of days later Ruth Ann gets a phone call at the office from Lute's secretary—"Yes, there would be a ticket for your husband."

I met Lute after the game outside the locker room—he told us to go out and find Bobbie (his wife) in the stands and wait with her until he got done with his radio interview. Lute came and we visited for 15 minutes. We had a photo taken of the four of us showing Ruth Ann handing the lefse to Lute. What a great memory. Thank God, Ruth Ann had the perseverance to stick to her plan or this never would have happened.

In 1984 the Hawkeyes were 8–4–1. We were invited to the inaugural Freedom Bowl in San Antonio. We played Texas and beat them 55–17.

Carlene Vavricek, Bob Hines and 11 others

Comments

Bret Lewison That Freedom Bowl was actually in Anaheim, CA in a downpour. Chuck Long threw for 6 TDs if I remember right and the 55 points scored by the Hawks was the most points scored on the Longhorns since beginning of the 20th Century. That game really catapulted the Hawks into that great 1985 season.

Mallory Jefferis Great story.

Brad Bungum Bret Lewison, you're right (of course ;-)). It was Anaheim. But did Long have 6, or 5 TD passes? I think you're right on that too…

PeteandRuth Ann Bungum

Saturday, May 9, 2020. Pete and Ruth Ann's journey through 59 years.

The year is 1985.

You, Yrsa Thom Chris, Alan Recker and 10 others

Comments

Tammy Feist Sletten Wow! What a blast from the past!!

PeteandRuth Ann Bungum

Saturday, May 9, 2020. Pete and Ruth Ann's journey through 59 years.

The year is 1985.

On June 18 we celebrated our 25th anniversary. We celebrated by getting together with our high school friends, Jerry and Elsie Narveson. We met at the Pink Elephant Hotel in Marquette, Iowa. They were celebrating their 25th anniversary also. We got to the hotel first. Ruth Ann had decided to bring her boots. She would then tell Jerry that the reason for the boots was that whenever Jerry and I got together our high school athletic heroics got bigger and better every time. Therefore, she needed to wear boots in order to walk through the deep *you know what*. We had a great time. We did some sightseeing along the Mississippi, went to Prairie du Chien and shopped, played cards, drank a few beers and did a whole lot of talking and laughing about our experiences as couples and friends.

Our big trip in 1985 was a month-long trip to Europe. It was not only our 25th but we were going to meet the parents of Inge Nielsen, Brad's future wife. We flew from Chicago to Frankfurt, Germany. During the flight I was a little uptight about driving in Europe. Brad had driven a lot in Europe—he told me not to worry because it wasn't that much different except for some signs.

We landed in Frankfurt at 7:00 AM. Went through customs and then to Hertz Rent-A-Car. They gave us a little Opal Corsa. Within 15 minutes I was driving on the Autobahn and Ruth Ann was the map reader and navigator.

We were going west on our way to Belgium to visit Rik Vlemmings who had stayed at our house in 1983 when he was in UWP. I knew we had to drive about 20 kilometers and then turn north. Ruth Ann was reading the map—I told her we have to turn pretty soon. She screamed at me, "I can't read this f-ing map—it's written in German!"

I turned around and went back to Frankfurt. I saw a guy (he was in the US Air Force) at a gas station and asked him, "What highway do I take to Belgium?" He told me. He said I wasn't the first one to miss that highway—it's a little hard to see. We made the correct turn and got to Bonn at mid-afternoon. We stayed for the night. We were very tired. Ruth Ann went to bed at 6:00 PM and slept till 8:00 AM for a total of 14 hours of sleep. We had breakfast at the hotel—no charge—as it was included in the room charge. Our destination was Bree, Belgium, to get to the home of Rik. We stopped at a bank to exchange dollars for Belgian francs. The exchange rate was wonderful, 33 francs to the dollar. I gave him $100 dollars—I got 3,300 francs. I felt rich. The banker told us how to get to Rik's house.

We had a picnic with Rik's family and then Rik took us on a walking tour of downtown.

The next day Rik and his brother drove us to Brussels, the capital. We saw the highlights, including the palace, the changing of the guard, the Atomium at the site of the 1959 World's Fair and the soccer field where 30 people were killed at a soccer game two months before.

We left Brussels by 3:00 PM and Rik stopped at a small town. Rik told us we were in Waterloo where Napoleon suffered his final defeat in 1815. We climbed up the 224 steps to the top of the earthen monument commemorating the battle. At the top they had maps explaining the fields below that would help us visualize the battle. What a thrill for me to see Waterloo.

That night Rik had to be the disc jockey at the local high school. He invited us along. What an eye opener for us. The parents were serving beer and pop. The kids, ages 15–17, could have either. We didn't see any kids who were inebriated. Needless to say, that wouldn't go over in the USA. We danced a few slow ones—the kids laughed at us.

Rik's job was something we don't have in America. He worked for a local brewery delivering beer door-to-door, like we used to have when milkman delivered milk.

On Sunday morning Rik had to leave early to go to a rock fest in western Belgium. We were left alone with his parents—they didn't speak English and we definitely didn't speak Flemish. We ate breakfast in silence. Then his mom packed a basket, handed it to us and said, "Picnic." That basket was filled with fruit and pastries which we ate later that day in Germany. That was so nice of them. When we got in the car to leave, his father said, "I love you." I'm guessing Rik taught them those words before he left. We still communicate with them every Christmas. Rik is married and has two adult daughters.

We left Bree and drove to Hamburg and stayed overnight. On the way we stopped at a rest stop and ate our picnic. From Hamburg we drove into Denmark. Our goal was to get to a city called Horsens and then put our car on a ferry boat to go an island called Samso. When on the ferry boat I saw a poster that caught my attention. It was entitled, "Fartplan." Ruth Ann took a photo with me standing by it. I asked Brad what it meant. He said it meant, "Schedule."

We got to the harbor to unload. We drove our car off the ferry. Then we saw Brad and Inge and her parents. They were waving a Danish flag, a U.S. flag and a black and gold "Go Hawks" sign. Arne, Inge's father, arranged for that to happen. We met her parents, Arne and Ellinor Nielsen. Then we followed them to their summer home. We sat on their patio, exchanged gifts and had a Tuborg, a Danish brewed beer. We gave them Hawkeye sweatshirts. They gave us prints of Samso Island.

One of our favorite photos was the two of them wearing their Hawkeye sweatshirts and holding up a Go Hawks sign and trying to say, "Go Hawks." It came out like Hoaks or Hokes. It was good for many laughs. After six days we left Samso and took off for Sweden.

I'll write about Sweden tomorrow.

You, Bret Lewison, Erland Christensen and 7 others

Comments

Phil Bungum ;~]

PeteandRuth Ann Bungum

Sunday, May 10, 2020. Pete and Ruth Ann's journey through 59 years.

The year is 1985, Part II.

After six days in Samso, we headed for Sweden. But first, I have to report on a favorite memory from those six days.

The morning after our arrival on Samso we had breakfast. When done we had a surprise. Arne brought out a bottle and poured us a shot from his bottle. He told us to sip it and drink it with our coffee. What he gave us was something called Gammel Dansk. It was bitter—I could hardly swallow it. Ruth Ann felt the same.

After we drank the shot Arne filled up our shot glass again. He announced, "The first shot got your left leg moving—now we have to get your right foot going." So that was our introduction to Gammel Dansk—a Danish tradition. The second shot went down easier than the first. By the third day we were looking forward to our two shots. It grew on us—we started to like it. The alcohol level is high—I don't know the exact amount but you do start out each day with a little buzz.

No wonder the Danes are the happiest people in the world. For the last 35 years Brad and granddaughter Alexandra have been giving us bottles of Gammel Dansk for Christmas.

Now on to Sweden. We were going to meet Bitte Larson, another of Brad's UWP friends who been to our house in 1983. We had written to her, so she knew we were coming. We met her in Stockholm. We ate with her at a restaurant in Gamla Staden (Old Town). We did a walking tour and then she helped us find a hotel. She had to leave but we made arrangements to meet the next day.

We took a boat tour of Stockholm. We learned that Stockholm was founded in 1250 AD. It was a city of 20 islands and several peninsulas connected by many bridges and ferry boats. The next day we traveled west to Molkom, the home of Bitte's parents. Their names were Ingvar and Bodil Larson. A memory of our visit was when Bitte and her father got into a heated discussion about Sweden selling iron ore to Hitler during World War II. Bitte was upset and embarrassed that Sweden had done such a thing—her father was much less vocal about it. Bitte said that Sweden's young people were not one bit proud of their country for doing what they did. She said there are still some hard feelings by Norwegians and Danes towards Sweden because of her actions. They haven't forgotten that Norway and Denmark were occupied by Nazi Germany and Sweden wasn't.

We headed west and drove to Oslo. We found a hotel on a cruise ship docked in the harbor. The next day we took the trolley to the world's most famous ski jump, Holmenkollen. Our next stop was the Viking ship museum. We saw a replica of the boats the Vikings took to Greenland around 1000 AD. Then we saw the Kon-Tiki museum and the original Kon-Tiki raft Thor Heyerdahl took across the Pacific Ocean in 1947. Next was Frogner Park. It is the huge outdoor sculpture park that contains over 200 sculptures. They were created by Gustav Vigeland who tried to tell the story of human life from birth to death.

The next day we drove north to Ringebu to find Ruth Ann's relatives and to find the gravestones of her ancestors. We found many of her ancestors. One of them was the grave of her great-grandfather Roen. We also found gravestones with the names Severud and Tangen. Her mother was a Syverud and her grandmother's maiden name was Tangen. So we found three sides of Ruth Ann's family. The name Roen was changed to Rain when the family came to America in the 1870s.

We asked a hotel clerk if she knew any Roens. She told us to drive up the mountain road until we got to John Roen's house. We lucked out, we found John, he spoke enough English so we could communicate. He told us to follow him to his house at the top of the mountain.

At the top we saw grass covered level land. It was all pasture with dairy cows all over the place and small barns and houses located five to ten acres apart. These were the summer pastures I read about as a kid. John owned 15 acres plus the house and the barn. In the house were John's two kids, 30-year-old Tirol, and 25-year-old Ole and wife Torva. They both spoke fluent English. John told us every

May they bring their 11 cows up and stay until September. John and Ole took turns milking in the summer months. John also owned that little farm where we found him. It was too hilly to grow crops except for hay for their cows. I asked Ole how his dad could make a living on that little farm. Ole explained that the Government subsidized farmers up to 12 times the value of their milk. He said if your milk was valued at $5,000 the government would pay the farmer $50,000 to $60,000. The reason for this was that the government wanted to keep people on these small farms so they wouldn't leave and move to the cities and cause unemployment.

Toril invited us to stay at her house in Vinstra. I'll finish Norway tomorrow.

You, Bret Lewison, Rhenee Grabau and 10 others

Comments

Elsie Narveson Interesting

Phyllis Michels I really enjoyed this post. When we took a Scandinavian trip way back when, we visited the stuff you mentioned in Oslo. Such an interesting place to visit. 😋

Phil Bungum ;~]

PeteandRuth Ann Bungum

Monday, May 11, 2020. Pete and Ruth Ann's journey through 59 years.

The year is 1985, Part 3.

After going to the grassy pasture on top of the mountain we went to Toril's house in Vinstra the next day. She had arranged a family gathering so we could meet more of Ruth Ann's ancestors. We met Thea, John's mother and his sister, Astrid, and husband, Herman, and another sister, Marta and husband, Hans.

We visited Thea's house—this is where Ruth Ann's grandpa Roen was born in the 1850s. Toril served us coffee and rosettes and krumkakke. Ruth Ann and I make those every year at Christmas.

Ruth Ann and Toril sat down and tried to figure out how closely related they were. They concluded they were fourth cousins. However, you could see a remarkable resemblance from the Roen genes. They both had rather square faces, complexions that were identical, and similar eyes, noses and smiles. They could have passed for sisters.

I had bragged to Ruth Ann for years that the Bungum family had a famous mountain named after them in Norway. Well, she got her revenge. Because she found out from Toril that there were three hills named after the Roen family. The hills were named Big Roen Hill, Middle Roen Hull and Little Roen Hill. We had driven on Middle Roen Hill. She got her kicks in by telling me she had three hills named after her family and at least there were roads you could drive on to get to get them.

It was time to leave Toril and head for Bungum Mountain. Before we left Toril told me to never drink when driving in Norway. If you get stopped and have to do the breathalyzer and if you have been drinking it will earn you a 21-day vacation in a Norwegian jail. There will be no trial—you go straight to jail. Toril said the government will allow you to do two weeks in the summer and the other three weeks in the winter. That takes care of the five weeks of vacation all Norwegians get every year. They call these "state vacations."

Then we drove west over the mountains to get to Sogne Fjord, the location of Bungum Mountain. When we drove into the town of Arnefjord, I stopped at the grocery store, went in and asked the girl working there if she could tell me where Bungum Mountain was. She said you must be from America. I told her my name was Bungum and I wanted to see where my grandpa was born in 1850. She got a big smile on her face and told me to follow her. She led me outside and pointed to the mountain I had just driven by and said look up, "That is Bungum Mountain right there." I was excited to think I was looking at grandpa's birthplace—this was the source of my name.

Brother Don had told me when I got there to "ask somebody to help you find the only schoolteacher living there because he would line up some kids to guide you up the mountain." The store girl told me how to get to his house. We found his house, introduced ourselves and he immediately remembered brother Don. We told him we would need some help climbing. So he calls two 12-year-old girls and a 16-year-old girl. We met them at the store, and they led us up to the Bungum farm buildings.

On the way up Ruth Ann had to stop and rest several times. I told her if she died it was the perfect place to end it all. For some reason she didn't appreciate my sense of humor. The original house and small barn were still there. Grandpa was born in that house in 1850. It was not flat land by a long shot—the only animals that could survive there would've been sheep and goats. I was told that the Bungum's did have cows. The only crop was hay. The main food had to be fish. We took a lot of photos. The view was fantastic—looking at the fjord below and mountains across.

Climbing Bungum Mountain was one of the highlights of my life and fulfilled one of my life-long goals and dreams. I could now scratch that off my Bucket List. The girls led us down to Arnefjord. I gave each girl 20 kroner for helping us out.

After seeing the Bungum homestead I know now why my grandpa and two of his siblings left that mountain home, in 1869, and came to Dodge County, Minnesota. The land there is flat as a pancake and you can grow all kinds of crops and raise all kinds of animals.

Grandpa's name was Peder—I was named after him. He married Martha Opheim on June 12, 1879. They would have ten kids—7 boys and 3 girls.

We left Bungum Mountain and headed for Bergen. A good memory from our stay in Bergen: we went to a nice restaurant. The guy waiting on us recognized right away we were from the States. He wanted to know where from so when we said Anamosa, Iowa, his eyes lit up. He said he was a foreign exchange student in Decorah in 1977–1978. We told him we lived on Winnebago street—he knew exactly where it was. He also knew where Anamosa was. He asked me if remembered the good basketball team Decorah had that year. I told him I sure did. I said, "Didn't you almost make it the state tournament that year?"

He said that was true—they got beat one game away from the state—Davenport Central beat them. He said he was the sixth man on that team. Talk about a small world!

Tim Bungum, Rhenee Grabau and 9 others

Comments

Phil Bungum ;~]

Bret Lewison That 77–78 Decorah team would have had Lon Olejniczak (probably Billy Broghammer too) on the team. Lon was all-state in 3 sports as a senior (football, basketball and baseball). I think Lon and Billy were both 79 grads. Lon & Bill both went on to play football for the Hawks in the early '80s (Lon at TE & Billy at WR).

PeteandRuth Ann Bungum

Tuesday, May 12, 2020. Pete and Ruth Ann's journey through 59 years.

The year is 1985.

We left Bergen and headed for Denmark via some driving and ferry boats. Our destination was Copenhagen to see Arne and Ellinor again before we went back to Anamosa. We stayed a couple days. We were grateful that they took us to Tivoli, Denmark's famous amusement park. It was one more thing I could cross off my Bucket List.

Then it was time to go back home. We took a ferry boat to Germany and drove to Frankfurt—returned our Opal to Hertz and within an hour we were on our plane heading for Chicago. We drove home. It was quiet when we walked in the door. Then Carron opened the patio door and in come ten people to welcome us home. Carron had arranged the party—we partied until 2:00 A.M. That was a nice gesture by Carron.

I have a few reflections about Europe.

It was the greatest learning experience of my life. Here are a couple more:

— The people of Europe seem to have a more relaxed approach to daily life.
— They aren't hung up on having a few beers or a glass of wine with their meals. Their attitude towards food is to eat real slow. Good food is one of the great joys of life and Europeans have learned how to enjoy it.
— The outdoor cafes caught my attention. Sitting outside and having a beer/wine and eating good food and watching people walk by is fun and relaxing.
— Another thing was seeing many people walking or riding a bike. As a result, I saw fewer people in the fat or obese category. On our first day in Europe we went to an ALDI store and there were 7–8 bicycles in front, all ridden by women. You don't see that very often in the USA.

— We have been to Denmark over a dozen times since 1985. We like it over there.

What an autumn we had in 1985. The Hawkeyes went 10–1. The Hawkeyes were co-champs in the Big Ten and went to the Rose Bowl. Yes, we did see the Michigan-Iowa game when Rob Houghtlin kicked the winning field goal with 2 seconds left. There was absolute pandemonium in Kinnick—screaming, hugging, high fives and thousands of fans on the field mobbing the players. What a happy night that was.

We made reservations to go to Pasadena to see the game. Brad came from Denmark to see the game. We also were joined by Paul and Verna Lewison from Anamosa. New Year's Day we got up at 4:30, ate breakfast and got on the tour bus by 6:00 for the hour drive to Pasadena to watch the Rose Bowl Parade which started at 8:00 AM. The parade was wonderful, and it was almost unbelievable to imagine all the roses on the floats.

When it was over it was back to the bus and a ride to the stadium. We got beat by 45–28 by UCLA. Ronnie Harmon fumbled 5 times. He had only one fumble all year. Yes, we were disappointed because we actually had the better team, but you can't turn the ball over 5 times against a good team like UCLA and expect to win. Brad took the loss seriously. I tried to cheer him up by telling him, "Hey, cheer up, there are a billion Chinese who could care less if the Hawks won or lost." It didn't do much good.

The next big event in 1986 was Brad and Inge getting married on October 18. Inge's parents and sister (Arne, Ellinor and Bente) flew in from Denmark. The next day we took them to a Hawkeye football game in Iowa City. They got to ride in The Hawkeye Fun Wagon—we won—beat Wisconsin.

The next day Paul Pinney and I took Arne to the Wapsi Country Club. We introduced him to 7–8 people. His memory was amazing. The next week, when he and Ellinor were taking a walk around town and they ran into one of those people he had met, Arne would greet them by their first name. I asked him how he could do this. He said he made a point of remembering names. As a businessman back in

Denmark he said it was important to remember names. One day he walked into T&D grocery store and said, "Hi Buddy, how's business?" He had met Buddy five days before. By the way, Arne was in the grocery business in Denmark.

Arne and Ellinor expressed a desire to see the Mississippi River. In elementary school they had read about Mark Twain's Huckleberry Finn and Tom Sawyer. They had never forgotten about life on the river with Tom, Huck and Becky Thatcher—they had to see the Mississippi. So off to the river we went. We took a photo of them kneeling by the river and putting their fingers in the water. They had big smiles on their faces. Then we took them on an evening dinner cruise on the Spirit of Dubuque. We had the guitar player play "Ole Man River"—we danced and sang. They really enjoyed their Dubuque visit.

I had Arne come and talk to my classes. They asked him a lot of questions—they enjoyed his accent.

On Thursday night, two nights before the wedding, Ruth Ann got a phone call from Colleen Guhl. She had been hired to make the wedding cake. Her husband had just died so she would not be able to make the cake. So, the three women decided to make a Danish wedding cake, called a kransakakke.

It looks like a pyramid. The cake dough is hand rolled into long, round sausage-like pieces and then laid one upon another until the 15–20-inch-tall cake was made.

But things weren't going right. The strips were not holding together as they should. Ruth Ann said Pete had a cousin in Minneapolis who had experience making these cakes. She called her and found out what they were doing wrong. The cousin told her you need to use powdered sugar rather than granulated. The problem was solved. Inge, Ellinor and Ruth Ann stayed up until 3:00 AM—the kransakakke was a success.

By Friday the wedding attendants were coming to town. Inge's attendants came from Arkansas, Texas, Denmark, California and Anamosa.

Brad's came from Colorado, Arizona, California, Pennsylvania, Minnesota, New York, Iowa and Anamosa.

Saturday morning the guys played a game of touch football. Eric, the African American, caught a knee to the eye. It swelled big time and he was to be singing a solo in five hours. As he was leaving to go to the doctor, he told Ruth Ann, "Don't worry Mrs. Bungum, the worst that can happen is that I'll have a black eye."

I'll finish 1986 tomorrow.

PeteandRuth Ann Bungum, Bret Lewison and 12 others

Comments

Bret Lewison Lots of great personal memories of people, places & events for me recalled in this post. Big smile on my face. Looking forward to tomorrow's finish to 1986.

PeteandRuth Ann Bungum

Wednesday, May 13, 2020. Pete and Ruth Ann's journey through 59 years.

The years are 1986–1987.

Brad and Inge's wedding was at 4 PM. My brother Paul performed the ceremony. He had also married us in 1960 so we decided he may as well marry Brad and Inge. He would also marry Carron and Dean on May 2.

The reception was held at the Holiday Inn in Cedar Rapids. It was a fantastic night. Paul Pinney served as MC and did a great job. The staff did a great job of serving the food and keeping the wine glasses filled. I gave a talk and Arne gave a talk. The guests loved his accent. By the time the reception was over many people had talked and told stories about Brad and Inge.

One talk I remember the most was from Bret Lewison. He was Brad's friend since age four. He winged it with no notes. This is what I remember the most from Bret's talk. He said that when Brad did something, he would do it also. He mentioned that "Brad went to Luther, so I went to Luther. Brad dated Kathy then I dated Kathy. Brad went into UWP then I went into UWP. Brad became a cast manager then I became a cast manager." There were several other things he mentioned. It was a great talk by Bret. All the talks were great—some funny and some more serious. We also sang some Danish wedding songs.

Then we got to watch a skit put on by my teacher colleagues. The skit's main theme was that Brad and Inge were going to get married on the 50-yard line at Kinnick Stadium. My principal, Walt Fortney, played the role of the minister. Paul Pinney was Hayden Fry. Darling Algoe and Bonnie Albertson played Brad and Inge. They ended the skit by singing, Climb Bungum's Mountain. I guess they wanted my family and friends to know that they weren't impressed with Peter and his famous mountain in Norway. The reception ended with a dance.

After the reception we went to our room and were joined by Jerry and Elsie Narveson from Chatfield and Connie and Carson from Des Moines. These two guys faced each other in a high school baseball game in May of 1956. You guessed it! They were arguing again as to how many hits Carson got off Jerry. Carson said he got 2–3 hits—*"I couldn't miss hitting that baseball because your fastball looked like a watermelon."* Jerry admitted Carson had one hit but definitely not 2–3. We went to bed at 5 AM. I don't know if it will ever be settled. It was a fun argument—all done in good humor.

The newlyweds went to Cancun for their honeymoon. By Monday night everyone had gone home. Ruth Ann and I were alone, we looked at each other and I said, "Well, it's all over, we can relax now." It's back to work tomorrow. That day I showed my students the video that Bob Algoe had taped for us. They really enjoyed it. We would soon start planning for Carron and Dean's wedding in seven months.

1987

This was a year of two major events—another wedding and a move to another house.

Carron and Dean set May 2nd as their wedding date. Dean was a local boy—he graduated with Carron in 1981. He was the son of LaVerne and Marian Rickels who were corn and soybean and hog farmers. Dean went to Lincoln Tech in Des Moines to get a degree as an automotive technician. He completed an 18-month course in 12 months.

One good memory was Carron calling from Cedar Rapids to tell me her and Mom had found a beautiful dress. She said, "I really like it, but it costs $600." I guess she was wondering if I thought it was too expensive. I told her if she liked it just buy it. It wouldn't have been fair to Carron if I said no.

Another fun memory is the rehearsal dinner. It was held at the Rickels farm. Brother Paul and wife Nellie rode with us to the farm. When we got out of the car, Nellie asked, "What is that smell?" Paul and I both said, "It is the smell of money." What Nellie was smelling was hog manure. I'm not sure she had ever smelled it before. The rehearsal dinner was different, relaxed and fun. It was typical Iowa, held in a farm basement with wonderful food and great people who were friendly, sincere, hard-working and as down-to-earth as you can find.

The wedding was at 4:00 PM. Brother Paul performed the ceremony. He now could say he had married the whole family—including Ruth Ann and me plus Brad and Inge. A disaster almost happened. When I walked Carron up the aisle and gave her to Dean I stepped on her train as I was trying to get to my seat. Thank goodness I saw what I was doing. I stepped back otherwise her train would've been ripped off and I probably would've tripped and fallen. I managed to avoid a real embarrassing situation. Carron didn't deserve to lose part of her wedding dress in front of 250 people. Sometimes the Good Lord looks over you.

After the ceremony I was standing by Mrs. Rickels and introducing her to all my relatives and friends. I did have a very embarrassing moment. When Walt Fortney, my principal, came through the line I did it. I said, "Marian, I want you to meet Walt and his wife, Bobette." The only trouble was that this was Carolyn, Walt's second wife.

He had divorced Bobette three years earlier. I quickly realized my faux pas and corrected myself, but the damage had been done. On Monday morning I talked to Carolyn and apologized to her. She told me not worry about it because it had happened before. The reason for the faux pas was Ruth Ann and I had known Walt and Bobette for over a dozen years, so it was natural to say, "Walt and Bobette."

Paul Pinney was MC again and did another good job. A lot of talks were given. Ruth Ann and I had written a poem about Carron. We had also written one for Brad. When I got up to read it I told Carron that her poem was twice as long as Brad's. She responded by saying, "That's because I did a lot more things than Brad."

Others giving talks were:

— Brother John, who was a godparent, gave a wonderful talk.

— Brad gave another—he told her his hardest job in life was cleaning her car. There is some truth in that statement.

— Preacher Paul told a joke. He said when he visited our house one time, Ruth Ann got upset with her. She told Carron to go to her room. She went and we didn't hear from her for an hour. Then Ruth Ann asked me to go check on her. I finally found her underneath her bed, and she didn't want to come out. So, I climbed underneath her bed to pull her out. As I was going under the bed to pull her out Carron says to me, "what's the matter Dad, did Mom get mad at you, too." This was good for some laughs.

— Dean and his brother Dan, did a take-off on the Smothers Brothers. It was hilarious. Bob Algoe did the video again. It was a fun evening.

Ruth Ann and I were so grateful we had two wonderful weddings.

The second big event in 1987 was moving. After 20 years living at 403 South Garnavillo, we bought another house. Those 20 years were the most memorable in our lives. It is where we raised Carron and Brad and all the memories that went with it. There would never be any future house that would replace or surpass the importance of that three-story, gold and brown shuttered house on Garnavillo street.

The question is, why did we move? I guess it came down to the fact that we needed a change in our life. The nest was empty now with both of our kids married. We were in a rut. To get out of the rut we bought another house. The house was on the east side of town. It was a one-story house with an antiquated swimming pool, and some cobbled additions built on. The inside of the house needed some updating and cleaning. This would be just what we needed. We needed a new project to occupy our minds. I had learned in my life that I was happiest when I had a project to work on. Ruth Ann felt the same. We bought the house from Jerry and Millie Fisher on Third Street. We would live there for eight years. We did numerous repairs and changes in those eight years. As a result, we were able to double our money.

We also changed our social life. We left Wapsi Country Club and joined Fawn Creek Country Club. We were due for a change in that regard also.

These two changes helped us get out of our rut. And it also turned out to be quite profitable.

As Ruth Ann and I looked back over our life together we both agreed we did the right thing in making those changes.

There is one more thing that took place in 1987. Ruth Ann started having upper back and neck problems. It was the beginning of a lot of pain she would have the rest of her life. One doctor wanted to do surgery—she said no—I want a second opinion. We asked Dr. Bailey to recommend another doctor—he recommended Dr. LaMorges in Cedar Rapids. Thank God for him. He had treated Kenny Fearing and was successful. He put her on pills and had traction done on her neck. Over the next year she became pain free. When it reoccurred in future years, she would take her pills and be good for another year. We were grateful to Dr. LaMorges for saving her from back surgery.

Tomorrow is 1988.

Erland Christensen, Yrsa Thom Chris and 9 others

Comments

Janice Blattie Good Memories

Bart Shindelar These are great! I look forward to reading them each day.

    PeteandRuth Ann Bungum Glad you're enjoying them

PeteandRuth Ann Bungum

Friday, May 15, 2020. Pete and Ruth Ann's journey through 59 years.

It is 1988.
We had no big trips this year.

It was Anamosa's sesquicentennial (150 years) so for the one and only time in my life I decided to grow a beard. It took a while to grow as I'm not the heaviest-bearded guy in the world. It was pretty ugly. I went from a full beard to a mustache. The only positive thing about it was that it was pretty much solid red and not filled with a bunch of gray (yet). I'm grateful that shaving devices had been invented because I did not want to look like that the rest of my life. By growing the beard, I could scratch growing a beard off my Bucket List. It was worth doing once in my life. I shaved it off at Christmas.

That summer I got help from Galen Harms (the school janitor and my friend) to help me deconstruct the house we had bought the previous October. Between the two of us we tore down the three additions to the back of the house and tore off the old shingles. Son-in-law Dean came on weekends and helped a lot. Bernie Keeney, my colleague, let me use his truck to haul the old shingles and scrap to the landfill. I hired Irv Graver to reshingle. The house had no shingles on it for several weeks. We lucked out because 1988 was the year of the drought. It never rained for 8–10 weeks so Irv didn't have to put on a tarp.

In the next several months we filled in the old pool, landscaped the back yard, built a privacy fence, painted and carpeted the interior, and remodeled the kitchen and both bathrooms. Now it was back to its original structure, as featured in the June 1949, issue of Better Homes and Gardens.

Now one of my favorite stories from 36 years of teaching seventh graders. This was an election year—Michael Dukakis was running against George H. W. Bush.

I subscribed to a weekly magazine called Junior Scholastic. An issue in September had an excellent article explaining the differences between the Republican Party and the Democratic Party. I took butcher paper and made posters for each party, explaining their beliefs, etc. Red ink for Republican and blue ink for Democrat.

I copied word for word from the magazine so I wouldn't be accused of bias. The next day I covered up the party names at the top of the posters and went through every word and phrase on each poster. I told the students to look and listen and then write down red or blue according to what they agreed with the most. They didn't know it, but if they wrote red, they agreed more with the Republicans. And blue meant they agreed more with the Democrats.

After writing their answer I took the blinders off the party names. The kids really got into it and many were surprised that their answer was different from what their parents believed. The biggest memory for me is what happened the next day.

Bobby raised his hand and said, "Mr. Bungum, I have changed my mind. Yesterday I agreed with the Democrats but today I am a Republican." I asked him why he changed his mind. He said. "I didn't change my mind, my parents changed it for me. I was telling them about class last night at the supper table and when I got done explaining they told me I was a Republican. 'Your grandparents are Republicans, we are Republicans and you are a Republican.'" I thought maybe his parents could have explained why they were Republican or maybe asked him what he saw in the Democrat poster that he liked or agreed with. It didn't sound like that any of that happened. It is one of my favorite stories from my 36 years in the classroom.

Now another favorite story from 1988. In November two high school female classmates (Joanne and Sharon) told us they were going to come to Anamosa and visit us. What we didn't know was what happened next. They put an ad in the Anamosa paper. Here is what they said in the article. "The Hawkeye Fun Wagon promises to be really fun this Saturday, November 12th. All single men over the age of 50 (no, that's not over the hill) are invited to join Pete and Ladies of the 50s. Call the Bungum's!"

Joanne had called the Anamosa paper and talked them into running it even though their policy was that it had to paid for in advance. Marna Ketelsen, the lady she talked to, knew us and decided to run it.

When they arrived, Ruth Ann and I decided to make Joanne's wishes come true. Bob Algoe was going to a birthday party attended by ten or twelve guys. He had read the announcement in the paper. I explained the details about the two ladies coming and asked him if he would bring all the guys and barge in the house and surprise Joanne and Sharon.

About 9:00 PM we were visiting with Joanne and Sharon and all hell broke loose. In the front door came ten guys yelling, "Where is the Minnesota meat—where are the hot ones from Minnesota?" The two gals were surprised. We took photos of them with the two ladies, told jokes and had a ton of laughs. The entire affair was a lot of fun. I actually got a call from a drunk who was at a local tavern. He had taken the announcement seriously and wanted to come and meet the Minnesota ladies of the 50s. I had to tell him it was a joke. He was disappointed.

Here are a few more happenings in 1988:

— Carron and Dean bought a house in Ely. They moved from Solon.
— Brad and Inge were in Tucson. Inge was working at UWP headquarters and Brad was a full-time student at University of Arizona.
— My brother Don was awarded the Distinguished Service Award for Education by Luther College. It was quite an honor.
— Ruth Ann and I turned 48.
— The Hawkeyes went 6–4–3. They lost to North Carolina State in the Peach Bowl. Score was 28–23.

Yrsa Thom Chris, Dean Rickels and 9 others

The
Hawkeye Fun Wagon
promises to be really fun this
Sat., Nov. 12.
All single men over the age of 50
(no - that's not over the hill!) are
invited to join Pete & Ladies of the
50's. Call the Bungums!

Invitation to join Pete and ladies of the 50's

You, Dean Rickels, Richard Stout and 8 others

PeteandRuth Ann Bungum

Saturday, May 16, 2020. Pete and Ruth Ann's Journey through 59 years.

The year is 1989.

We had one sad event and one happy event in 1989. The sad one was the death of Inge's father, Arne Nielsen, in Denmark. He had a heart attack at age 61. At that time, Brad and Inge were Cast Managers of an UWP cast.

They got the call while in Rochester, Minnesota from Bente, Inge's sister. They had a long and sad flight back to Denmark knowing that Arne had passed away. Ruth Ann and I sent a card and wrote a letter expressing our condolences and recounting the wonderful memories we had of Arne. We had only known him for four years, but we had such great memories because he was such a sincere, funny and likeable human being. We think of him often. If this world was made up of more people like Arne it would be a wonderful world.

The happy event in 1989 was Brad graduating from the University of Arizona. He got his degree in secondary social science education. He graduated magma cum laude. Magma cum laude is the second highest degree of merit for academic work. Ruth Ann and I flew to Tucson to attend the ceremony. The speaker was Senator Barry Goldwater. It was probably one of the shortest speeches ever for a graduation—it was ten minutes.

After the ceremony we went to Brad and Inge's apartment for a party. Brother Jim and wife Verleen, Brad's godparents, were there. They had moved to Fountain Hills, Arizona, from Rochester two years before. Jim worked for the Mayo Clinic and was transferred to Scottsdale to work at the Mayo Clinic there. There were many in attendance—most were UWP friends.

Carron and Dean were there also—they had driven from Iowa to surprise Brad and Inge. On the way down they stopped at a gas station in New Mexico. Carron recognized a guy standing by his car. She went to him and asked if he was Sam Donaldson, the ABC news guy. It was him—she had her picture taken with him.

We flew home on Monday. In July Brad and Inge became Managers of Cast A. That means they were the bosses. They traveled for the next year except for a two-week interruption in September because of Arne's death.

Here are a few other memories from 1989.

We finished off the back yard, dug up the old patio, poured a new one and built a privacy fence.

In October Ruth Ann and I went to Dyersville to visit the baseball field where the movie *Field of Dreams* was filmed. I ran the bases and walked out of the corn field. In my opinion, the most famous line in the movie was "Is this heaven? No, It's Iowa." What a line, one for all Americans to know! In fact, it should be taught to all kids in kindergarten through high school. Seniors should be made to write an essay on the significance of those six words and their importance to America. It should be made a graduation requirement.

When looking in the mirror in 1989 I could see my body was changing. My pants were getting harder to snap, the numbers on the scale were getting larger. In other words, I was getting a gut and the scale was reading 190 pounds. I had gained 25 pounds in the previous ten years. My eyes weren't seeing things like they used to. I couldn't do anything about the eyes, but I could do something about the waist. The next year I did something about it.

Tomorrow I do 1990.

PeteandRuth Ann Bungum, Erland Christensen and 15 others

Comments

Sharon Wykle Twedt You are a great writer Brad.

 PeteandRuth Ann Bungum Sharon—did you mean me?

Sharon Bungum Shupe I agree with Sharon, your writing is very good.

Brad Bungum It's all Dad here, Sharon Bungum Shupe and Sharon Twedt!! I'm only the editor and archivist ;-)

PeteandRuth Ann Bungum

Pete with Beard about to kiss Ruth Ann

You, Tim Bungum, Rhenee Grabau and 13 others

Comments

Jan Siebels Wow!! What a great pic!! ♡

Brad Bungum Nice hair Pops... Love those afro-days of the 80s...

Herbert Stufflebeam How old were you there! Mr. B just curious 20ish.

Brad Bungum Herbert Stufflebeam LOL! He was 48...

Herbert Stufflebeam no way. One hell of a man and Teacher! I would like to see him again. My favorite!

>**Brad Bungum** Herbert Stufflebeam, stop by on your next trip to town!!

Herbert Stufflebeam Brad i might just do that thanks!

PeteandRuth Ann Bungum Herbert Stufflebeam I was 48

PeteandRuth Ann Bungum Any time—I'd like to see you also

Herbert Stufflebeam Thanks Mr. Bungum

Tom Beadle Do I know these people? 😌 Years ago I drank beer with people that looked just like them.

PeteandRuth Ann Bungum what kind of beer did we drink in those days?

PeteandRuth Ann Bungum

Sunday, May 17, 2020. Pete and Pete and Ruth Ann's Journey Through 59 years.

The year is 1990.

This was another memorable year for us. We both turned the big 5-0. Hers was on April 4 and mine on November 20. For Ruth Ann's birthday, our neighbors, Bob and Bonnie Walderbach, put a big sign on our yard saying, "Honk—Ruth Ann is 50." On my birthday Bob got 250 empty beer and soda cans from Family Foods. He came over at 4:30 am and spelled "Happy 50th, Pete" on the front yard with those cans. A couple of my students saw the greeting when riding the bus to school. They were wondering if all the cans were mine.

On Easter break we decided to go cruising. On Friday we flew to Ft. Lauderdale, got on our cruise ship and went to the Bahamas. We spent Saturday touring Nassau. One memory is we were driven through the poorest area. The poverty was unbelievable. It made Ruth Ann and I count our blessings. On Saturday evening we had our dress-up dinner. Our dinner tablemates were a mother (a teacher) and daughter from New York City. The other couple was from Ohio. He was a mail carrier and his wife a homemaker. He talked too much and wouldn't shut up. His poor wife didn't say a word. On Sunday I took my morning walk and explored the whole ship. The thing about a cruise ship is you can eat 24 hours a day. It is not a place to lose weight. On Monday we flew home.

On Wednesday, April 19, about 5 pm, we received a call from Carron. She was screaming and crying. She was pregnant, not with one baby but with THREE. She knew she was carrying triplets. Her water had broken—she had called Dean to come home right away. Ruth Ann told her to have Dean take her to St. Luke's as soon as possible. We stopped and told Dean's parents about the situation. Carron was already admitted when we got there. The doctors had already decided to send her to University of Iowa Hospital. We and Dean's parents drove to Iowa City. The University doctors were already examining her. The doctors told Dean and Carron the bottom baby was already dead but the other two had heart beats. The doctors told all of us that they could probably keep those two alive for another five or six weeks but if they were born at 27–28 weeks, they wouldn't be looking at college material. They more than likely would have lung and eye problems.

By this time the doctors had discovered that Carron had only one kidney and half a uterus. Ruth Ann and I never had a clue that she had this problem when growing up. Carron and Dean had a lot to think about. So, the choice was one that Carron and Dean had to make. We and the Rickels left at midnight. That night Carron and Dean discussed the situation and made the decision to abort and start over. The doctor told them it would be best if she got pregnant again as soon as possible because her uterus was stretched, and she would have a better chance of carrying the next one to full term.

On Thursday Carron delivered. The three were laid on Carron's tummy. There were two girls and a boy. They weighed 11, 13 and 15 ounces. I picked them up and all three fit in the palm of my hand. Carron then picked up the three babies and laid them on her chest. She said, "I want one more look at them before they are gone." Carron and Dean named them Alex Bradley, Hayley Sue and Blaine Marie.

The hospital chaplain was such a big help. She suggested they be cremated and then have a memorial service at St. John Lutheran Church in Ely on Sunday. The babies were cremated on Saturday. The memorial service was very emotional. The urn with the triplet's ashes was on the altar—she still has it at home. Carron left the hospital to attend. I felt sorry for her. She was not only physically exhausted but emotionally as well.

The service was attended by many from the congregation. Also attending were Rick and Patty Delagardelle and their two daughters. Rick was a colleague of mine. It was so thoughtful of them to come and was much appreciated by Carron and Dean and Ruth Ann and me. The weeks ahead were not easy for them—many tears were shed. However, good news came in August. She was pregnant again.

We took a mini vacation in August. We went to Eau Claire to visit Jim and Pat Cooley, Ruth Ann's cousin. Then we traveled to Green Bay. We drove around Lambeau Field and then to the Packer

Hall of Fame. It was very interesting because our high school secretary was from Green Bay. Her dad played for the Packers from 1934–1945. He was in the Packer Hall of Fame. His name was Joe Laws. I found his plaque and took a photo. We also hit some of the adult beverage places. I would love to be at one of those bars after a Packer victory. I should put it on my Bucket List.

I want to end 1990 with a favorite story about my Mom. She was 85 years old when this happened. In June I went to visit her at the Martin Luther Home in Bloomington, Minnesota. While visiting, the conversation had slowed a bit so I thought I would liven it up. I asked her what Dad and she did on their first date. She got this smart-alecky grin on her face and told me, "It's none of your business, Peter." I absolutely lost it. The more I laughed the more she laughed. That comment was precious. I still think about her answer and laugh as much now as I did then. That was probably the last laugh we had together. She passed away in November of 1991.

Tomorrow it will be 1991.

Yrsa Thom Chris, Richard Stout and 7 others

David L. Eaton, Laurie Emery and 24 others

Comments

Bonnie Walderbach Wonder who did that?? 😆 😆

    PeteandRuth Ann Bungum Bonnie Walderbach guess who?

PeteandRuth Ann Bungum

Monday, May 18, 2020. Pete and Ruth Ann's journey through 59 years.

Today is 1991.

A big project in 1991 was remodeling our master bedroom. We tore out walls to the old bathroom and started over. The big addition was installing a whirlpool. The whirlpool became our Friday night entertainment. We would rent a movie, order a pizza, have a few beers handy, get in the whirlpool and enjoy the movie and the beers. We would just relax. It was a good way to unwind after a week of work. That whirlpool is the one thing we missed the most when we moved to a mobile home in 1995.

On April 10th our lives changed forever. We became Grandpa and Grandma. Within nine days of what would have been the triplet's first birthday, April 19th, Carron delivered an 8-pound, 3-ounce boy. They named him Wesley Dean. Ruth Ann and I were so happy. We had almost reached the conclusion that we would never be grand-parents. We didn't know if Brad and Inge in Denmark would have any kids. And would Carron, after losing her triplets and having half a uterus and only one kidney, be able to carry a baby long enough to survive. But that was not to be—by October of 1992 we had three grandchildren.

But there is something special about the first grandchild. Grandpas and Grandmas usually go bonkers with gifts and atten-tion. I bought a camcorder. I thought that any grandson of mine was going to be President someday, so I better record his every move for his future campaigns. The birth of Wesley Dean made it possible for Carron and Dean to get on with their lives after the death of the trip-lets. In May we babysat for the first time. That was really different. We hadn't taken care of a four-week-old since Carron was a baby. We managed just fine but there is a reason young people have babies. I don't think Ruth Ann and I could have handled it on steady basis.

My 51st birthday, on Wednesday, November 20, was one I will never forget. The reason is that my Mom died that day.

Brother Don had called me at school to tell me Mom was on her death bed. I chose not to go that day to see her die. I couldn't stand to see her take her last breath. I got a call before midnight that she had died. I told my siblings we'd come tomorrow. We went to Rochester on Thursday and met sisters Jan and Betty and brother Chuck at the funeral home. We picked out a casket. The funeral was on Saturday at Zumbro Lutheran Church in Rochester.

The weather was nasty, almost blizzard conditions. After the service we had to drive 15 miles to West St. Olaf Lutheran Church near Hayfield. She was to be buried beside Dad, who had died in 1961. The committal was like something I had seen in a movie (I think it was *Dr. Zhivago.*) The wind was blowing, the snow was stinging my face and the wind chill was 10 degrees below zero. I remember thinking as the casket was lowered into the ground, "Mom, you were always so cold in your home with your poor circulation, even when the thermostat was set at 90 degrees and you had on three sweaters, plus an Afghan. It just isn't fair that you are buried in this kind of weather."

Mom would've been 87 in a week. She had a strong religious faith which kept her going and kept her strong. Raising nine kids was no easy task, especially seven boys. She had had lung surgery and both legs amputated below the knees in the late 1970s and early 1980s. She had had diabetes since 1945 and had given herself a shot twice a day for over 40 years. Mom met every task/challenge thrown at her in life. Mom's reply was that she always figured that the Lord would help her and Dad raise nine kids. The nine of us kids had done well in life and there was nothing that made Mom happier or prouder than her successful kids. All nine of us have been positive contributors to society.

In her later years she had a saying that I've never forgotten. She would say, "Peter, in 100 years you'll never know the difference." I now say that more and more as I get older. It really is a good piece of wisdom and it makes me realize that I'm not going to live forever. I have become a little more philosophical about life. I have used those words after a bad golf game, deciding whether to buy something, consoling myself when the Hawkeyes lose a close game, and helping friends make decisions.

At age 79 I don't worry about as many things in life as I used to. I try to enjoy each day. Learning the following sentence has helped me. "Yesterday is a memory, tomorrow is a promise, but today is a gift and that is why it is called, The Present."

I have put a photo of Mom on Facebook. I took this photo in 1980. She was living alone in her Rochester home at the time. I asked her if she was ever scared that a burglar would come in and rob her. She said, "No, I'm not. If a burglar breaks in and sees me with no legs, just stumps, my prostheses, my hair net and my coke bottle glasses, they'll turn around and run out that door in a hurry."

Thank God she had a sense of humor.

The Hawkeyes were 10–1–1 in 1991. We played against BYU in the Holiday Bowl—we tied.

Tim Bungum, Rhenee Grabau and 16 others

Comments

Jill Darrow Your mother seems to have overcome many challenges with a positive outlook on life. I am really enjoying reading your memories. Your children are so lucky to have them written down for them to enjoy!

Dee Ihlenfeldt I so agree! Good job Pete!

Mark Holub Mr Bungum, I continue to greatly enjoy your daily posts. Thanks for the comments concerning aging and mortality. Something we should all take to heart.

Pat Cooley I remember your mom's spunk ♡

Bret Lewison You think the "in a 100 years" line would work with Brad Bungum in the unlikely event the Hawks lose to the Gophers this fall?

  Brad Bungum not likely to work, Hound Bret Lewison…

Bret Lewison Brad Bungum hopefully, we won't have to try it out. Hawks have never lost to the Gophers in September. Let's just hope we're able to see it live.

Kimberly Bungum I remember this vividly. I also remember as a child about 7 or 8 cleaning her stumps and putting her stump socks on and helping her with her prosthetics. I think this is when I knew I wanted to become an RN. Wow, now that I know what I know about diabetes etc, I know how incredibly brave and strong Grandma was ♡.

Mark Blattie Grandma B was one tough women. I was a pallbearer for her, and uncle Pete's description of the day was not exaggerated. In my opinion, Elsie went out swinging:)

  Brad Bungum Mark Blattie, we'd all be swinging at something if we had 10 kids and 7 of them were Bungum Boys! 😂

Brad Bungum Dad PeteandRuth Ann Bungum, did you guys actually all sit down for dinner together (or any meal) as kids, or was it just a buffet and survival of the fittest?

Mark Blattie Brad Bungum that is true.

Phil Bungum Mark Blattie In a blizzard…

Shelley Bungum DeBernardi Grandma was an incredible woman!

PeteandRuth Ann Bungum Brad Bungum—we sat down—but remember all nine of us weren't home at the same time.

PeteandRuth Ann Bungum

Tuesday, May 19, 2020. Pete and Ruth Ann's Journey Through 59 years.

Today is 1992.

In 1992 Ruth Ann and Pete went from one grandchild to three. On October 14, Carron gave birth to a 7-pound, 11-ounce girl—she was perfectly healthy. She was named Ellyn Sue. On October 23 in Copenhagen, Denmark, Inge gave birth to a 4,030-gram girl. She was named Alexandra—no middle name. The girls were only nine days apart.

Ruth Ann and I decided we needed to go see Alexandra as soon as possible. We had seen Ellyn, the future first female President of the USA. So, it was only fair we go to Copenhagen to see a future Prime Minister of Denmark. We flew to Denmark on Christmas Day. Alexandra was every bit as cute as Ellyn. Ruth Ann and I felt we had the cutest granddaughters in the world. Not only were they cute but we could see they were super intelligent! By the way, that wasn't just wishful thinking on our part. As adults Alexandra is a medical doctor and Ellyn has a master's degree in hydrogeology and environmental studies. She works for the National Park Service.

During our week in Denmark, Alexandra was baptized at their Lutheran Church in Lyngby (a suburb of Copenhagen.)

Two days after the baptism Ellinor (Inge's mother) invited us to her townhouse for a Danish Christmas meal. It was an eight-hour affair. We started eating at 1:00 pm and finished about 9:00 pm. Ellinor would serve a course, then we'd take a break, drink some wine and visit. An hour later we would eat another course, take a break again, visit and drink a different kind of wine. This went on and on until 9:00.

No one loses control because of too much wine since everyone is eating constantly. What a fun day and a great memory.

I'll say this about the Danes. They know how to throw a party—they know how to enjoy food—they know how to enjoy wine—they know how to enjoy life. There's a reason they are considered the happiest people on earth.

One other memory of that trip to Copenhagen is our stop in Amsterdam. We had a six-hour layover until the next flight. We decided to take the train downtown to kill some time. When we left the train station we started walking, not paying much attention to where we were walking. We soon realized we weren't in Anamosa anymore.

We were kind of window shopping when Ruth Ann says, "Pete, look at that window display." It was a sex shop with every kind of sex toy you could imagine. We continued to walk and soon noticed bikini clad women sitting inside the windows. It finally dawned on us we smack-dab in the middle of Amsterdam's Red-Light District. It was 10:00 am on December 26th and some of the girls were open for business. They probably needed some extra cash to pay for Christmas presents.

Then we stopped at a restaurant to have a bite to eat. I went to the toilet—on the way back I stopped at a table that had a newspaper covering it. Being the curious person that I am I picked up the paper to look it over. When I did that, I noticed about 20 plastic bags with a white powder in them. I realized I shouldn't have done that. There was a guy sitting about 15 feet from the table. He was staring at me—I quickly replaced the paper. He didn't say a word. I think he realized I was an American tourist and had done it in total innocence. We decided to get back to the airport before we got into any more trouble. When we told Brad about our experiences in Amsterdam he was flabbergasted. He wasn't sure his Mom and Dad should be let loose in big cities without a guide or bodyguard.

The summer of 1992 was a fun time. We hosted a retirement party for Paul, my oldest brother. He was retiring from a 36-year career as a Lutheran minister. Seven of the eight brothers and sisters came. We had asked all of them to have some memories of Paul to tell. Here are some of those memories:

Sister Betty was one year younger than Paul. Her memory was Paul saying he was going to marry Shirley Temple. And he was going to be millionaire.

202

Brother Don was four years younger. He said he loaned Paul $130 in 1952 and never got repaid. So, Don figured he should get paid now but the bill now would be $1310 figured at 6 percent annual interest. He didn't get paid.

Sister Jan said she should get paid for all the free meals she gave him when he was in the seminary in St. Paul. She mentioned also about their adoption of Kim and how it had changed their life.

Brother Chuck remembered Paul was going to build an artificial lake on the field behind our house. He mentioned Paul's business ventures like raising rabbits and hamsters and then freezing them to death. He said that whatever he did as a kid, Paul seemed to see him do it or knew about it. Paul was definitely my Master while growing up. He ended his talk with a real zinger. He mentioned a guy from Mantorville named Coon Anderson. I guess Paul had once asked Coon if he would ever amount to anything. Coon answered by saying, "No, I'm going to be just like you."

Brother John started his memories by telling Paul that he didn't know if he should call him God or Mr Gopher. John said that Mom "read a letter to me she had gotten from you when you were a missionary in Iran. You mentioned you had met an angel in Iran." Then Mom said, "I think Paul is going to get married"—and he did. Then John said, "One time you sold me some powder that came from Nigeria. You said the people in Nigeria who used this powder never got colon cancer. I've tried your powder and can't stand it. I don't care, I'll get colon cancer before I'll use that stuff again."

Brother Mark mentioned about all his business ventures. He rattled off 10–15 of them including raising worms—none of which were successful. He said that Paul always loved to call and talk and give advice.

I brought up about Paul asking me as an eight-year-old if I would ever amount to anything. I told him I would keep trying. He also told me that when a man got married, he should be the boss. When a man tells his wife to jump, she should ask, "How high?" And she wasn't to come down until the husband tells her to. For some reason that angel from Iran didn't agree.

Ruth Ann mentioned that he was always free with advice on how to raise kids and save money. The only problem was he didn't have any kids and since he was a minister, he had very few bills.

Then Paul got his revenge. He was actually very nice about it. He brought up memories of each of us and did a good job of ad-libbing the entire thing.

We had all chipped in and bought Paul a Minnesota Gopher cap and sweatshirt. Carron's husband Dean served us a glass of wine and we all stood up and gave Paul a final toast. I made a VHS tape for everyone.

That retirement party was one of the best and happiest family gatherings we ever had.

The Hawkeyes were 5–7—no bowl game.

Tomorrow is 1993.

You, Yrsa Thom Chris, Linda Blattie Smaby and 5 others

PeteandRuth Ann Bungum

Wednesday, May 20, 2020. Pete and Ruth Ann's journey through 59 years.

The year is 1993.

A family reunion was held at brother Don and wife Joan's home in Lindstrom, Minnesota. Almost the entire family was there. My nephew, Phil, who was attending Iowa State at the time, thought he had the "funny" of the day. The Hawkeyes and Cyclones do not like each other very much. Phil brought out a tee-shirt that he thought was hilarious. On the front was Cy, the Iowa State logo, with the words, "THIS IS YOUR BRAIN." On the back was the Tiger Hawk with the words "THIS IS YOUR BRAIN ON DRUGS." Below the Tiger Hawk was "ANY QUESTIONS?" It was pretty funny to tell the truth. Phil and all Gopher fans there could hardly stop laughing. I think Ruth Ann and I were the only Hawkeye fans.

Now Phil, this is what I call trash talk. So, I will take this opportunity to do some trash talking of my own. We Hawk fans have been known to call Iowa State Moo-U. We have also said it is better to flunk out of Iowa than to get a degree from Iowa State or Minnesota. You might say that there is no love here. As I see it, there will be no Cyclones, Gophers or Hawkeyes in heaven. They are all violating the Eighth Commandment. According to Martin Luther's Catechism that commandment says, "Thou shalt not bear false witness against thy neighbor."

What does this mean? According to Martin Luther, "We should fear and love God so that we do not deceitfully belie, backbite, nor slander our neighbor, but apologize for him, speak well of him, and put the most charitable construction on all that he does."

So, there it is. I guess I'll see all of you Cyclones and Gophers in HELL.

But then I read the Tenth Commandment and changed my mind. It says, "Thou shalt not covet thy neighbor's wife, nor his man-servant, nor his maid-servant, nor his cattle nor anything that is thy neighbors."

Again, Martin Luther says that this means, "We should fear and love God so that we do not entice away Hayden Fry or Kirk Ferentz or any of our assistants or any of our All-American football players, but seek to have them remain and discharge their duty to all Hawkeye fans."

According to this, I, as a Hawkeye fan, have a much better chance of going to Heaven because I have never coveted any Cyclone or Gopher coaches or players to come and be a Hawkeye. I'm sure glad I read that Tenth Commandment.

This is the end of my trash talk.

Other things we did in 1993 include:

We flew to Tampa Bay to attend nephew Tim's wedding. He married a gal named Lisa. She was a Hawkeye. She had been a trainer for the Hawkeye football and wrestling teams. Tim was the only son of brother Jim and wife Verleen. Tim had gotten his PhD in Public Health at the University of South Carolina. He is now a professor at UNLV.

The 1958 high school class had its 35th reunion. Chatfield has the tradition of honoring the class that graduated 35 years ago—so we went to the graduation ceremony at the High School. It was hard to believe we had had been out of school 35 years. It is even harder to believe now that I have been out of school 62 years.

I'll end today's post by going back to 1991. I mentioned in that post we had installed a whirlpool in our remodeled bedroom. This photo shows the whirlpool with my Friday night partner. We had a lot of good times in that whirlpool. Some really good memories, especially now when she is gone.

Ruth Ann in hot tub

You, Tim Bungum, Yrsa Thom Chris and 10 others

Brad Bungum Dad, PeteandRuth Ann Bungum, you were pretty mild in your trash talk! Must be mellowed in your old-age. When we talked yesterday, you were all ramped-up to "bring it on"… I was disappointed, to be honest, but in the spirit of ending divisiveness in our world, I'm glad you chilled…;-). At the end of the day, we're all midwesterners (ISU/UI/UM fans), and I was cheering as loudly for the Gophers to beat PSU and Auburn last season, as I've ever cheered for the Hawks (almost). Not sure I can say the same for my Bungum Cousins, but I'll leave that one alone ;-). I'll leave this with a joke we used to tell back in the day of stupid jokes and when we really had fun trash talking each other around IA/MN games: Q: "What's the difference between a Minnesota cheerleader and a bag of garbage?" A: "At least a bag of garbage gets taken out once a week."

That was about as good as it got…we're all pretty close as cousins these days and seemed to have survived the trauma of the '70s and '80s and '90s when we took this stuff a lot more seriously… Bret Lewison wouldn't agree that I've mellowed, but I have…

Mark Blattie "What's the best thing to come out of Iowa? Interstate 35!" Ha

Bret Lewison Why is Iowa so windy? Because Missouri is full of hot air and Minnesota sucks.

Mark Blattie Bret Lewison that one is good.

Mark Blattie Bret Lewison always loved my cousins and family coming out of Iowa but trash talk is fun.

Phil Bungum And you know I think in the 80s they came up with that new Hawkeye logo. But there was something strangely familiar about it. If you turn it so the hawk's beak is at the bottom, and the neck will be on the topside...what do you see!?!? Yabba dabba doo!!!!!

Phil Bungum Right on campus near the tracks there were horses, the student farm was right on the Southside with the dairy, and I would fetch hog manure across the street from our campus apartment to put in our student garden patch.

Phil Bungum Iowa reeks of $$$$$$

Phil Bungum http://4.bp.blogspot.com/.../s280/KY+logo+iowa+-fred.jpg

Phil Bungum ISU also has the Vet school and out north of Ames along I35 is the USDA National Animal Disease Center that collaborates much with ISU. And you know, it's harder to get into vet school than medical school, like Iowa City has. Vets students learn

medicine from pigs to poultry and everything in between. I remember Dad telling how when he was young the nearest doctor was the horse doctor, who was also their dentist.

PeteandRuth Ann Bungum

Thursday, May 21, 2020. Pete and Ruth Ann's journey through 59 years.

The year is 1994.

We took a trip to Denmark and a side trip to Berlin. We went to Tivoli Amusement Park in Copenhagen. Before Walt Disney built Disneyland in the 1950s, he went to Tivoli for ideas. Darla Algoe, a teacher colleague of mine, was also in Denmark at the time so we had made arrangements to meet at Tivoli and dine together. We also met Ruth Ann's cousin (Toril Roen) from Norway. Ruth Ann had called her before we went and arranged the get-together.

Then we took a trip to Berlin. On the bus going into Berlin I was excited—because I am a lover of history. We saw many of the famous attractions of Berlin. The most memorable are as follows:

- Olympic Stadium—where Jesse Owens kicked butt in 1936.
- Brandenburg Gate—and all the Middle Eastern immigrants peddling everything from pieces of the wall to watches, necklaces and old Nazi army uniforms.
- Kaiser-Wilhelm-Gedachtnis-Kirkwall—it is the war-ravaged church that was left in its bombed-out state as a reminder of WWII.
- Checkpoint Charlie—where U.S. and Russian tanks faced each other in 1961.
- Potsdam—where from July 17 to August 2, 1945, Truman, Stalin, and Clement Attlee made final decisions for postwar Germany and Berlin.
- Reichstag—it was burned by the Nazis in 1933.
- Holocaust Museum—built on the grounds where the last battle was fought between Nazi youth and the Russian Army.
- Statues on city streets—When I saw the first one, I thought it was a real statue. But when I saw one blink, I realized

they were real people. Of course, they had a container in front of them for tourists to drop in some German marks.

- Berlin Wall—it had been four years since reunification so most of the wall had been torn down. But a few parts were still standing. Brad and I actually chipped out a few chunks. I still have mine.
- Loretta's Beer Garden—after a day of touring we stopped at Loretta's for a beer and some brats. We enjoyed the beers and the brats and just watching people. One conclusion I've reached in life is that people are pretty much the same all over. They all like to be with friends, relax, laugh and have a good time. When leaving Loretta's Ruth Ann saw a little Ferris wheel outside the entrance. She stopped and insisted that she ride on it. She had had too many beers because it was 3:00 am and nobody was working. Brad and I told her we didn't have any German money either. Then she said, "If Carson Ode was here, he'd be on my side and let me ride the Ferris wheel."

Brad and I started walking back to the hotel—she finally joined us. Brad said, "I'm going to call Carson in Des Moines and see if he would let you ride the Ferris wheel." He called but got the answering machine—he left a message. When we got home to Iowa, he told Ruth Ann he agreed with her and she definitely should have been able to ride that Ferris wheel at Loretta's.

We had some very sad news in 1994. Ruth Ann's oldest brother passed away. His real name was Cyrus Vergel Rain, but he went by Bud. Between working on farms, at a plastics factory and smoking too many Pall Mall cigarettes Bud had developed a bad case of emphysema. His quality of life was gone—he could only walk 20 feet and couldn't dance anymore (his favorite activity). He was so short of breath he couldn't make it to the bathroom on time. He was home alone one morning, and he decided life wasn't worth it anymore. He got out his single shot .22 and ended his life. He was only 63.

Richard Stout, Stephen Zimmerman and 1 other

PeteandRuth Ann Bungum

Friday, May 22, 2020. Pete and Ruth Ann's journey through 59 years.

The year is 1995.

We had no big travels in 1995. But Ruth Ann and I did make a big change in our journey through life. We turned 55 and it made us more aware that we were getting closer to retirement age. We made a major decision to get ready for retirement. We needed to cut our expenses and the best way to do that was to sell our house and get rid of that big monthly payment.

In August we went to look at mobile homes. We chose one to purchase. Carron came the next Saturday and we showed her the one we liked. She pointed out something that made sense. The one we had chosen had a separate family room. She said from observing us over the years we were definitely happier when the kitchen and family room were one big room. We followed her suggestion and changed our mind. I'm glad we did.

So, we bought one with the kitchen and family room as one big room. Now we could sit at the kitchen table and watch television, listen to music and entertain guests. I jokingly told Carron "Thanks a lot kid, you just cost us another $4,000." We bought a 28 x 70 foot Fleetwood, 1,900 square feet, three bedrooms, two bathrooms, formal dining room and the 24' x 28' kitchen/family room. The next summer we added a shed, carport and deck. We loved it and it has been perfect for us.

Our next job was to sell our house. We chose Warren Wortman as our realtor. He knew our neighbors across the street were interested. He told us to up our asking price by $10,000. He said with all the improvements we had made there would be no problem getting the higher price. Warren sold it in two weeks. We got our price. Thank You Warren, for the extra $10,000.

We made enough profit from our eight years in that house to pay cash for our mobile home. We have never regretted making the move. And thanks again to Carron for talking us into buying this one. Ruth Ann and I lived here for 25 years.

Another good memory from 1995 is when we went to Minnesota for a reunion with Ruth Ann's family. Brad and three-year-old Alexandra had come from Denmark. Alex was sitting at a picnic table talking to her Minnesota cousins. She was talking in English when all of a sudden, she told everyone, "I'm from Copenhagen, Denmark, and I speak a little bit of English." That was good for the laugh of the day. She was less than three years old when she came up with the line. What a comedian! Brad and Inge insisted that she learn both English and Danish. What a blessing. She is very fluent in both.

Another good memory is when Ruth Ann and I took the three grandkids to Chuck E. Cheese and the Play Station. At the Play Station there was an elevated structure that had tunnels and slides. It was easy for the kids to climb and crawl, but it wasn't for Grandpa. They talked me into going with them. Here was this 54-year-old Grandpa crawling on his hands and knees through tunnels and going down slides with 20–30 preschoolers. The grandkids thought it was pretty funny. I was just happy when it was over. I never did that again.

The Hawkeyes had an 8–4 record in 1995. We played the Washington Huskies in the Sun Bowl in El Paso. We kicked butt. We won 38–18. They had beaten us in the 1982 and 1991 Rose Bowls, so this was a sweet victory.

The photos are Ruth Ann and her cousin Toril from Vinstra, Norway. They were fourth cousins. I think they could pass for sisters.

The other one is the Berlin Wall. Brad and I chipped some souvenirs.

Rhenee Grabau, Richard Stout and 4 others

PeteandRuth Ann Bungum

PeteandRuth Ann Bungum

Saturday, May 23, 2020. Pete and Ruth Ann's journey through 59 years.

The year is 1996.

In July we traveled to Denmark again.

Brad had bought a summer house in the northwest corner of Denmark. We spent most of our time there. While at the summer house four-year-old Alexandra told Ruth Ann she had a trick to play on Grandpa. She told her that she had brought some nail polish with her to paint Grandpa's toenails. Ruth Ann told me to sit on the patio, then pretend I was sleeping so Alex could do her trick. I obliged. When Alex saw me sleeping, she got her polish and with Ruth Ann's help they painted my toenails red. I woke up, pretending to not know what had transpired and proceeded to read my book. Of course, Alex was waiting for a reaction from me. When I didn't say anything she finally said, "Grandpa, do you see anything different with your toes?" I looked and pretended to go into hysterics. Alex also went into hysterics from laughing so hard.

She thought it was so funny that she did it every time we saw each other for the next five–six years. The routine was the same every year—except in 2002. That year she used green polish with sparkles in it. Actually, I liked green the best. I thought she had outgrown it, but I was wrong. When she was home for grandma's funeral, she recruited her two cousins, Wes and Ellyn, to help her. They painted them red when I was really napping. Their ages were 29 for Wes and 28 for the girls. They thoroughly enjoyed it. At that time, it was good to have something to laugh about.

I have another good memory about the painted toes. I had the green toes in 2002. When I got home, I had to see Dr. Vernon for a physical. I had forgotten my toes were green. So when I took my socks off, I saw my green toes. I thought I better explain why they were green. I told Dr. Vernon my granddaughter in Denmark had painted them. He then said with a smile, "Now, that's a pretty poor excuse." We both had a good laugh.

About two or three times a day Ruth Ann I would walk with Alex to Olga's Market. She would ride her bike, which had training wheels. It was a small grocery store and they had all kinds of ice cream. She loved ice cream. Alex loved to tell the store owners that her Grandpa and Grandma were from America and didn't speak Danish so she would interpret for them. The little twerp wasn't quite four years old, so she was pretty proud to help us by interpreting. What she didn't know was that the store owners spoke English.

During Thanksgiving we took a four-day trip to Branson. We saw Bobby Vinson, Tony Orlando, Charlie Pride and Yakov Smirnoff. Tony sang his most famous song, "Tie a Yellow Ribbon around the Old Oak Tree." All the shows were very enjoyable.

Grandson Wes entered kindergarten and became computer literate at age five. On Grandparents Day we visited his class and he showed us how he used the computer. I asked him a question about his computer. He didn't think it was a very intelligent question. He said, "Grandpa, are you retarded?"

We spent a Sunday in May, from 10:00 am to midnight, wallpapering our family room. And believe it or not there was no divorce, not even a fight. I had never been a believer in miracles, but I changed my mind after that day.

In August Ruth Ann's mother went into the Good Samaritan Nursing Home in Preston, Minnesota. She was 84 and needed the security of someone around all the time. Other than her arthritis, she was in good health. She would die in 2002 from brain cancer.

The Hawkeyes went 9–3 in 1996 and were invited to the Alamo Bowl in San Antonio for the second time. We beat Texas Tech 27–0.

Tomorrow will be 1997.

Yrsa Thom Chris, Richard Stout and 4 others

Brad Bungum Dad PeteandRuth Ann Bungum, I also remember how Alex Alexandra Bungum weaseled you and mom out of spending a few kroner many times a day on those little toy vending machines up at Olga's…;-)

Alexandra Bungum Good times 😄 🐊 😍

Alexandra Bungum I love reading your posts!!

PeteandRuth Ann Bungum

Sunday, May 24, 2020. Pete and Ruth Ann's journey through 59 years.

The year is 1997.

When school was out in June Ruth Ann and I boarded a plane for Los Angeles and on to Hawaii. We had never been to Hawaii, so we were excited. We had enough frequent flyer miles for a free trip. We lined up an itinerary with a travel agency in Cedar Rapids. They made reservations for us at the Pacific Beach Hotel in Honolulu, across the highway from Waikiki Beach and a half mile from Diamond Head.

The first thing we did in Honolulu was visit the Arizona Memorial, watched the video of Pearl Harbor Day and examined the list of those that died that day. The second day we enjoyed the beach. The third day we flew from Oahu to the island of Maui. Maui is made up of two volcanic mountains joined by a low-lying isthmus. Both volcanoes are now dormant and one of them, Haleakala, has one of the world's largest extinct volcanic craters.

Ruth Ann had told me that she had a surprise for me. I found out what it was when we checked into Hertz Rent-a-car. The lady handed me the keys to a Chrysler convertible. We were busy in Maui for the next three days. The first day we went sightseeing in our convertible. The second day we took a guided tour of the eastern part of Maui. It is called the Hana Tour because you stop at a famous little town of Hana, on the eastern tip of Maui. We drove through Haleakala National Park but didn't get to the top of the volcano. Our tour guide was the best. He stopped frequently to let us try native Hawaiian fruit. He also explained about many of the 2,500 kinds of plants found in Hawaii and not found elsewhere on earth. The tour cost each of us $90 but I was so impressed with him I gave him a $20 tip.

We went to a luau our second night. It cost $65 each—we both felt it was a rip-off. They advertised it as the best in Maui and you could have all you wanted to eat and drink. That wasn't exactly the case as the drinks were very limited—so was the food. But the entertainment was enjoyable.

The third day we bummed around on the beach and ate and drank at the beach bar. I got into several conversations with some of the employees. Many were born and raised on the U.S. mainland. I asked why they were living in Hawaii. The typical answer was: "We vacationed here when we were young, had fallen in love with the climate" and people and decided to come back and live and work here. I really enjoy talking to people and just listening to their stories. I have kind of become a Barbara Walters.

We flew back to Iowa via Seattle and Minneapolis. The Hawaii trip was fun and educational. I wouldn't mind going again.

Now a word about the grandkids. Wes and Ellyn took Tai Kwon Do lessons. They were really pretty good. They looked so cute in their uniforms and colored belts, a green belt for Wes and a yellow for Ellyn. They learned a lot but had to quit when it became too expensive.

When they were five and six, they had learned how to play Monopoly, the adult version. Their Dad, Dean, had taught them the real game after first playing the kids' game. I couldn't believe they could do it. They even knew how to mortgage property. Pretty good I would say, for kids that age.

I bought them a globe for Christmas. I wanted them to learn about the big world they lived in, and also to know where their cousin, Alexandra, lived.

Brad and Lene came in July. They brought Alexandra and Lene's two kids, Mathilde, age five, and Mads, three. The most enjoyable thing we did was take them to the July 4th parade in Monticello. Wes and Ellyn were also along. All five of them thought it was a pretty good deal to have a bucket and fill it with candy thrown from the floats. None of the kids were shy about staking out their territory and collecting the goodies. We also took them golfing, let them drive the golf car and had them look for lost golf balls. It was Lene's first visit to our house. We all had a good time.

Brad took a new job in 1997. He joined Eaton Consulting, headquartered in Boston. Eaton Consulting was owned and operated by Dave Eaton, a former colleague of Brad's in UWP. The company was in the business of contracting with multinational corporations to train their employees that were going to work in another country. It was called cross-cultural training. The goal/objective was to train the employee, the spouse and the kids so the culture shock would be less when they relocated. The biggest goal was that the employee would be a better businessperson in his/her new location. He/she would know how business was conducted in that nation and therefore be more effective and successful.

Brad had no customers when he started. His first one was a good one—it was the LEGO Toy Company in Billund, Denmark. Brad did well with Eaton—then they were sold to a San Francisco firm.

That changed things—when they downsized in the 2000 teens he was laid off. He and another guy started their own consulting firm. Then UWP came calling—he became a Vice-President in 2015.

In December a new student came from Oregon. His parents were divorced so his mother sent him to Anamosa to live with dad. He was not a happy kid, was shabbily dressed, had long straggly hair and didn't smile. He refused to do anything. On his third day I gave him an assignment I thought he could handle. He tore it up and threw it on the floor right in front of me. He caused some trouble in the hot lunchroom, so I gave him an assigned seat. He didn't like that at all. The counselor called him into her office and had a talk with him. In the conversation he divulged that after a week he wanted to kill two people—the Principal and Mr. Bungum. He wanted to kill me because of that assigned seat in the lunchroom. That was the first time I had ever been threatened with death. I can honestly say I had trouble sleeping for the next week or two. The counselor didn't think I had anything to worry about—she did nothing about the threat. I was relieved when he went back to Oregon after a month. I felt sorry for that boy—I wonder what happened to him.

Tomorrow will be 1998.

Yrsa Thom Chris, Emilie Bungum and 2 others

PeteandRuth Ann Bungum

Monday, May 25, 2020. Pete and Ruth Ann's journey through 59 years.

Today is 1998.

In July we went to Denmark again. One of the highlights was going to LEGO Land in Billund. It is an amazing place. Everything is made of Legos. We saw replicas of the U.S. Capitol, the Statute of Liberty, a German city to European castles. An amazing thing happened when we were standing in line to get something to eat. Brad, Lene, Ruth Ann and I were talking with each other when a lady in line ahead of us, came to Brad and said, "I recognized your voice, you're Brad Bungum, aren't you?"

This lady was from Belgium, on vacation at Lego Land with her husband and three kids. She had been in UWP and had traveled with Brad in 1982. She hadn't heard Brad's voice in 16 years. For her to recognize Brad's voice after those many years is amazing. What are the odds of this happening? I could only venture a guess on one in a million. She told us she remembered her host family in Anamosa. We learned that she had stayed with friends of ours, only two blocks from our house. We concluded it was the Orville Spilde family.

Some other good memories from 1998.

We stopped in Aarhus to eat at Billibong's Restaurant. Their sign said, "Billibong's Restaurant is famous for live music and bullshit."

I went to a public rest room. I was in there with ten other guys when a lady walked in and replenished the paper towels. She visited with a couple guys, but I just stared at the wall. I was the only one uptight about the lady in the men's room.

Lene was teaching school in a town called Mellerup. She taught Danish and Gymnastics. Ruth Ann and I visited her classroom and teacher's lounge. Classrooms are the same as here but the big difference I noticed was in the teacher's lounge. The refrigerator in the lounge was stocked with Tuborg Beer and Gammel Dansk, a Danish liqueur. Lene and her colleagues would relax on Friday with a couple of Tuborgs and a shot of Gammel Dansk. Sounded good to me. I don't think it would fly in Anamosa or any place in America.

I want to include this story before I forget. It is almost another one of those unbelievable things that happen in this world. It took place in 1994 when Brad was running a language school in Copenhagen. Brad was interviewing people to teach English at his school. He interviewed a guy named Bryan Akers. In the midst of the interview, Bryan told Brad he had cousins living in Iowa, near Central City. Brad's eyes lit up and he told Bryan he was raised in Anamosa, only 15 miles from Central City.

As it turned out, his relatives were the Hendersons. They belonged to our church and I had taught his cousins. Bryan's mother and Mrs. Henderson were sisters. Bryan used to spend a month or two in the summer visiting his Henderson cousins. Brad hired him. Again, what are the odds of hiring a guy to teach for you in Copenhagen, Denmark, and then finding out that you know his Aunt and Uncle and went to school with his cousins? It is another one of those one-in-a-million deals.

Now it is back to 1998.

We drove to Spjald in western Jutland. We met Lene's parents, Paul and Jytte. He was retired from his car business, selling Peugeots, the French car. Jytte had worked in the local care center and taught swimming at the local high school. They took us to the west coast so could we see the bunkers the Nazis built on the beach to prevent a possible invasion. The walls of those bunkers were over a meter thick. There was no way our bombs could have destroyed them. We were amazed at the size of these bunkers.

They also took us to a windmill farm built by the Vestas Corporation. There were over 100 windmills twirling away, producing electricity for Danish towns and cities. Denmark is perfect for wind energy because wind is blowing constantly due to the North Atlantic Drift.

We were back in the states by August.

We went to our 40th class reunion in Chatfield, Minnesota. We were all 57–58 years old. There were some obvious differences from how we looked on graduation day, June 5, 1958. The women had bigger butts, the men had bigger guts and both sexes had more gray hair. The most disappointing thing about all our reunions is that so many of our classmates that live in the area have never attended. I guess they have their reasons. I would guess their reasons are more likely negative than positive.

In September I submitted my resignation. I was ready. After 36 years of teaching seventh graders the time had come to say goodbye to the classroom. Every day that year I told myself that this is the last time for this or for that. It was a good feeling.

The Hawkeyes went 3–8 in 1998. It was Hayden Fry's last season as coach. He had developed prostate cancer and it was sapping his energy. He was 72 years old and losing the recruiting battle to younger coaches. He wisely retired before fans and rich alumni money-givers got on him. In 20 years as Iowa's coach he won or shared three Big Ten titles, won 143 games, lost 89 and tied six. We went to 14 bowl games. He won six, lost seven and tied one.

He had won more games than any other coach in Hawkeye history. He could leave a proud man. Hayden had prostate surgery in 1999 and made a full recovery. He and his wife, Shirley, retired to Mesquite, Nevada. Hayden passed away in December 2019.

You, Bret Lewison, Yrsa Thom Chris and 1 other

John Spilde Always enjoy reading about your travels!

PeteandRuth Ann Bungum

Tuesday, May 26, 2020. Pete and Ruth Ann's journey through 59 years.

The year is 1999. This is Part 1. It is about Ruth Ann's retirement. Mine will be tomorrow.

This was a life-changing year for us. We both retired from our public service jobs. I had been teaching for 36 years and Ruth Ann had been at the Treasurer's Office for nearly 22 years. The month of June was monumental because that is when both of us walked out the door. I will write about Ruth Ann's last days first.

Her official farewell was June 12th. Jan Miller, her boss, started out the morning by calling in a Deputy Sheriff with a set of hand-cuffs. He went to her desk, put a handcuff on her wrist and locked the other cuff to her desk drawer handle. It was Jan's way of telling Ruth Ann she didn't want her to leave and wasn't going to let her leave. After a half hour the Deputy was kind enough to let her go.

Then they pinned a beautiful corsage on her, and the party began. The corsage consisted of a few flowers surrounded by miniature tax receipts, license plates and money, the three things the Treasurer's Office was noted for and hated for. Then Ruth Ann had to go to both banks with deposits that morning and there was a rose waiting for her at both banks. She went to the post office and there was another rose in the Office mailbox. This was all arranged by Jan and the gals.

Photos were taken of Ruth Ann with her colleagues. She also had a photo taken with the five men on the Board of Supervisors. Throughout the morning every employee in the Courthouse stopped to say farewell and enjoy the food served by her colleagues.

On Friday night the gals had her official retirement party at Club 528 in Cascade, Iowa. The funniest incident happened as we were sitting down. The waitress came to Ruth Ann and loudly stated, "Robert called and said he would be ten minutes late." The story behind that statement is that Robert was a guy who had a part-time job as a male stripper. Over the years Ruth Ann had joked that she would love to see him perform. It was good for a laugh.

After the dinner she was given a large bag of goodies. The first thing she pulled out was a XXX pair of black panties. I guess the insinuation was that she would get a fat butt as she aged and would need them someday. There were two gifts I refuse to mention because only a group of women could have thought of those. The last two things were actual license plates. The first one was an Iowa State plate. They all knew we were big Hawkeye fans but two of the gals were Iowa State fans. They thought it would be hilarious for her to have a Cyclone plate—it was. The second plate was a personalized Iowa Hawkeye plate. It had a Tiger Hawk and Iowa on top and in the middle in big letters was "BUNGUM." On the bottom, in smaller letters, was the word "RETIRED." Jan had talked to Tom Stelzer, the head of Prison Industries at the Reformatory, about having a plate made. He had to get permission from the Iowa Department of Transportation to make the plate. It is a piece of history—there will never be another plate like it in Iowa or the U.S. Who knows, maybe the Smithsonian will come calling. We put the plate on our golf cart.

Carron came and did a wonderful job of reading the poem she had written about her and Mom. Brad had written one also—Carron read his. They both brought up tons of memories about Mom. They had many kind words about their Mom and related many humorous happenings. I finished the speaking by sharing many of my favorite memories I had with her since we were 15 years old.

On her final day at work I had started a paint job and was scraping away when a car pulled up. It was Jan. She wanted me to quit scraping, go home and get my camcorder and come to the Treasurer's Office. I followed her orders. Neither Ruth Ann nor I knew what was going to happen.

When I got to the Office the gals led us out to a pick-up. There was a tarp over something in the back. Mike, Jan's husband, flipped down the end gate, tore off the tarp and there it was. It was a 300-pound stone with engravings on the smooth side. The top third had the Tiger Hawk, the middle third said "BUNGUM" and the bottom third said "EST. 1960." What a wonderful farewell gift. It was something we could display and cherish the rest of our lives. Mike told us that Jan had spent an entire day looking for the perfect stone in their farm pasture. She had it engraved by an artisan in Monticello. We have the stone in our front yard so it can be seen 24/7/365.

All of the kind words said to Ruth Ann and the gifts and parties given to her were a tribute to her professionalism and expertise on the job. Her relationship with her colleagues and the public was one of kindness and respect. In fact, many customers wanted her to wait on them because they felt comfortable with her and she would never put them down. Jan asked her many times if she would like to come back part-time—her answer was always "no." She felt she retired at the right time because no one wanted her to leave.

Tomorrow will be Part 2 of 1999. I will write about my retirement.

Stone with Bungum est. 1960. Ruth Ann with BUNGUM license plate

Bret Lewison, Rhenee Grabau and 17 others

Comments

Bret Lewison That must have been some party. Pretty telling when Jones County officials and employees throw the party just outside of Jones County's boundaries.

PeteandRuth Ann Bungum It was a fun night

Elsie Narveson Great memories of a great gal

Phyllis Michels I am really enjoying your saga!

Michelle Andresen Toenjes I sure did miss seeing Ruth Ann retire! She was a great, kind, and fun lady. I learned alot from her! Miss her lots!

PeteandRuth Ann Bungum I agree Michelle—I miss her a lot too.

Brad Bungum Dad PeteandRuth Ann Bungum, who is the little kid in the picture?

PeteandRuth Ann Bungum It is Mike Millers son.

Amy Tobiasson Picray Thank you for sharing! I had forgotten a lot about her last day. I was so fortunate to have started my career with Ruthann! Definitely brings back a lot of smiles and good memories!

PeteandRuth Ann Bungum glad you're enjoying my/our journey—I miss her a lot. Thanks for your kind words

Sharon Wykle Twedt Always liked your rock...

PeteandRuth Ann Bungum

Wednesday, May 27, 2020.

The year is 1999—Part 2—Pete's retirement.

My last day of school was June 8th. When I got out of bed that morning, I was thinking of my first day of teaching in August 1962. Another thought was that these 36 years had really gone fast. I sat down with Ruth Ann and had a funny feeling. I couldn't believe it was actually going to be my last day. I finished my coffee, gave Ruth Ann a kiss and told her, "Well, I guess this is it." I headed for the door, got a lump in my throat, and actually shed a few tears. I had taught 36 years, been in the classroom 6,479 days and this would be day 6,480. I probably should have jumped with joy but that feeling wasn't there.

That last morning my colleagues and I took our seventh graders to the swimming pool. We brought the kids back to school at 11:15. We dismissed the town kids and I was on bus duty for the rural kids. Then Cheri Francis, the math teacher, came running down the sidewalk toward me and said, "Pete, you have a phone call and I think it is Brad in Denmark." She took my bus duty and I went in the lounge to take the call. He had timed the call perfectly. I had emailed him and told him I would have my last minute of duty at 11:30, June 8th, 1999. I looked at my watch and the numbers on my watch were 11:30. In Denmark it was 6:30 pm. He congratulated me and asked how I felt. I told him I felt funny and couldn't believe it was over. So, Brad was the first person I talked to as a retired teacher at 11:31.

That afternoon I went golfing with Paul Pinney—he had retired two years before. We talked about our careers. I asked him how he had adjusted—he said it wasn't a problem. He said when he retired, he was ready to do something different. He got a job mowing at the Fawn Creek Country Club—a stress-free job. I told him I was going to paint. It would not be as stressful as the classroom. The paint brush wouldn't be a discipline problem.

That night was the official retirement party for the three of us retiring. The other two were Darla Algoe, 7th grade English, and

Marsha Ketelsen, Consumer Education. The party was held at the lodge in Wapsipincon State Park. Walt Fortney, our retired principal, had been asked to say few words about the three of us. Walt said I was always very professional, was willing to innovate and try new things and even when we didn't agree on a major decision or change at the Middle School, he knew I would always be on board. I appreciated his words—they were true.

The next speaker was Dale Reck, our highly talented art teacher. Dale's job at all the retirement parties was to do a drawing of the retirees. He was also a funny man. He had the following to say about me before he presented me the drawing. He said almost every day this year I would make a comment that this was the last time I had to do this or that. Using that as his launching he said he was going to add to my list of "lasts." Here they are:

> *Pete, you've had your last SHIT—Special High Intensity Training.*
>
> *Pete, you've had your last DEEP SHIT—Departmental Employee Evaluation Program—Special High Intensity Training.*
>
> *Pete, you've had your last EAT SHIT—Employee Attitude Training—Special High Intensity Training.*
>
> *And Pete, you've had your last DIP SHIT—Director of Intensity Programming—Special High Intensity Training.*

He went on to mention I had always been known as the Number One Norwegian—Mr. Norsky—at the Middle School. I had managed to educate the entire staff on that magnificent mountain in Norway, "Bungum Mountain."

Using my Norwegian ancestry as the theme he came up with a memorable drawing. He drew an 18 x 24 drawing using colored pencils. Since I was recognized as the King of the Norskies he printed "Peter the Great" on top. I was also known to drink a beer or two, so he incorporated that. Across my chest he printed "Patron Saint of Brewsky." He had me dressed in papal clothing with a little mug of beer hanging on a necklace. Needless to say, it brought tons of laughs. I have it hanging in my office—I look and smile at it most every day.

Rick Delagardelle spoke next. Rick was a friend, former colleague and principal my last year. He said that when he started teaching in 1973, he looked at me as his mentor. He also mentioned that he looked at me as being very professional. He brought up my ANAD project, my willingness to volunteer at athletic events, being advisor for the Raider Review, our school newspaper, for 31 years and being a lunchroom supervisor. His words were much appreciated.

Both Carron and Brad had written memories about me. Carron read both of them. Brad wrote about some of his memories in the 1970s when all four of us would be on the patio listening to Ron Gonder broadcasting Hawkeye football games. Carron brought up having me for her teacher. She said I never gave her any favors.

The next day we went to the Casino in Dubuque. It was a fun way to unwind.

In mail the third day I received a congratulatory message from Iowa Senator Chuck Grassley. His niece, Gwen Wiegmann, was a colleague—she must have told him.

On the third day of retirement I went to my classroom and cleaned. It was necessary for me to clean my stuff out of the desk, closet, filing cabinets, and bookshelves to make it ready for Mr. Schultz, my replacement. I had one more thing to do. I went to the office and turned in my school key and room key. I told myself, "Well, this is really it. I can't get into the school anymore."

When I was driving home, a serenity came over me. I told myself it was over, and it was time now to look at the future and a new life. My new life would be one of no more pre-school workshops, no more preparing lessons, no more correcting papers, no more teacher meetings, no more in-service meetings, no more conferences with parents, no more hall duty, no more lunch room duty, no more angry parents to deal with, no more writing to legislators urging them to adequately fund Iowa schools. I had a feeling of joy. I was ready for my new life.

One more good memory is getting a letter from a former student. The letter was from James Russet, a high school and then a college chemistry teacher in Crown Point, Indiana. James was in my seventh geography class and again in my eighth grade American History class from 1972–1974. He said that Darla Algoe, Rick Delagardelle and I were the three that made him think and explore ideas for himself. We were also partially responsible for how he taught high school and college chemistry. He said he learned much more than history and geography from my classes and that they were the beginning of his teacher education program. I got several more—pretty much the same message from all of them.

Alexandra Bungum, Bret Lewison and 15 others

Comments

Jill Darrow Pete, in reading the names of your fellow teachers, I am reminded of what a positive impact so many of you made on your students. As an AHS grad, I think fondly of nearly all of the teachers I had.

PeteandRuth Ann Bungum Thanks for the kind words. I remember fondly when you babysat Brad and Carron.

Brad Bungum I also fondly remember that, Jill Darrow and Dad...;-)

Jay Blattie Love the pic!!

Bernie Paulson That was also the year I retired. No regrets.

Phil Bungum ;~]

Sharon Wykle Twedt Good picture...

Elsie Narveson Quite the retirement

PeteandRuth Ann Bungum

Thursday, May 28, 2020. Pete and Ruth Ann's Journey through 59 years.

The year is 2000.

This was a memorable year for Pete and Ruth Ann. We turned 60 and had been married for 40 years. To celebrate we booked a trip to Jamaica from June 28 to July 3. But that was going to create a problem for Brad and Carron. We didn't know it, but they had planned a surprise celebration on July 1. Carron was contacted by friends of ours that told her we were going to Jamaica at that time. She called Brad in Denmark to tell him. He came up with a lie that he would use on us. He called us and said he and Alex were coming to Anamosa from June 30 to July 6. He already had paid for it and couldn't get his money back. We believed him. Then we had to cancel our journey to Jamaica. We had already paid for it also. But thanks to Kris May, our travel agent, she got ours changed to August.

The kids told us we would celebrate our anniversary on July 1 by going to the Amana Colonies for some fine dining. On the morning of July 1, they told us to dress casually. They told us we would have to pick up Wes and Ellyn at the lodge in Wapsi Park because they were camping with their other grandparents. When we got there, things didn't look right. Why was Paul Pinney there with a camcorder? When we saw some of our friends standing around, we knew we'd been had. They took us in the lodge—waiting for us was six of my siblings plus Ruth Ann's cousins, several of our high school classmates and numerous local friends.

Throughout the day other people showed up. The biggest surprise was Paul and Sharon Twedt from Huntington Beach, CA. and Carson and Connie Ode from Des Moines.

The speeches began at 4:00. The first to go was seven-year-old granddaughter Alex from Denmark. She had memorized her speech—here it is:

> *Hi grandpa and grandma. I'm glad to see you. I'm glad to see Wesley and Ellyn and Aunt Carron and Uncle Dean. Grandma, did you have a good birthday? I hope Grandpa will have a good birthday, but now when you don't have to work anymore you can come to Denmark to see me. Happy Anniversity (sic) Grandma and Grandpa. I love you both. Skoal, and if you don't know what that means it means "Cheers." Lift your glass, look at each other and then say "Skoal."*

She got a rousing ovation.

When she sat down Grandson Wesley yelled to her, "Tell everyone about Grandpa's underwear." She gets up, grabs the microphone and tells the story.

> *When I was sleeping with Grandpa and Grandma one morning Grandpa had to go potty. I saw that he had a hole in his underwear. I tell Grandma and we laugh. The next day me and Grandma go shopping. We don't know what to buy Grandpa. Grandma says, "Maybe a jar of peanuts," but then she says he will get fat if he eats all those. We still don't know what to buy Grandpa and then Grandma says, "Maybe a new pair of underwear." She bought him five pair.*

The next day she told me that I had holes in the front of my underwear too, but she didn't look.

There were about 15 speeches—I'm only going to mention one more.

My brother Chuck, four years older than me, gave an interesting one.

He said when I was age five, I threw a butter knife at him and it stuck in his leg. He said when he showed Mom what I had done she said, "Chuck, you deserve it." I don't remember doing that.

Between those people who were at the lodge and those who sent greetings by mail we heard from about 110 people. Carron took all the cards and letters and put them in two huge scrapbooks. The end result was fantastic, a truly professional job. Those scrapbooks were wonderful keepsakes for us.

These are my final thoughts on the party. Ruth Ann and I couldn't imagine how Brad and Carron pulled it off when many people in Anamosa knew about it for at least four months and the grandkids also knew. We were in awe over the friends and relatives who came from Minnesota, Wisconsin, California, Colorado, Texas, Arizona and Iowa. And we had messages from Georgia, Florida, Denmark, Texas, Washington, Australia, and Iowa.

Tomorrow I'll write more about 2000.

Yrsa Thom Chris, Carlene Vavricek and 9 others

Comments

Elsie Narveson That was a fun day. Hats off to your kids for pulling off a great surprise

PeteandRuth Ann Bungum

Pete and Ruth Ann with grandkids at our 40th anniversary

Friday, May 29, 2020. Pete and Ruth Ann's journey through 59 years.

The year is 2000—Part 3.

This is my last post on 2000.

Other than the celebration for our 60th birthdays and 40th anniversary we did a lot of traveling.

In February we went to Mazatlan, Mexico, with brother John and wife Lorna. It is on the Pacific side. They have a timeshare there, so it is a frequent vacation spot for them. The highlight for me was going parasailing for my first and only time. I really wasn't afraid. I did what the instructor told me, and I had a perfect take-off and landing. The landing is the trickiest part. First, you have to find your instructor on the ground because he gives you hand signals on whether to pull the ropes on the right or left side of your parachute. I spotted my instructor on the beach—he guided me down to a perfect landing. I was charged $20 for a ten-minute flight. I was pulled by a high-powered motorboat.

We spent a lot of time on the beach—it had numerous vendors. One of the them was a tattoo artist. I got a tattoo for the first time—it was one of those that last ten days. I had it put on my forearm. It was a heart with "I Love Ruth" written above the heart. It was really cool.

The next day Lorna and I took a walk on the beach. We decided to leave a message for Ruth Ann in the sand, right below our 14th story window. We carved 12-foot letters in the sand. It said, "I love Ruth," with a heart for the word "love." When we got back to the room, I told Ruth Ann to go to the window and look down on the beach. She was so touched that she melted in my arms!!!!

On July 12 we finally started our delayed Jamaican second honeymoon. It was one of those all-inclusive trips.

My main memory is a negative one. Ruth Ann and I went swimming. Soon we were surrounded by five Jamaican kids. They spoke English so we could easily communicate. I asked them about school, girlfriends, boyfriends, jobs of parents, etc. One of the parents snapped a photo of me with all the kids. Then came the disappointment and I was upset. The seventh-grade girl asked me if I knew what KFC stood for. I said I did.

Her next line: "We are really poor, and would you like to take us to KFC to eat tonight?" The entire thing was a set-up, obviously taught to them by their parents and most likely something they did many times. I refused. I talked to one of the Jamaican hosts and she was hoping I said "no." She said the Jamaican government was encouraging tourists to not spend money on the locals. The intent was to stop the mentality that begging was okay. I was disappointed because I was having such a good time visiting with those kids. One more of their ploys was that the youngest boy was deaf. It was a lie.

One more memory is when we were being driven to our resort, I noticed the poverty. We noticed that on the north beach side of road were the hotels, condos, tennis courts, swimming pools and restaurants surrounded by wealthy white people from Europe and the U.S. On the south land side were the tiny cardboard shacks occupied by Jamaicans. I saw many men sitting on the porch in the middle of the day, doing nothing except watching the traffic.

I had several thoughts as we drove by. How did they survive from day to day with no job and no income? Was there any hope for a better tomorrow? Would their kids have a better life? My biggest thought was how lucky I was to have been born a little white-skinned Norwegian on a farm in southeast Minnesota. If there is one thing traveling has done for me, it is to open my mind and make me grateful for the wonderful life I've been able to live.

In October we went to Denmark to help Alex celebrate her eighth birthday. She had all her 22 classmates there. The rule in her school is if a girl has a party all the girl classmates must be invited. If she chooses, she can invite the boys. The same rule for the boys. Alex decided to invite all the boys. Another rule was gifts would not cost more than 15 kroner, about $2.50. The party lasted from 1:30 to 5:30. Brad and Inge kept the kids busy with games, music, dancing and food. They escaped with only one shattered window—a boy did it. Ruth Ann and I were glad Brad and Inge were in charge. Alex said she would never invite the boys again. The reason for inviting all the kids of the same sex is that they are taught at a young age that no one is better than anyone else. There will be no snobbish cliques in their classroom or at their parties. I like that.

The Hawkeyes were 3–8 in 2000. The good news was they improved every game. We could've had seven wins with a little luck going our way. Things were looking positive for 2001.

Alexandra Bungum, Bret Lewison and 6 others

PeteandRuth Ann Bungum

Saturday, May 30, 2020. Pete and Ruth Ann's journey through 59 years.

The year is 2001.

In March we went to Tunica, Mississippi. On the way home we stopped in Steele, Missouri, and visited a local bar. We sat at the bar and started visiting with the locals. Soon a guy walked in, saw Ruth Ann and took the seat next to Ruth Ann. I think he thought she looked pretty nice. He wasn't used to seeing an attractive, well-dressed lady sitting at that bar. His name was Sonny and he was a native of Steele. He was smooth, easy to talk to and funny. We told him we were from Anamosa, Iowa. Sonny said he knew where it was because he had driven through Anamosa when delivering watermelons to Minneapolis. He referred to watermelons as "ghetto apples."

As we were talking to Sonny, some other guy at the end of the bar was getting louder and louder, using many four-letter words. Sonny had had enough of his foul mouth. The guy's name was Tony. Sonny yelled, "Tony, shut your rotten mouth! We have a nice lady sitting here." Sonny whispered to Ruth Ann that she had to excuse Tony because he was from the bayou.

Then we met Jake. He had some definite opinions about the law enforcement officials in the area. He had no time for the sheriff, the police chief in Steele and the police chief in the neighboring town of Cooter. He said they were all harassing him. For some reason he also knew where Anamosa was. When we got ready to leave Sonny invited us to stay and get a room at the bed and breakfast and come back for the dance that evening. We politely declined and told everyone it was nice to meet them.

When we drove out of Steele the first thing Ruth Ann said was, "I think Sonny and Jake are ex-cons." She had learned while working at the Reformatory that inmates knew about prisons in other states, especially the good ones. Inmates considered Anamosa a good one.

When we returned home, we told Carron about our experience in Steele. She and her husband took a trip south the next year. We told them to stop in Steele and stop at that bar and ask about Sonny and Jake. When they stopped Carron explained to the bartender her parents had stopped in February and had met Sonny and Jake and they were wondering if they were around. The people at the bar said they hadn't seen Jake lately, but they knew Sonny was back in prison in one of the "M" states. Carron could hardly keep from laughing. My guess is Sonny was in Minnesota—he probably delivered more than ghetto apples to the Twin Cities.

In October Brad, Lene, Alexandra, Mads and Mathilde came to Anamosa. We took them to a Hawkeye football game. Mads fell in love with the Hawkeye drinking cups/containers. He wanted to take some home to give to his classmates. So, we started collecting them in the south end zone bleachers. We collected 123 cups. When we got home the cups needed to be cleaned. We went to the bathroom and set up an assembly line. I scrubbed them in the bathtub, Alex and Mads dried them and Mathilde stacked them. They took them to Denmark and gave each classmate a Hawkeye cup. The end result is there are 90 new Hawkeye fans in Denmark. It is amazing how Hawkeye mania is sweeping world—there is no end to it.

We had a big party in October. We planned a surprise party for Brad's 40th birthday. They almost didn't come from Denmark because of an anthrax scare. Thank goodness they decided to come anyway, because we had invited his UWP buddies from New York, Boston, Montana, Colorado, Kansas, Iowa, South Dakota and northern Minnesota. The party was a total surprise (*shocked* is a better word) for Brad. The party was a big success. It was fun to listen to all the guys recall their days with Brad in UWP. Some of them had not been together for 17 years.

On Christmas Day we boarded an airplane in Cedar Rapids with five people. Ruth Ann and I decided we would treat Carron, Wes and Ellyn to a trip to Denmark. The kids had never been on an airplane before. As we lifted off Wesley said in a rather loud voice, "Mom, I'm really hyper, I need some Ritalin."

One of the highlights in Denmark was Brad and Lene treating us to a Danish Christmas Lunch. What a treat! Let me explain:

Course 1. Two kinds of herring, bread, curry sauce, hard-boiled eggs, tomatoes, mackerel and tuna spread. Then drink some wine and conversation.
Course 2. Red cabbage and frikadelle (meat balls). Then drink a different kind of wine and conversation.
Course 3. Liver paste and pickled beets. Then more wine-conversation.
Course 4. Pork roast and potatoes. More wine-conversation.
Course 5. Pastries. More wine-conversation.

It was a three-hour dinner with several kinds of wine between courses and a lot of conversation. What a wonderful way to spend an evening. It is another example of one of the many things I like about Denmark. They know how to enjoy life. Keep in mind the kids did not get wine.

We took a tour of Copenhagen. The kids got to see the Little Mermaid, the round church, the entrance to Tivoli, the walking street, the Queens Palace. And we took a photo of them standing by one of the Queen's guards. We ate at the Hard Rock Cafe.

On New Year's Eve the five kids blasted away with fireworks until 1:30 in the morning. They are legal in Denmark. But the kids had to put on safety glasses.

We flew home on New Year's Day, 2002. We went from Denmark to Amsterdam to Minneapolis to Cedar Rapids. In Amsterdam the European Union had just converted to the EURO—so it was the first day. It was a little challenging for some of the workers in the restaurant.

Also, before we boarded in Amsterdam, we told the security lady to ask Wesley if he was always nice to his sister. He said, "Some of the time."

Tim Bungum, John Spilde and 3 others

Comments

John Spilde Thank you for your service as a teacher Mr. Bungum! The longer I live the more I appreciate growing up in Anamosa! So many great people! It took a village to raise us Anamosa kids! Sincerely, John

PeteandRuth Ann Bungum

Sunday, May 31, 2020. Pete and Ruth Ann's journey through 59 years.

The year is 2002.

I'm going to divide 2002 into two posts.

In January I took on a monstrous paint job. I was hired to paint the medical clinic in Anamosa. It had 36 rooms. I could only paint on Saturday afternoon from noon to 8pm and Sunday from 7am to 7pm. It took me four hours to paint my first exam room. After that first room I worked out a system and got my time down to two hours and 45 minutes. By the time I finished, after eight weekends, I had painted 32 of 36 rooms. It was a good payday.

The downside of 2002 was on November 17 at 3:15 am when Ruth Ann's mother passed away at the Preston Nursing Home in Minnesota. We were with her when she took her last breath. She opened her eyes, took a huge sigh, and had her last breath. Her eyes had not been open for two days. Her eyes were so glazed I'm not sure she saw anything. An EMT told us later that opening the eyes in the last minute of life is a normal phenomenon. As I left the room, I kissed Myrtle on the forehead and said goodbye. It was 3:15 am on a Sunday morning. That was the first time I had seen anyone die. Ruth Ann, her brother Roger, and I were by her side when she took that last breath.

Ruth Ann called the Riley Funeral Home in Chatfield. They picked up the body at 4:30 am. Mr Riley wanted us to come see him at 10:00 that morning to make final arrangements.

Roger and Ruth Ann scheduled the funeral for Wednesday, November 20. For some reason that date is familiar—yes, it would be my 62nd birthday. I would guess there aren't many people in this world who have their mother die on their birthday and their mother-in-law buried on their birthday.

The funeral was at Root Prairie Lutheran Church in rural Fountain, Minnesota. Carron gave a wonderful eulogy. She based her eulogy on the theme, "Everything I Needed to Know I Learned

in Kindergarten." Brad came from Denmark and was one of the pall-
bearers. She was buried beside Cyrus, her first husband. She lived 90
years and 66 days, about ten years longer than the average female in
the U.S.

Here are a few more memories of 2002.

Walt Fortney, my principal for 25 years, died from lung cancer.
I went to see him about two weeks before he died. I hardly recognized him—he was an 80-pound bag of bones. There was no casket
and no viewing of the body. He donated his body to the University
of Iowa Medical School. I've missed Walt a lot over the years.

In September we went to Iowa State University in Ames, Iowa.
Grandkids Wes and Ellyn were being recognized as State of Iowa
Scholars along with 200 other kids from Iowa. What I remember
the most are some words from the main speaker. The speaker was
an assistant football coach. He told the 200 kids, "You don't have to
apologize to your classmates for getting good grades and being recognized as an Iowa Scholar. Just remember this, 'Tiger Woods, after he
has won a golf tournament doesn't go up to his defeated opponents
and tell them he is sorry he beat them.' Tiger has worked hard to be
so good and you have too. So be proud of your accomplishments." It
caught the attention of the kids.

The Hawkeyes won the Big Ten Championship with a perfect
8–0 record. I was ushering in church that November. I was eating
breakfast on the last Sunday of November when I had a brainstorm.
I told Ruth Ann I was going to call my three partners and see if they
were in favor of all of us wearing a Hawkeye Big Ten Champion
sweatshirt when ushering. They were all in favor. I brought four to
church with me and we all got decked out in our black and gold.
When we took offering, everyone could see us. As we passed the
plates most all of the congregants had big smiles. And a few of the
younger ones gave us "thumbs up." That was the happiest bunch of
Lutherans I had ever seen at a Sunday worship service. I can tell you
one thing for sure—more people remember our Hawkeye sweatshirts
than what was said in the sermon that Sunday. Now you know why
you see those bumper strips all over America—you know—the ones
that say, "It's Great To Be Hawkeye."

In November I made a big decision to lose weight. I had gotten up to 195 pounds. My pants wouldn't fit anymore, I would get dizzy trying to pick something off the floor plus Dr. Vernon told me to lose weight. I googled Mayo Clinic. Their message was this:

1. Exercise. Take 5–10 minutes to warm up. I would do some yoga stretches and breathing exercises.
2. Then for 15–20 minutes do some calisthenics, use the inflated exercise ball to do sit-ups and lift weights three days a week.
3. Walk briskly for at least 45 minutes, preferably longer. Some days I would stretch it to 60–70 minutes.
4. I learned I could burn off 5 calories a minute by walk-ing—60 minutes x 5 = 300 calories per day. Each pound contains 3,500 calories so in 12 days I could rid myself of a pound. With my extra minutes it amounted to 2–4 pounds a month. I made a line graph to keep track of my lost pounds. On my graph I recorded numbers from 195 pounds down to 155 pounds. It was fun to watch the line on my graph head downward.

By May I was down to 163 pounds. My original goal was to lose 30 pounds. I made it. Dr. Vernon told me to not get carried away. He said I should stay in the 165 range.

The other big thing the Mayo booklet told me to do was change my eating routine. Instead of eating three big meals a day, eat five times a day, but smaller portions. It said I could eat anything, includ-ing carbohydrates—but don't be a pig. I have been eating five small meals a day since I read that in November 2002. I eat at 9 am, noon, 3:30 pm, 6 pm and 7:30 pm. The idea is to keep your body on an even keel, so you have no big spikes in your blood sugar. I'm writing this on May 31, 2020—my weight this morning was 166.6 pounds. The first thing I do every morning is weigh myself—and I still keep my line graph. I'm proud to say I've kept my weight off since 2003 😊 17 years.

My second major decision was to start writing my autobiography. It took me three years, but I finally finished in March 2006. I have a lot more respect for authors after being one myself. Writing forces a person to have patience and self-discipline and motivation. It makes you do research and take notes and makes you think about grammar, punctuation and capitalization again.

Tomorrow I'll write about our trip to London, Paris and Amsterdam.

You, Richard Stout, Ellyn Rickels and 3 others

PeteandRuth Ann Bungum

Monday, June 1, 2020. Pete and Ruth Ann's journey through 59 years.

The year is 2002—Part 2.

In July Ruth Ann and I took a vacation to London, Paris and Amsterdam. I'm going to mention a few of the highlights in each city.

LONDON:
On a bus tour we saw/visited:

- Kensington Palace—where Princess Di lived.
- Westminster Abbey
- Hyde Park
- #10 Downing Street
- Piccadilly Circus
- Trafalgar Square
- Buckingham Palace and changing of the guard
- Scotland Yard headquarters
- Lloyd's of London
- St. Paul's Cathedral
- Harrod's Store—we didn't buy any baby octopus
- Had "fish and chips" at a pub
- Tower of London—we saw the spot where Anne Boleyn and Katherine Howard had their heads cut off in 1536 and 1542. They were wives #2 and #5 of Henry VIII.
- Millennium Ferris Wheel—each bucket holds 25 people, there are 25–30 buckets and it takes about an hour to take the ride
- Tower Bridge, the Pub where Shakespeare used to hang out
- 10 Bells Pub where several of Jack the Ripper's victims had their last drinks.

PARIS:

We took the EuroStar train to Paris—we went through the Channel and got up to 187 miles per hour.

Our guide warned us to securely hang on to our purses and wallets because the Gypsies waiting for us were catlike quick and would work in teams to pick our pockets. And they can spot Americans right away.

Our hotel was four blocks from the Eiffel Tower.

We took a tour and we saw:

- Arc of Triomphe
- Champs Elysees
- French Assembly
- Sorbonne
- Latin Quarter where Jackie Kennedy had lived
- Place de la Concorde where Marie Antoinette and Louis XVI were guillotined
- The guide told us that some tax collectors were guillotined—Ruth Ann, being an old tax collector, was relieved to not have lived at that time
- We stopped at the Eiffel Tower—our group got up to the first level. Pretty amazing structure. They paint it every seven years, so I thought about putting in a bid.
- Notre Dame Cathedral. It burned last year.
- Versailles. Went into the Hall of Mirrors where the end of World War I treaty was written
- Lourdes—saw the *Mona Lisa*

Paris is a fascinating city; the architecture is remarkable and the way the streets are laid out is awesome.

AMSTERDAM:

We took a guided tour of the Red Light District. Our guide was Linda, a 22-year-old university student. We walked through the whole district. The girls were in the windows and gave all of men big smiles as we walked by. There were white, black and Asian girls.

The average age was 18–26 and many go on to being escorts as they approach 30. Average price was 25–30 euros for 15–20 minutes. This is the minimum and prices double if you want a half hour and special services will cost even more. Condoms are included in the price. The girls are taxed, and they also have to pay their landlords (pimps) for renting the room. They work eight-hour shifts and they rotate shifts, so they all get a chance to work at night which brings in the most money. There was a condom museum and a sex museum—we didn't go to either one.

- Rik's Museum—we saw original paintings by Rembrandt, Vermeer, Van Gogh and Steen plus others.
- Diamond factory—we got to see diamonds being cut and polished. Ruth Ann and I got to hold a $100,000 diamond.
- Wooden shoe factory. I tried a pair on, and they fit good.
- 400-year-old Dutch windmill with the original lumber in perfect condition
- Anne Frank's house. We saw the original rooms and book-cases that hid the annex where they hid. We saw the marks on the wall measuring the heights of Anne and sister Margot as they grew over the 25 months of secrecy. We saw Anne's original pictures and posters on her bedroom wall and her diary entries. We saw father Otto's letters to relatives and friends after the war trying to find out if his daughters were still alive. Otto was the only one of the eight to survive.
- We went to Madame Tussaud's, the wax museum. It is amazing. I had Ruth Ann take a photo of me with Winston Churchill.

It was great vacation—one of most memorable. We got home on July 29, 2002.

Tomorrow it will be 2003.

You, Erland Christensen, Carlene Vavricek and 8 others

Comments

Brad Bungum Great memories Pops PeteandRuth Ann Bungum... but for the sake of history for you and I, I need to write this now, as I read your 1 June post in real time with what I'm watching on CNN from Denmark... I'm literally crying for right now...for the United States, for those who can't get justice, and in the immediate real-time, for the peaceful protesters who just got attacked by DC cops just so DT could move over to a church with a bible in his hand for a photo opp. I'm sure he needed Google Maps to find out where to walk... My question is, "Are we going to sit on our asses for 5 months and let him get re-elected (watch-out for real if that happens!), or are those of us who believe in what's right gonna get off our respective asses and do something—seriously something—to make sure that doesn't happen?" Those of you who don't agree with me can de-friend me now and I'll be forever forgiving and grateful. But I honestly cannot live with myself any longer if I don't speak out on this. Helicopter video doesn't lie...our president does. 100 times a day. And this is bull-crap. Excuse all my bad language, but enough /is enough. I'm tired of holding back for professional or personal reasons... DO SOMETHING! Do what you know is right. I think most of the people who read this will know what "right" means...

PeteandRuth Ann Bungum Well written Brad—I agree 100%. Our only hope is he doesn't get re-elected. He acts more like Hitler all the time.

Cindy Meyer Norton Thanks so much for writing what I've been avoiding saying as to not stir controversy. What ideas do you have? I was a precinct captain for Joe and donate to his campaign but really feel helpless right now as what more to do. I am astounded that people think tRumps behavior is ok. I understand those with Republican ideals but supporting him is so beyond anything I can even fathom trying to rationalize.

Brad Bungum Cindy Meyer Norton Cindy, just start by getting people to vote. Talk to them calmly and fairly about the consequences of not doing so (even if they vote for Trump—that's why it's called democracy...but that is seriously at risk right now in America IMO). Disagreement doesn't have to mean a fight or anger. Though current leadership makes it a zero-sum game, I admit. But start there—get out the vote in any upcoming primaries, and more importantly in November. And maybe one more thing that I read the other day... "More importantly, in the US political system, do your homework on your local, county and state election options." They have (in many ways) way more influence on our daily lives than Washington. And we have easier access to them than we do to national candidates. By local, in terms of importance, I mean state reps/senators, mayors, sheriffs, and perhaps most importantly District Attorneys and judges. Don't just rubber stamp the incumbents. Do the homework and know where they stand on the issues important to you as an individual. That's a great start in terms of making the change any individual might want…

Elsie Narveson Sounded like an outstanding trip.

Cindy Meyer Norton, Cindy, what is your email address? I have an article I'd like to send you with additional solutions as to what we can do (other than complain)…

Cindy Meyer Norton Brad Bungum cnorton38@aol.com. Appreciate that. Complaining gets me nowhere but feeling really negative. I recently read a wonderful article written by President Obama which sounded like your original response. Getting informed and involved in all levels of elections.

PeteandRuth Ann Bungum

Tuesday, June 2, 2020. Pete and Ruth Ann's journey through 59 years.

Today is 2003.

January 1, 2003, found Ruth Ann, me, Brad and Alexandra at the Orange Bowl in Miami. We played USC and got beat 38–17. That game is still too painful for me to talk about so I sure can't write about it.

The third Wednesday of January was much happier for me. I received my first Social Security check. Several of my colleagues died in their 40s and 50s so I decided to go for it at age 62.

In March we took a trip to Branson, Missouri—it was one of those time-share deals where you pay $300 and get three nights in a motel, some free meals and free shows. The third day is the sales pitch day. They want you to buy a share in a condo in which you can spend a week or two once a year for a vacation. But you have to pay a monthly fee all year. We didn't buy and they put us threw pure hell. They tried three salespeople on us. We didn't buy. We were happy to leave that place.

Carron turned the big 4-0 on April 24. We had a surprise party for her. Brad and Lene came from Denmark. Other invitees were Diane (sidewalk shit) Norton, Carlene Pinney, Lisa Heitland Williams, Mark Lubbock, Janet Norton, and Dave Kerton (her boss at Kirkwood). Ruth Ann and I learned a lot of things we didn't know about Carron. She was totally surprised, and a good time was had by all.

Brad came home in September by himself for two Hawkeye games. He flew around the world to see his beloved Hawkeyes beat the Gophers. Here is how he did it: On a business trip he flew from Copenhagen to Singapore to Shanghai to Tokyo. Then it was Tokyo to Seattle to Chicago to Cedar Rapids. He may be the only guy who has flown around the world to see the Hawkeyes.

We ended the season with a 9–3 record and went to the Outback Bowl in Tampa on January 1. We played the Florida Gators—we kicked butt by a score of 37–17.

In October we took a two-week bus trip to New England. What follows is a list of what we saw, visited and learned.

- West Point
- FDR's Hyde Park home on the Hudson River and burial place
- Lexington, Concord, old North Bridge
- Site of the Boston Massacre
- Site of the Boston Tea Party
- Paul Revere's Home
- Kennebunkport, Walker's Point (Home of H. W. Bush)
- Learned to speak with a Boston accent—Boston/Baaston, Cuba/Cuber, cars/caas, Harvard/Havard
- Franciscan monastery
- White Mountains
- Bretton Woods
- Plymouth Notch (home of Calvin Coolidge)
- Maple sugar museum
- Robert Todd Lincoln's home
- Norman Rockwell museum
- Morgan horse farm
- Fort Ticonderoga
- Finger Lakes
- Niagara Falls
- Our guide in New Hampshire didn't like people from Massachusetts so he called them SPORS—it meant (Stupid People on Rental Skis). He also confided in me that he calls them Massholes.

It was a great trip and ranks in a first-place tie with London, Paris and Amsterdam.

Tomorrow is 2004.

You, Rhenee Grabau, John Spilde and 3 others

PeteandRuth Ann Bungum

Wednesday, June 3, 2020. Pete and Ruth Ann's journey through 59 years.

The year is 2004.

On Valentine's Day we headed for New Orleans. It was Mardi Gras time. We found a hotel one block from Canal Street. This is where the parades take place. We watched parades for two nights. Each float threw beads. Ruth Ann received 54 strands of beads. We had a fun time telling friends and family Ruth Ann had to flash 54 times in order to get 54.

On the second day we walked to the French Quarter and had brunch at Brennan's. We both had Eggs Benedict. It tasted out of this world—the price was out of this world also—$35 each. We also had a bottle of wine and a piece of their famous banana dessert. Our total bill was $121. A little pricey for a breakfast but it was vacation time. I thought about Mom's words of wisdom. "A hundred years from now you'll never know the difference."

On the third morning I got up at 6 am and took a walk through the French Quarter. At 6:30 am many of the bars were open. I was invited into three of them. They wanted me to enjoy a Bloody Mary. I politely declined.

After four days we headed East on I-10, our destination was Daytona Beach. We took a tour around the Daytona Racetrack. We went through the race museum. We are not race fans, but it was very interesting. We learned a lot about NASCAR.

That night we had another first for us. We went to a Hooter's Bar. The servers wore some eye-pleasing outfits. They were very nice young ladies. We talked to several of them. They were typical young people trying make a living or get through college. It was another example of having an image of something but when you actually see it, they are two different things.

We went to the Kennedy Space Center. We had a great day viewing the launch pads. We saw an actual Saturn rocket in the museum. It is unbelievably huge.

Then we drove to Kissimmee. I fulfilled one of my lifelong dreams. We got to see the Houston Astro's training site and I got to see a Major League Baseball team in spring training. I was excited, much more than Ruth Ann. As I was looking at Biggio, Bergman, Bagwell, Everett, Valentine, Ausmus, Oswald, and Pettite work out I was thinking how young they look. I really wanted to see Roger Clemens, but he was a no-show. Ruth Ann's impression of spring training was a little different than mine. Her comment was "What's the big deal? All they did was throw the baseball around." I assured her there was a little more to it than that. Seeing spring training allowed me to scratch one more thing off my Bucket List.

On March 1 we drove to Marietta, Georgia to visit Ruth Ann's cousin, Terry Trogstad and his wife, Patti. They took us to CNN headquarters, Stone Mountain, the 73rd floor of the Westin Beach Tree Plaza to have a drink in the rotating bar/restaurant. Then it was on to the famous Mary Mac's Tea Room for dinner. I had pot likker, corn bread, black-eyed peas, turnip greens, and chicken. Pot likker is the liquid left over after meat and vegetables have been cooked, often used for broth or gravy. Mine was broth. I enjoyed the food but can't say I would say I would like a steady diet of it.

The CNN tour was great. It was fun to see Wolf Blitzer do his broadcast. It was fun and an educational two days.

I have a fun story to tell about Terry. He is a big man and weighs about 320 pounds. Terry said he went to his doctor for a physical. After the exam the doctor pronounced him in perfect health, even at 320 pounds. Terry went on to explain his doctor also weighs 320 pounds.

In October we went to Denmark again to celebrate Alexandra's 12th birthday. We spent a day visiting her school. Some of the similarities between our schools and Danish schools are tests, textbooks, attention spans, homework, playgrounds, backpacks, class sizes, and school boards. Some differences are that teachers are called by their first names, the teachers dress more casually, there are no hot lunches and the students eat in their classroom. And on Fridays, after school, the teachers get to have an adult beverage in their lounge. Also, more foreign languages are taught at younger ages and there are no athletic teams. They have fewer computers, the teachers are all bi-lingual and by the age of 13–14 most Danish kids can speak English and some French and German. They start learning English in 1st to 3rd grade.

In June Ruth Ann's brother, Roger and wife Linda came to Anamosa to visit the world-famous J&P Cycles. It is the largest supplier of after-market parts and accessories for Harley Davidson cycles. Roger owns a Harley. It is also the home of the National Motorcycle Museum. We took Roger and Linda through the museum and to J&P's display room. They really enjoyed seeing a motorcycle used by Evel Knievel, Peter Fonda's Easy Rider and Steve McQueen's personal Indian Chief. There were old cycles from the early 1900s, BMWs from Germany, Italian and British cycles and new Harleys plus many others. The museum and store have had visitors from all 50 states and over 30 countries. It is a very interesting place to visit.

I'm going to end 2004 on a humorous note. One day Carron took a dress out of her closet. It was somewhat wrinkled, so she sprayed water on it and put it in the dryer. Wesley was watching and asked what she doing.

Carron explained that with the water and the heat of the dryer, the wrinkles would disappear. Wes looked at her and said, "Would that work on Grandma's face?"

Ruth Ann thought it was a riot.

It was one of the best years in our 59-year journey.

Tomorrow is 2005.

Brad Bungum

Carlene Vavricek Enjoy reading your posts Pete. You and Ruth Ann made a lot of beautiful memories throughout your marriage! ♡ Thanks for sharing with all your FB friends and family.

PeteandRuth Ann Bungum

Thursday, June 4, 2020. Pete and Ruth Ann's journey through 59 years.

The year is 2005.

We had a quiet year in 2005—no big trips.

In May we did something we had been thinking about for a long time. We bought our burial plots. We decided we would be buried in Anamosa. We couldn't think of any reasons to be buried in Minnesota. Anamosa had been our home for 41 years and was the only home Brad and Carron had ever known. Our lots cost $200 each. We chose our lots next to two of my teaching colleagues. And we would be buried only 100 steps from the famous artist Grant Wood. He lived in Anamosa until age 12. His most famous painting is *American Gothic*. You know, I'm talking about the pitchfork guy. One of the main reasons we did it is Carron and Brad wouldn't have to do it when we pass.

In October Brad and Alex and Mads came from Denmark. One of the things I did was take them to the Cedar Rapids Museum of Art to see the Grant Wood exhibit. We were able to see the originals of eight of his paintings, including *American Gothic*. It was on loan from the Chicago Museum of Art.

It had a guard on duty every minute of the day. I asked the guard if he knew the value of it. He said no one will tell him. *American Gothic* is the second most recognized painting in the world and to think Grant Wood got his start in Anamosa, Iowa. *Mona Lisa* is number one.

The day was exciting for me. Having some artistic talent myself, I really studied his paintings. I particularly looked at the eyes, nose, mouth, wrinkles as facial expressions. *Absolutely fantastic* are the words I would use to describe his talent.

We had had a wonderful first five years of our retirement. Then it started falling apart.

In July Ruth Ann started having achy leg muscles so bad she was unable to sleep. She was diagnosed with Restless Leg Syndrome—the

Doctor prescribed Requip. It appeared to be helping. In early August she went for a refill—the pharmacist screwed up, big time. They mistakenly gave her Resperdal which is prescribed for Alzheimer's, bi-polar and psychotic problems. The pill bottle was labeled Requip, but it was really Resperdal. She took the pills for ten days—and felt worse every day. Ruth Ann discovered the mistake herself.

She called the pharmacist and described the color and shape of the pills. He told her a mistake had been made. He told her to come right away. He apologized and told her to take half a pill the next day and then quit. He said it hadn't happened before and he was taking precautions to see it didn't happen again. He gave us our money back, $77.02. She got the correct pills this time. In September she switched from Requip to a drug called Carbadopa. It was much more effective and by October she felt fairly normal.

This was just the beginning of four more years of medical hell.

The first week in November Ruth Ann developed stomach cramps and severe diarrhea. It was back to the doctor. The first diagnosis was diverticulitis. In a couple of weeks, she had a CT scan and the new diagnosis was colitis. She was put on antibiotics, showed no improvement so she was admitted to the Anamosa Hospital on November 21.

Her colitis was so bad while in the hospital that her bowel movements were pure blood. She spent a week there with IVs and a liquid diet. The doctors put her on a high dose of prednisone. It helped bring her colon and diarrhea under control. She was released on November 28. In the next weeks she had a colonoscopy, was weaned off prednisone, put on nine pills of Asacol per day rather than Prednisone. She lost 25 pounds and a lot of muscle strength. She started physical therapy to rebuild her strength. By April her health was much improved. She was put on antidepressants—they helped her whole outlook on life. Most people would get depressed if they hadn't felt well for eight months.

In August we took a trip to Minnesota for a family wedding. Ruth Ann didn't feel well but she said she'd go for my sake. After the wedding we went to Mantorville to see my old home—I had lived there from age two to eight. The years were 1942–1949. My old two-story home had been torn down and replaced with a ranch style. Everything seemed so much smaller than it looked when I was eight years old. That included the yard, hill, driveway, barn, creek, river, pasture—everything. I drove around the school I went to in grades 1–3. Mantorville has really grown. There are housing developments all around.

Then we went to a Bungum family reunion in Oslo. It was a fun day. I always get a kick out of going to a Minnesota reunion and listen to people talk. When you are away for years it is really noticeable. The Norwegian accent is so obvious. When we left that day, I told Ruth Ann that many of my relatives could have had roles in the movie *Fargo*.

The first week in December the Hawkeyes played in the Outback Bowl. We lost to Florida Gators—we lost 31–24.

Tomorrow will be 2006. Our struggle with health problems continues.

Erland Christensen, Rhenee Grabau and 8 others

Comments

Rhenee Grabau My sisters and I all have RLS. Miserable. But sero-quel, oh my god. 😳 😔

Pat McQuaid Schoon I remember when Ruth Ann received the "wrong" pills!!! What a bummer!!!!

PeteandRuth Ann Bungum

Friday, June 5, 2020. Pete and Ruth Ann's journey through 59 years.

The year is 2006.

By February 2006, I really thought Ruth Ann's medical problems were over. And I didn't have anything to worry about because I didn't ever get sick. How wrong I was. Ruth Ann and Pete became the 21st century version of the Job in the Old Testament.

In 2005 Ruth Ann had been through Restless Leg Syndrome and colitis. By March 2006, she was pretty decent. She was gaining her weight back—she no longer looked like an Auschwitz survivor. Her weight had gone from 104 pounds to 120. There were two positives in her weight loss—she got a bunch of new clothes and her blood pressure went to normal. Her colon had settled down and things went back to normal in that domain. But it was only a temporary respite.

In April Ruth Ann came down with back pain plus pain in her butt, neck and head. The doctor diagnosed it as an arthritic spine—she was put on pain pills. In June she was admitted to Saint Luke's Hospital. She ended up in bed, flat on her back for five days. After an MRI, a CT scan, X-rays and blood tests they determined she had an arthritic spine, an upper vertebra touching a nerve, possibly a cracked tailbone at some time in her life, and low potassium. They treated her with pain pills and shots to the neck. She came home on June 11th and felt the best she had in a year.

My turn started on April 14. I awakened with a bad cough and extreme shortness of breath. I could not walk 100 steps. After visits to Dr. Vernon for X-rays he sent me to Saint Luke's to see a pulmonologist. After a couple different doctors, I ended up seeing Dr. Paynter. My left lung was going to hell. He drained a quart of bloody fluid from around my left lung. He did it by inserting a needle through the left side of my back. It did not tickle when he inserted the needle even though he had given me a shot of Novocain to numb the insertion of the big needle.

Dr. Paynter gave me some pills for my cough—they looked like little nuggets of gold. They really worked—in three days I quit coughing. Then he put me on prednisone for 20 days. They worked and I felt better. But I had to see Dr. Paynter again in June. A CT scan was given to me—it showed my left lung was cleared up, but my right lung was clouded over. He wanted me to take no more pills and see him the end of July. He was hoping the cloudiness would disappear by itself.

On September 3, at 2:00 am, I awakened with pain in my right lung. I could not get comfortable and didn't sleep the rest of the night. The pain increased during the day to the point where I could hardly breathe. I called Dr. Paynter's office—they recommended I go to the ER at St. Luke's. I had a chest X-ray. The doctors told me it appeared to show that fluid had solidified around my right lung. They put me on a pain reliever and sent me home. They worked. Dr. Paynter moved my next appointment from October 24 to October 4th.

I had a CT scan. Dr. Paynter said he was sending me to Dr. Levett, a surgeon, to let him make a decision as to whether to do surgery or not. I saw him again on November 6 after he had studied all my X-rays and CT scans.

He came right to the point. His words were "I need to do surgery to see what is wrapped around your right lung. Also, I want a biopsy of the masses in that lung to see if it is cancer—that will change my strategy when operating. This operation will be major surgery."

Two days later his nurse called and told me I would have surgery on November 16. I would have a busy eight days with preparation appointments for surgery.

On November 10 I would go to St. Luke's for a biopsy on my right lung.

On November 13 I would go to St. Luke's for lab work and an electrocardiogram.

On November 14 I would go to Dr. Vernon for a physical.

On the 15th I was very nervous about tomorrow. I asked Ruth Ann if she would go to a movie with me to make the time go faster.

We went to Talladega Nights. It wouldn't win any academy awards, but it was funny.

I went to bed at 9:30 and slept until 3:30. I was awake from then on. I got up at 6:00 and took a shower with the antiseptic soap they had given me.

Ruth Ann and I left for St. Luke's at 8:05 am. As I drove, I was thinking about the next 12–15 hours of my life and my life in the coming weeks and months.

The surgery was called a decortication of my right lung. I asked my nurse what that word meant. She said a decortication means to scrape or peel something off an organ, usually a lung. We reported to the reception desk at 8:50. They told us to wait in the lobby. The nurse came in 9:15 and called for Peter. My thoughts were "Okay Pete, this is it so be strong and have faith everything is going to be alright." By 9:20 I was in my hospital gown. My day for surgery had commenced.

Nurses were putting IVs on my arm. Jim, the pre-surgery barber shaved my chest, stomach and arm pits. The anesthesiologist came and started prepping me.

That morning Brad flew in from San Francisco. Carron picked him up at the airport. I was so happy they were there.

The nurse came in and said, "We can go early because everything is ready." About 10:15 I said my goodbyes. The last thing I remember is getting hugs from Ruth Ann, Carron and Brad. For me it was "lights out" for the next 9–10 hours. For the three of them it was to the lobby until 6 pm to wait and pass the hours by talking, reading, laptop, eating and napping.

I'll finish this tomorrow.

Comments

Pat McQuaid Schoon Pete, I'm really glad that I already know that your family got the good news they were hoping for.

PeteandRuth Ann Bungum

Saturday, June 6, 2020. Pete and Ruth Ann's journey through 59 years.

The years are 2006 to 2008.

In this post I'm going to do the rest of our three years of medical hell with only a few details.

After my lung surgery I left the hospital on November 21, 2006, six days after my surgery. Getting back to normal was painful. I had pain daily for the next three months. I had an 11-inch incision under my right arm. See the photos. In three months, I was close to being pain free.

Our next ordeal with medical problems was in March of 2007. Ruth Ann slipped on a melted ice cube in our kitchen. She breaks her femur and shatters the hip ball. She has surgery on March 12, 2007. Doctors insert a titanium femur and hip ball.

In April of 2007 my PSA starts to go up rapidly and a biopsy comes back showing I have prostate cancer. I have my cancerous prostate removed on May 15. I found out what a catheter was all about—I had one in for 15 days. I rapidly healed—only took pain pills for two days.

In September 2008, medical hell returns. Ruth Ann awakened me at 4 am to tell me she had horrible pain from hip bone to hip bone. We go to the ER—the diagnosis is appendicitis. She goes by ambulance to St. Luke's and has surgery at 4 pm. Dr Lawrence tells me he had perforated the appendix, but it shouldn't be a problem because he cleaned all the poison up.

By October Ruth Ann's pain from the appendectomy had gotten worse.

On October 25th she had a CT scan again. She had a serious infection in her kidney and uterus. We switched doctors at this point and ended up with an OB-GYN doctor named Dr. Joy Olson. She determines Ruth Ann has MRSA staff-infection. She does surgery the next day—she performs a complete hysterectomy. She removes every female organ that was possible to take. She had a lot of cleaning to do but was confident and optimistic this would solve Ruth Ann's problem. The next day I went to see Ruth Ann—she shows me the incision—it was over six inches long and ran from her belly button to her pubic bone.

The good news is that Dr. Olson's optimism was correct—it solved her problem. We have not had any more surgeries. I'm forever grateful to Dr. Olson for what she did for us.

This ends my story about our three years of medical hell. I will admit I read the Old Testament book of Job. The good news about Job is that he was finally healed and so were Pete and Ruth Ann. So, in three years we had five surgeries—she had 3 to my 2.

I really wondered what we had done to deserve this. There is no answer, but I admit I did wonder. The good news is we never had them at the same time. So we were there for each other when the other needed our support. Right now, I'm sitting here looking at the urn and thinking about all the things we went through together in 59 years and how we supported each other in times of need.

I've got tears right now. I miss her so much.

The photos show my 11-inch incision for my lung surgery—and Ruth Ann after her hysterectomy.

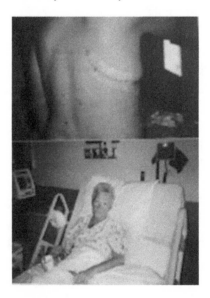

You, Erland Christensen, Rhenee Grabau and 20 others

Comments

Bonnie Walderbach Thinking of you ♡

> **PeteandRuth Ann Bungum** Thanks Bonnie

Sharon Bungum Shupe As you must have read in Job, God allows hard times but not because I deserve or have done anything wrong. I must remember God created everything. God created the earth (I belief) with actions and reaction. Positive thought, belief in the creator will allow me to get through this life.

> **PeteandRuth Ann Bungum** Thanks Sharon

Jill Darrow I am glad you two had so many wonderful years together. Your memories are priceless, and a reminder of the love you shared.

> **PeteandRuth Ann Bungum** Thanks Jill

Jena Costello GOD BLESS YOU

> **PeteandRuth Ann Bungum** Jena Costello thanks Jena—I appreciate it.

Elsie Narveson That was quite an ordeal. It was a blessing that you weren't on one of your trips!

> **PeteandRuth Ann Bungum** Elsie Narveson you are so right. Thanks for your comment

Carlene Vavricek Thinking of you Pete. May all the beautiful memories sustain you until you one day meet again. Hugs to you my friend.

> **PeteandRuth Ann Bungum** Thanks Carlene

Shelley Bungum DeBernardi Thinking of you Pete. Take care ♡

Kimberly Bungum I love these stories

John Spilde Thank you for sharing this information! I often wish work opportunities in western Iowa could have been closer to Decorah, my birthplace and Anamosa, where I spent most of my growing up years. (From my second semester of kindergarten through high school/college summers.) Glad God brought you two together! Trivia to tell you Mr. Bungum, but my Dad's name was spelled "Orval." Most people spelled it "Orville." Those "damn" history teachers taught everyone in the world about Orville and Wilber Wright. LOL! (That was a loving "Damn."). By the way my mom's name was "Bernadean" and most people spelled it "Bernadine." Soooo, I could get in on the FUN, my parents spelled my middle name "Samual." Most people spell that name as "SamuEl." God love ya! I always enjoy your news, but not the suffering parts! Sincerely, John

Bret Lewison Well I suppose God knew you & Ruth Ann were going to go through these health problems and he figured, we might as well bunch em together and get em over with in 2006–2008 since the Hawks didn't play very well in those years (at least '06 & '07 so you wouldn't miss any great bowl game destinations).

He had you through all that mess & ready to enjoy that wonderful 2009 season.

I've been thinking, it's a good thing you turned your life around and became a Hawk fan. You could still be a Gopher fan. Talk about Job. You'd have had a lot more years good could have spread those health issues out over. Go Hawks. Hang in there #1 Hawk.

Phil Bungum ;~]

Carson Ode I was aware you dealt with some tough medical issues. I was not aware of the extent and timing. Those were definitely trying times. We miss Ruth but are glad you are still with us.

PeteandRuth Ann Bungum Carson Ode thanks Carson—I appreciate it

Sharon Wykle Twedt Not the best time in your lives, but you dealt with it. Thanks for sharing...

PeteandRuth Ann Bungum

In Sunday, June 7, 2020. Pete and Ruth Ann's journey through 59 years.

The year is 2009.

By late December Ruth Ann was feeling well enough to have some fun. So, we signed up to go see the Hawkeyes play in the Outback Bowl in Tampa Bay on January 1, 2009. We beat South Carolina 31–10. It was a fun time and so relaxing for both of us. Ruth Ann held up super and had no pain from her hysterectomy.

By February she was still feeling wonderful, so we said let's make up for the last three years and do some more traveling. We called our travel agent and told her we wanted to go to Cancun, Mexico, for a week or two—we had never been there. She lined up a 10-day tour. It was great. The highlight was visiting the Maya structures in Chichen Itza. They were built around the 800s. My thoughts were "How could they build something like those without modern engineering?"

We met a lot of tourists—there were a lot from Canada. One story I remember is while eating at an outdoor restaurant I saw a five-year-old girl from Montreal. She had beautiful red hair, so I went over to her table and told her she had beautiful red hair. I said I love red hair because I have red hair. So I took off my hat and said, "See, look at my red hair."

She looked at my hair and said, "But your hair is all white." I laughed my head off. Leave it to kids to tell the truth.

The grandkids reached some milestones in 2009. Granddaughter Alexandra finished her foreign exchange school year in Anamosa. She loved her year in an American school. The things she learned were that our schools are a lot easier academically but more fun with all the extra-curricular activities. In Denmark there are no extra-curricular activities—it is strictly academic and much more homework. She flew back to Denmark in June. She would be in Gymnasium for three years and then to university to study to be a doctor. She made a lot of friends.

Granddaughter Ellyn became a senior at Prairie High School in Cedar Rapids.

Grandson Wesley graduated from Prairie and enlisted in the Air Force. He left for San Antonio on September 14. After basic training he would go to Keesler Air Force in Biloxi, Mississippi, to become an Air Traffic Controller.

We went there for his graduation in November. He played drums in the band. Our hotel was two blocks from the Alamo. We went through it. There is only a small part of the original structure left. The most fun times we had were at a grill/bar called Dick's on the river walk. The employees used butcher paper to make hats for us. The fun part was what they wrote on them. On mine they wrote, "I pop Viagra like Skittles." And another one was "All I can get up is my blood pressure."

On Ruth Ann's they wrote, "Miss America 1910." Another lady's said, "I was a waitress at the Last Supper." Her husband's said, "I fought in the Great War—Civil War." They had many more—it was a fun place.

One other memory: Across the street from our hotel was a city park occupied by homeless people. I got up early and took walks, so I got a first-hand look at these people. It was mainly white men and one woman. They all had their garbage bags filled with their earthly possessions. I watched them and all they did was walk around or through the block time after time and then take a break. They slept on park benches. It must have been pretty chilly when the temperature dropped into 30s and 40s.

Across the street was a Methodist Church. They provided a breakfast and a supper for these homeless people. I guess that is what Jesus Christ would do. I wanted to talk with a couple of them to find out how they got into this situation. But I didn't. I was grateful that I wasn't one of them.

We took no more trips in 2009.

Tomorrow will be 2010.

Yrsa Thom Chris, Dean Rickels and 4 others

Comments

Jill Darrow I'm so glad we got to meet Alexandra during her time in the states. She is a beautiful girl and will be a wonderful doctor.

> **PeteandRuth Ann Bungum** I agree—by the way she got her MD degree last January

Pat McQuaid Schoon Loved the red/white hair story. (I'm sure that the little girl was just wanting to "brag" about knowing her colors. Ha!)

PeteandRuth Ann Bungum

Monday, June 8, 2020.

The year was 2010. We celebrated 50 years of marriage.

2010 was a special year for Pete and Ruth Ann. It was a year of celebrating.

Our first celebration was to spend the first week of January in Miami. It was a family get-together with Brad and Lene coming from Denmark and Carron and Dan joining us from Springville, Iowa. We watched the Hawkeyes defeat Georgia Tech in the Orange Bowl.

We won the game and it was the first time Brad got to see the Hawkeyes win a Bowl game. When the game was over Brad gave me a hug that nearly broke my ribs. After seeing us get beat in the 1986 Rose Bowl and the 2003 Orange Bowl he was one happy Hawkeye fan. Back at the hotel we all celebrated with some adult beverages— then he bought me a Hawkeye victory cap and a souvenir football. I still have both of them and wear the cap all the time.

We got to bed at 2 am. We all went to bed with smiles on our faces.

With both of our kids and spouses with us it was a great way to start celebrating our 50th anniversary.

Our second celebration was in March when Ruth Ann and I spent ten days at the Punta Cana Resort in the Dominican Republic. It was a wonderful way for us to relax and reflect on our 50 years together. It was one of those all-inclusive vacations. That means we didn't have to pay for anything when we ate or sat at the bar. We really like the Dominican Republic—the people are so kind and helpful. They are just nice people.

Our third celebration was on our anniversary date of June 18 when Carron arranged for us to enjoy a meal at the Rainbow Supper Club in Anamosa. Carron worked there and upon our arrival she escorted us to table that was decorated with flowers, balloons and cards. The big surprise came when someone patted Ruth Ann on her shoulder and said, "May I have this empty seat at your table?" She turned around and it was Brad. He had flown in from Denmark to surprise us. What a SURPRISE. Carron and Brad planned the whole affair and it worked to perfection. The other diners watched everything unfold and gave us a big ovation. One guy volunteered to take a photo of the four of us with our camera. I have included that photo plus another. It was a memorable night. Thank You Carron and Brad.

Another gesture to help us celebrate was a card shower orchestrated by Carron when she put a notice in the local paper announcing our 50th anniversary. We got 87 cards. For about two weeks it was fun to get the mail every day.

Some other events happening in 2010 included Ruth Ann and I turning the big 7-0. She did it on April 4 and I did it on November 20. I guess if you have been married for 50 years you would probably be 70 years old.

The rest of 2010 was pretty mild. No surgeries and no trips. Tomorrow will be 2011.

Ruth Ann and Pete trying to give each other a glass of wine

You, Inge Bungum, Yrsa Thom Chris and 12 others

Comments

Inge Bungum Wonderful pictures!

Pat McQuaid Schoon Great stories and great memories!!!!

Shelley Bungum DeBernardi Love the pics

Sharon Wykle Twedt Great pictures...

PeteandRuth Ann Bungum

Tuesday, June 9, 2020. Pete and Ruth Ann's journey through 59 years.

The year is 2011.

I'm going to start today with something that happened to me on my 68th birthday on November 20, 2008. We had just been through five surgeries in three years.

That day I was grateful we had survived those five surgeries. That day I was grateful we had both achieved 68 years of age. I was also grateful that we were living longer than many deceased in the obituary pages. I was grateful we were fortunate enough to have lived our lives in 20th and 21st century America. I was grateful for the wonderful medical care we had received that saved both our lives. If we had lived a hundred years ago we both would've been dead. I told myself that we really had a lot to be grateful for.

So I made a decision that day to express my gratitude in a book. My goal was to express my gratitude every day for/to someone or something that enhanced my/our journey through life.

I had read an article in AARP Magazine by a professor at the University of California-Davis. His name was Dr. Robert Emmons. He had researched on how keeping a gratitude journal could lead to a happier life. His research revealed that people who did this were more optimistic, their self-esteem was better, exercised more, slept better, felt more refreshed and were better able to cope with daily problems, especially stress. With all the plusses to be gained I said, "I'm going to do it." I ended up with a 147-page book.

Before I started i made a list of what I would be grateful to or for. Here is my list:

— Government/laws/court decisions
— Organizations/institutions
— Inventions/discoveries/ideas
— Memories/thoughts/words
— Events

— People
— Other things

I started on January 1st, 2009. My first expression of gratitude was my wife, Ruth Ann. For every expression I wrote a paragraph explaining why. My last expression on December 31st was "I'm grateful I completed this Gratitude Journal." Then I went on to list seven things on how it helped me become a better person.

So I did it. It was the most life changing thing I ever did. It was such a good experience that I wrote a sequel in 2014. I used quite a bit of the 2009 book, but I concentrated more on the people who had enhanced my/our life in some way.

It has definitely changed my life. Every day when I awaken and when I take my walk, I express gratitude for many things. And I also keep a copy in the bathroom to see what I wrote on that day in 2009 and 2014.

I encourage others to try expressing gratitude—it'll make you feel better.

Now to 2011 and our journey through 59 years.

It was a great year in that we made it through the year with no major health problems. We were able to get "Out of Dodge" on several occasions.

In March we spent four days in Laughlin, Nevada. My brother Chuck and wife Marlys drove up from their winter home in Arizona and spent several days with us. They took us to Oatman, Nevada, an old silver mining town, where the donkeys still roam the streets. We gambled some and lost but didn't lose the house. Laughlin has about ten casinos, so it is not a Las Vegas. We enjoyed our visit.

In July we spent ten days in Boston. Brad and Lene did a house swap with one of his Boston colleagues. These colleagues were living for ten days in Brad and Lene's house in Denmark. Two of the fun things we did were take a "WW2 Duck boat" tour of downtown Boston.

The second thing was a guided tour of Fenway Park, home of the Red Sox. While taking the tour our guide asked if there were any Yankee fans in the group. Well, one older guy raised his hand. The guide then said, "Since we have a Yankee fan in the group, for the rest of the tour I will talk slowly and use small words." Do you think there is any truth to the rumor that the Red Sox and Yankees do not like each other?"

In 2010 Brad had surprised us for our 50th anniversary. So this year we reciprocated by surprising him on his 50th birthday. With the help of Lene we pulled it off. We flew to Billund airport and Lene picked us up on November 13, and we drove to their house.

She had us walk around to the back of the house. Brad was sitting in front of the sliding glass door. When he looked up, we were standing there—the look on his face was one of shock.

On the 19th Lene has an open-house for Brad—over 60 of his friends, colleagues and neighbors came to help him celebrate.

The Danes know how to have fun—the first guests came at 1:30 pm on the 19th and the last ones left at 3:45 am on the 20th. In true Danish style we had food about every two/three hours—and there was a little wine and beer in between to pass the time until we ate again. What a fun day and we were so glad we went to help Brad celebrate his 50 years.

We turned 71 this year. But we were grateful for no health issues.

You, Erland Christensen, Rhenee Grabau and 9 others

PeteandRuth Ann Bungum

Wednesday, June 10, 2020. Pete and Ruth Ann's journey through 59 years.

The year is 2012.

First and most important we were blessed with another year of good health. In March we flew with brother John and sister-in-law Lorna to San Francisco. We stayed in John and Lorna's time-share near Union Square and a short distance from Chinatown. The reason for the visit was greatnephew (our Godchild) Matthew Bungum's wedding near Modesto. His mother is Kim, daughter of my brother Paul and sister-in-law Nellie.

The beautiful wedding was the #1 highlight while #2 was a bus tour of San Francisco. The bus guide was knowledgeable and humorous. His most humorous remark was when he drove by Lombard Street and said, "This is the most crooked street in the world, but some people disagree. They say the most crooked street in the world is Wall Street."

We also drove by O. J. Simpson's high school. There used to be a sign which said this was Simpson's high school. But it no longer exists—they aren't very proud of it anymore. We also drove over the Golden Gate Bridge and went through Chinatown. It was a fun tour.

Another highlight was a 19-day trip to Denmark in late June and early July. The occasion was granddaughter Alexandra's graduation from gymnasium (high school). The ceremony for the 300 students was much the same as here except the grads do not wear gowns—they wore anything from shorts to jeans. They also have special caps instead of mortarboards.

The biggest difference was how they celebrate after the ceremony. When the ceremony was over the 300 grads marched to the parking lot, and in groups of 30, climbed onto the back of 10 trucks, covered with canvas in case of rain. For the next 13–14 hours the driver gets directions from each student on how to get to his/her house. At each house the parents are prepared to give all 30 kids food and drink. They spend about 20 minutes at each house and then onto the next one. Alexandra was #17 and they arrived at 7:30. They still had 13 stops to go. A tired Alex told us the next day they arrived at the 30th home at 1:30 am—about 14 hours after the ceremony was over.

Another difference was when she had finished her final exam several days prior to graduation. Ruth Ann and I were there to witness it. She was in a room with two teachers who told her she had passed her exam. Then they gave her the cap that all successful grads get. She came out of the room with her cap on and a huge smile.

Waiting for her in the hallway were not only us but Mom Inge, Dad Brad, Aunt Bente and her other grandma, Ellinor. We all gave her a hug and a rose. Then we all went to the commons and out came the champagne—we all had a glass of champagne and a cookie. Even the Principal stopped for a glass. For some reason I don't think that would go over in the USA.

The third highlight was my 50th class reunion at Luther College in Decorah, Iowa, on October 5, 6, and 7. What made this reunion so great was getting together with my three best friends and roommates from Luther in 1958 to 1962. The three couples were: Paul and Sharon Twedt from Huntington Beach, CA., Terry and Suzanne Sorom from Wenatchee, WA., and Carson and Connie Ode from Des Moines, IA. Friday night was the most special as Terry received a Distinguished Service Award from Luther along with eight other distinguished alumni. Terry was an ophthalmologist and practiced in Wenatchee his whole career.

Paul was a teacher and principal in Huntington Beach. Carson was an artist and graphic designer in Des Moines.

We stayed at a BnB in Lanesboro, MN—which was the hometown of Terry and Carson. Sunday morning, we had breakfast in Lanesboro and then it was time for hugs and goodbyes. I can tell you one thing—we had a ton of laughs in those three days. The photo is of the four of us along with the wives. From left to right for us guys is Carson, Terry, Pete, Paul.

The four wives left to right are

— Sharon goes with Paul

— Suzanne goes with Terry
— Connie goes with Carson
— Ruth Ann goes with guess who?

The other photo shows her graduation cap and the six of us who drank champagne with her. From left to right are grandparents Pete and Ruth Ann, Dad Brad, Alexandra, Mom Inge, grandma Ellinor and Aunt Bente.

The sad news is brother Chuck died from a stroke in July. He collapsed in a casino while playing a slot machine. He was 75. He was four years older than me. He was #2 to die in our litter of nine—sister Betty was #1 in 2008. At the funeral in Alexandria, MN, several of my siblings and I were talking about who would be next. After all we were getting up there. There were 7 of us left with 4 in their 80s, 1 in the 70s and 2 in the 60s. So, in the next 5–10 years we would be attending more funerals of our siblings.

Sad but true.

Pete's college friends and our wives at 50th college graduation

Bob Hines and Kristine Pittman Kilburg

Comments

Sharon Wykle Twedt We did have a lot of fun at your 50th college reunion. Cherish those times we were together…

PeteandRuth Ann Bungum Thanks Sharon—Ruth Ann and I were blessed to have you and Paul as such good friends through all of our 59 years. God Bless.

PeteandRuth Ann Bungum

Thursday, June 11, 2020. Pete and Ruth Ann's journey through 59 years.

The year is 2013. It was a good year in the fact we had no major health problems. But it was a sad year because my brother Paul, the oldest kid in our litter of nine, passed away on January 15 in Modesto, California, due to numerous health issues, including lupus. He was 86. We had a memorial service in August for Paul at West Saint Olaf Lutheran Church in Hayfield, Minnesota. His daughter, Kim, and widow, Nellie, and grandson, Javon, brought his ashes back to be buried there. It is the church where he was baptized and confirmed. Paul was a Lutheran minister.

Sister Jan's 80th birthday was celebrated in Bloomington, Minnesota. She gave a great talk on how life had changed since her birth in 1933. She was born in the farmhouse—and after being potty trained she had to use the outdoor potty and get used to using the Sears catalog for toilet paper. And she went to country school which also had outdoor toilets. I gave a talk about my memories of her when growing up. Jan sure didn't look to be 80—more like 60.

Ruth Ann and I had our 55th class reunion in Chatfield, Minnesota. We stayed with our high school friends, Jerry and Elsie Narveson. Jerry and I talked baseball and it got a little deep when we talked about our great baseball exploits in 1957–1958 when we won the district both years and almost went to the state tournament. Put your boots on now—I don't think Chatfield has ever had a better pitcher-catcher combination than Jerry Narveson and Pete Bungum.

One morning I got up early and took a walk to my old home from 1952 to 1958. My parents made it into a private nursing home. It is still green. Some additions have been made since my mother sold it in 1963. It is a fabulous structure built by a doctor in 1895. I'm putting a photo in so you can see what I mean.

The absolute greatest highlight was from September 1 through September 17. Son Brad, my brother John and I took off on a "Bucket List" dream of going on a Major League Baseball trip. We left on the morning of September 1 and visited 10 major league stadiums. Here is the order: Milwaukee Brewers, Chicago Cubs, Cincinnati Reds, Cleveland Indians, NY Yankees, Philadelphia Phillies, NY Mets, Baltimore Orioles, Pittsburgh Pirates and Kansas City Royals. We also went to Arrowhead Stadium on the 15th to see the Chiefs beat the Dallas Cowboys. A real bonus was grandson Wesley got to join us from his Air Force base in New Jersey. He came for the Yankees, Phillies and Mets. As a 22-year-old I think he really enjoyed being around us old duffers—we were 72, 70 and 52.

From Pittsburgh we drove to Anamosa on the 13th, stayed overnight and took off for Kansas City. For three nights we stayed with Rusty and Angie Russel, he was an UP WITH PEOPLE friend of Brad. They were the perfect hosts with wonderful food, great hospitality, including lots of laughs. We visited Harry Truman's Library. It was so interesting and educational. We even saw the letter Harry had written to a reporter who had written a negative article about his daughter's singing ability. It was handwritten. Harry's wife told him not to send it, but he did it anyway. I was only eight when he did it, but I do remember.

I've been asked what my favorite stadium was and my answer is always the same—all of them.

We stayed at 35th street In Manhattan. It was three blocks from Times Square. I took a walk every morning before John and Brad woke up. One morning I stopped at Macy's and looked around and saw neckties for $85 each. I didn't buy. I also tried some midwestern friendliness by saying "Good morning" to everybody I met. Not one person responded. They wouldn't even look at me—they just stared straight ahead and kept walking. They did give me some strange looks as if to say, "Are you nuts or something?"

I tried the same thing in Pittsburgh and 9 of 10 responded with "Good morning." What does that say about the people of Manhattan?

One day all three of us walked to the NBC Today Show. Very interesting. During the commercial two women came out and refreshed the lipstick and make-up on the two women. Al Roker was the friendliest—he would visit with people. Brad got on TV.

We weren't the only ones to take a trip and have some fun. Ruth Ann and sisters-in-law Marlys and Lorna took a casino trip. They visited five casinos in six days. They went to Waterloo, Dubuque and the Quad Cities. We were hoping they would make enough money to pay for our trip. But that was not the result. I have a feeling that the casinos came out ahead. The three gals didn't talk. They said they had fun.

One other event I want to mention is a former student came home to be honored at the high school. The new weight room was named after him. It was now called the Marshal Yanda Weight Room. Marshal was a former Hawkeye player and had become an All Pro in the NFL. He was the starting right guard for the Baltimore Ravens. I talked to Marshal and he shared some memories of my seventh-grade geography class in the 1990s. He wasn't very interested in studying while in seventh grade. Coach Kirk Ferentz was the guest speaker. Then Marshall talked and gave a great talk.

When I had Marshal in seventh grade, I thought he would be a farmer like his Dad. He didn't get serious about his studies until he was in junior college at Mason City. Then he realized he could probably play for the Hawkeyes if he got better grades. He did get serious—his grades had improved enough to be able to get into the University of Iowa. He played two years for the Hawkeyes and then was drafted by the Ravens in the third round of the 2007 draft.

I guess it pays to get serious—he is now a millionaire.

Ruth Ann and I were grateful we had no serious health issues in 2013.

Tomorrow will be 2014.

You, Erland Christensen, Yrsa Thom Chris and 2 others

Comments

Brad Bungum Dad PeteandRuth Ann Bungum, isn't the old Chatfield home also on the National Registry of Historic Buildings? I'm pretty sure there is a sign out front still, acknowledging that?

PeteandRuth Ann Bungum

Friday, June 12, 2020. Pete and Ruth Ann's journey through 59 years.

The year is 2014.

Compared to previous years, 2014 was a pretty mild year.

The only travel was in January when we flew to Tampa Bay to see the Hawkeyes get beat by LSU in the Outback Bowl. The score was 14–21.

Despite rumors to the contrary Ruth Ann did not join the LPGA Senior Golf Circuit. Just kidding—she gave up the game in April 2004. She hates the game. I spent much of my time writing Gratitude Journal #2.

In October a little orange and white kitty met me on our deck and wrapped himself around my leg. I brought him in the house and showed Ruth Ann. She said, "Pete, you know how to get to me. I love cats." So we adopted.

We hadn't had a pet since 1981. We took him to the vet for shots and had him declawed and neutered. We named him Jordan because we live on Jordan Drive. We think some farmer dropped him and his sister off in the mobile home court. They must have figured somebody would adopt—they were right because someone up the street adopted his sister.

As a kitty he was a terrorist. He loves to destroy stuff—like chewing through the wires on the Christmas tree lights. The good news is he has given us a lot of laughs, loves to sleep with us and loves to lick Ruth Ann's hair when she is sleeping. As I write this in 2020, I will admit he has gotten obese. He needs to go on a diet. Now that Ruth Ann is gone, he has become my best friend.

The highlight in 2014 for several Anamosa Norwegians was a lutefisk supper at Bob and Darla Algoe's home on December 15. Attending were Vic and Mary Hamre, Jay and Arlie Willems, Paul and Verna Lewison, the Bungum's and the hosts, the Algoe's.

The rules are you or your spouse must have some Norwegian blood. Then everyone must bring one or more Norwegian foods they ate in their homes at Christmas time. Ruth Ann always got the job of baking the lutefisk because she was the only one who knew how to do it right. Not all Norskies had the exact same foods at Christmas so it was fun to eat some different foods. And not all liked lutefisk. The big lutefisk eaters were Bob Algoe, Mary Hamre, Arlie Willems, Ruth Ann and me. Most of the rest would eat a little or none at all. A person has to acquire a taste for lutefisk—it is definitely different. We always have a good time—it is a fun way to spend an evening.

Yesterday I mentioned I had lived in a green mansion in Chatfield, Minnesota. It was my home from seventh grade to graduation. Brad called me yesterday and told me it was now on the National Registry of Historic Homes. I Googled it and found it. It is now a "bed and breakfast" and is really something to see and even better would be to spend a night there. You could sleep in one of the bedrooms I slept in. You can find it by Googling "Oakenwald Terrace.com" or "Oakenwald Terrace Bed and Breakfast."

The front looks the same but there have been many additions to the north side and back. The inside is completely different.

Tomorrow is 2015.

Green house. Pete's home from 1952-1958

Bret Lewison, Erland Christensen and 9 others

Comments

Kimberly Bungum That's so cool!! I would love to stay there!!

Linda Blattie Smaby Kimberly Bungum It was cool and I remember staying upstairs with Laddie, someone's dog. Grandmas?

Kimberly Bungum Linda Blattie Smaby idk! I remember the Rochester house but not this one. Maybe have driven by here with dad at some point. That's all I Remember

Linda Blattie Smaby Kimberly Bungum Probably before you were born! It was in Chatfield.

Mark Blattie Linda Blattie Smaby grandma had that mean little Dachshund. Don't remember the name.

Linda Blattie Smaby Mark Blattie I think it was Laddie!

Brad Bungum Mark Blattie and Linda Blattie Smaby, you're a bit before my time… :-). I don't remember ever being in the house, or the dog, Laddie. Don't remember Gramma ever having a dog, actually. I've seen the Chatfield house many times, and Dad took us on a tour there once so I've been inside (he knocked on the door and explained who he was—we got a tour!). But I'm with Kim… Rochester is my only memory.

Linda Blattie Smaby I was pretty young too but do remember how pretty it was. I can't believe Grandma had a dog. Didn't think she liked them 😳. Laddie was a chewer!

PeteandRuth Ann Bungum

Saturday, June 13, 2020. Pete and Ruth Ann's journey through 59 years.

The years are 2015, 2016, 2017

2015 was a good year—no major health problems. The best thing all year was the Hawkeyes were undefeated with a 12–0 record. We lost the Big Ten championship game to Michigan State. We were invited to the Rose Bowl and got beat by Stanford. We didn't go but watched in horror on TV as Stanford took us to the cleaners.

So, I'm going to do 2016 today also. There is a lot to say about Ruth Ann's health.

On November 26 Ruth Ann and I went to Minnesota to visit relatives. Our first stop was at brother John and Lorna's in St. Peter. That's as far as we got. That night Ruth Ann slipped and fell in the bathroom and fractured two small bones in the pelvic area plus her tailbone. Her pain was so bad we had to call the ambulance at 4:00 am. She spent the next 18 days in the St. Peter Hospital.

Unfortunately, the first orthopedist prescribed walking, as much as possible. She tried to walk every day, but the pain got worse. The head nurse decided we needed a second opinion, so she referred Ruth Ann to another orthopedist in Mankato. He completely reversed the treatment and said no more walking and keep all weight off the left leg. I asked the doctor if I could take her on a five-hour ride to our home in Anamosa. He said I could but get a walker in case she has to go to a bathroom—I don't want her trying to walk by herself.

So John took me to Mankato to a Salvation Army Store and they gave me a walker for free. It was back to St. Peter. John and I got her in the car and Ruth Ann and I took off on our five-hour drive to Anamosa. Thank God she didn't have to go. I had called Carron from St. Peter and told her to get a wheelchair—I was going to need it to get her in the house and then when she was in the house.

When we got to Anamosa, I called Carron and told her to have her friend Steve come and help me get her up the five steps to the deck. We were back home on December 15. For the next several months I was a full-time caretaker. I was the chief cook, bottle washer and housekeeper.

I had to dress her, help her shower, get her in and out of the wheelchair to go potty and to make it to the kitchen. She felt more comfortable sleeping in the recliner so when she had to go potty, she would blow her whistle. One night I got up five times. It is not much fun going to bed knowing I'll be hearing a whistle in a couple of hours. One evening for supper she wanted shrimp alfredo—she told me what to do and she had her shrimp alfredo. She was happy.

It was over 56 years since we had said to each other "for better or for worse" and "in sickness and in health." We were finding out what that meant.

I decided if I was ever going to get her out of the house in a wheelchair, I would need a ramp. I called a guy named Denny Wilson to build it. He had it up in three days. So, we only had less than a week to be house bound. It was expensive but worth it.

There was bad news this year. Jim, my 82-year-old brother, died on December 17, in Rochester. He had lung problems. That meant that out of 10 kids, 5 had died. The five living are Mark (73), John (77), Me (79), Jan (86), and Don (88). The five deceased are Karen, Betty, Paul, Chuck and Jim.

Jim worked for the Mayo Clinic as a urological technician. He was a great athlete in his youth. He liked sports so much that he played softball at their retirement village in Arizona when he was in his seventies. His wife was Verleen and they had three kids: Pam, Shelley and Tim.

I'm going to do 2017 also.

The ramp was lifesaver. I could wheel her down, help her get in the car and go to Happy Hour. And reverse the process when leaving.

The Mankato doctor had lined her up with an Anamosa orthopedist. His name was Dr. Hill. She met with him in January. He simply said to take things slowly and don't do anything stupid. In other words, use common sense. By March 8 he released her from further care.

On Valentine's Day I gave her ten roses and a box of chocolates. I also cleaned the whole house. I thought it would perk her up and make her forget about her problems. For a little while anyway. It sure helped—it was a good day. Her bones were healing but it was a slow process.

She was still weak—on April 14 she fell off the stool and pooped on the floor. I helped her get up and back to bed. Then I cleaned the floor. I remember thinking at the time—"for better or for worse." I guess that fit into the *worse* part.

She must have had more pain than she told me about. Every day she would take many Tylenol plus blood pressure pills, anti-depressants pills, calcium pills and a muscle relaxer. This would continue until she passed away.

The rest of 2017 was noneventful. We didn't travel any further than twenty miles from Anamosa.

Yrsa Thom Chris

PeteandRuth Ann Bungum

Sunday, June 14, 2020. Pete and Ruth Ann's Journey through 59 years.

The years will be 2018 and 2019.
This post will be a tough one for me. Our journey comes to an end.
On May 17, 2018, Ruth Ann fell on the deck and injured her back. An ambulance took her to the ER. The doctor gave her some hydrocodone and sent her home. I had to get a wheelchair again. I took her back to the doctor on the 25th. She is referred to a specialist, Dr. Eck. He does an MRI and decides he has to do a kyphoplasty on her back. He said she has two vertebrae touching each other that need to be separated. He does the surgery on June 8th, 2018. I brought her home on the 11th. The surgery worked and her pain disappears. She even wanted to go to Happy Hour again. She was pretty healthy until February 2019. Then she gets the flu and spends two nights in the hospital.
In April 2019, her back-pain returns—the doctors do an X-ray and discover a growth in her right lung. She has a biopsy—the doctor calls and said she has cancer in that growth. She has surgery on May 24, Dr. Levitt says they got it all. She comes home on the 29th. For pain they give her oxycodone.
It was a fairly okay summer. But on September 10, 2019, she slips on the kitchen floor—I take her to the ER again. Her back pain was so bad she couldn't walk. The ER doctor says she needed to go to the newly built Transitional Care Center in Robins—a small town five miles north of Cedar Rapids.
For those suffering constant pain this was the place to go. Their only purpose was to relieve pain. On her second day they pumped her full of oxycodone with a pill at 4 am, 8 am and noon. When I got there about 2 pm she was incoherent. Her arms were flailing, and she didn't even know me. They had given her too much. From then on, she refused to take any oxy. They relied on Tylenol. They also

took her on walks—trying to strengthen her legs. Her stay there was cheaper than a hospital. She stayed for 20 days.

She was still in pain every day in October. By November she figured another kyphoplasty would relieve some of the pain. We went back to Dr. Eck to see what he thought. Dr. Eck agreed. So he performed surgery again in December. Kyphoplasty is when two vertebrae are touching each other. He explained to me that he would inflate the vertebrae in order to separate them—then insert some plaster between them to keep them separated. It worked the last time. When I got her home, the pain was still there. It didn't work this time.

Between late November until after Christmas she started having pain in her right leg. And she was going to bed at 6 pm and not eating enough. This was new and I was concerned. Plus, she also was having stomach problems. She was back in the hospital around December 28. They diagnosed diverticulitis.

On New Year's Eve I was sitting in her hospital room when the head nurse came in carrying some x-rays. She said, "I have some good news and some bad news. The good news is the diverticulitis is under control. The bad news is that five cancer doctors studied your x-rays and found two more cancer tumors. One is embedded in your left rib and the other one in your right hip.

"The doctors said you can have a biopsy done to see if they are related to your lung cancer. Your other choice is to go to hospice." Ruth Ann listened and said, "I'll go to hospice and get it over with." The nurse said, "It is your decision. We can call Monticello Nursing Home (ten miles north) right now to see if they have room. They have a hospice unit."

I was not really surprised—she had mentioned to me she was sick of having pain all the time. I asked her if she was positive she wanted to do this. She said yes.

So, I told her I would go and have the nurse call Monticello. She called and they did have room. The Monticello lady told me to come over this morning and pick out a room. Carron and I went and picked out a room. We came back and checked her out of the

Anamosa Hospital and took her to Monticello. Two nurses came to the car with a wheelchair and got her in the room.

On the way to Monticello she said something to me I will never forget. She was crying and said, "Pete, are you taking me to hospice?" I said I was "because you told me that is what you wanted." When we left, she told me to bring her some clothes and she would like a TV. The next day I brought her clothes, but I forgot one item. She told Carron, "I'm not surprised because he never did listen to me." I also went to Walmart and bought a TV.

I talked to the head hospice nurse. I asked her what I could expect in terms of time. She said, "Some die in less than a week—we've had some that lasted 8–9 months. Our job is to make them as comfortable as possible with no pain." Ruth Ann was put on morphine and a 72-hour pain relief patch on her back shoulder. They would squirt the morphine in her mouth every hour or two.

Tomorrow I'll write about her final hours and minutes in our journey through 59 years.

You, Alexandra Bungum, Erland Christensen and 14 others

Comments

Erland Christensen Very touching. Both my parents died from cancer at 53 years.

John Spilde I am saddened by the story, but sincerely appreciate hearing the details! You can never take the smalltown concern and caring out of me!! Sincerely, John

    PeteandRuth Ann Bungum Thanks—I appreciate it.

PeteandRuth Ann Bungum

Monday, June 15, 2020. Pete and Ruth Ann's Journey through 59 years.

The year is 2020.

We took Ruth Ann to hospice on December 31, 2019. We had to take her to Monticello (10 miles north) because Anamosa did not have a hospice unit. She had a lot of visitors in the next nine days and numerous phone calls. Visitors included her family—Brad and Lene and Carron, grandkids Ellyn and Wesley. Others included Carson and Connie Ode, Brett and Verna Lewison, and Dean and Dana Rickels.

The nurses were putting powerful pain patches on her back shoulder every three days and squirting morphine into her mouth every 1–2 hours. She was going down-hill every day. The only thing she would eat was ice cream. Brad, Lene and Carron would spoon feed her. Her ability to talk and communicate was getting less and less. All the kids would take turns trying to talk to her. By January 7 her eyes were getting glassy and she just stared straight ahead and could not make eye contact. We all knew the end was getting closer. She didn't talk either.

On the 9th everyone left the room and let me talk to her by myself. She was laying on her right side. Her eyes were open, and she appeared to be looking at me, but the stares were not eye to eye. I don't know if she heard me because she never responded to anything I said with a smile or any words.

I talked to her about meeting in seventh grade, flirting in eighth grade, starting to date between our 10th and 11th grade years, and getting engaged at age 18.

I mentioned the picnic she had at her farm in 1956 and going to the outdoor theater that night and holding hands for the first time. I continued with brother Paul marrying us in 1960, going on our honeymoon to Canada and then to Luther in Decorah to begin her two years as secretary to the college treasurer.

I went on to talk about the birth of Brad and Carron. I also talked about our life in Martelle, Rochester, Dubuque and back to Anamosa in 1967. I mentioned about raising the kids there. And her jobs at the Reformatory and as Deputy Treasurer for 22 years in Jones County.

I also mentioned the wonderful trips we had taken. I kind of went through our whole life together. She kept her eyes open but never acknowledged one thing. The nurse told me that the last thing that goes when people are dying is their hearing. So, she probably heard me.

I knew the end was coming that day. Her mouth was open as she would breath heavily through her mouth. I gave her a kiss on her open mouth and told her I loved her, always had and always will for the rest of my days. I left the room and shed some tears. I knew they were my last words with her.

Brad was not there because he flew back to Denmark on the 8th to see his daughter, Alexandra, graduate from medical school. She would officially be an M.D.

Carron and Ellyn left about 7 pm. So, it was just Lene and me in her room. We both knew she wouldn't make it through the night. We pulled up chairs beside her bed. Lene held her hand and I patted and rubbed her tummy.

By 9 pm her breathing was getting harder and harder and louder. At 9:28 it was getting worse. I knew she wouldn't last much longer. I told Lene I'm going to start timing her breaths to see how long between each one. The first one was 11 seconds, the second one was 25 seconds, the third one was 45 seconds and it was 62 seconds in her final breath.

I didn't need to do anymore timing. The time was 9:30 pm on January 9, 2020.

I went and got the hospice nurse. She came and took her blood pressure. Another nurse said she would wash the body. After the washing I went and gave Ruth Ann a final kiss.

I talked to the head nurse and told her we needed to notify Cedar Memorial in Cedar Rapids for funeral arrangements. She called them and they came and picked up the body at 11:30.

Lene had called Ellyn earlier and told her to pick up Carron and come right away because Ruth Ann would not make it through the night. They got there at 9:35. I told them, "She just died five minutes ago." Carron and Ellyn both lost it.

On the 10th we went to Cedar Memorial to make funeral arrangements. We got everything in order for the funeral. The funeral was on Wednesday, January 15, 2020, at St. Paul Lutheran Church in Anamosa.

Some final thoughts on our journey of 59 ½ years.

We were married for 21,720 days.

In those days we had a few ups and downs. But we always got things patched up. We were so grateful in our retirement years that we didn't do anything stupid. We were set financially and had a wonderful retirement as a result.

My final word on our journey through 59 ½ years is: I am so grateful I had Ruth Ann for my wife, my lover and my best friend for all those years. I was blessed.

Alexandra Bungum, Bret Lewison and 33 others

Comments

Bret Lewison Blessed indeed. And so was she.

    PeteandRuth Ann Bungum Bret Lewison thanks Bret

David L. Eaton We are with you, Pete…every step…you're never alone, so glad I could share this journey with you, a great writer and storyteller. But most of all, thank you for being a friend to me, and for your special son, who is my best friend for life.

    PeteandRuth Ann Bungum Thanks for your kind words

Bonnie Walderbach The Best! ♡

    PeteandRuth Ann Bungum Thanks Bonnie

Kelley Bantz Wells Oh Pete!! ♡♡ thank you for sharing your story of your life with Ruthann! Jerry and I feel so blessed to have gotten to know each of you over the past few years. You are both very special friends and we miss seeing you. We truly miss Ruthann also, what a beautiful lady. Hugs

> **PeteandRuth Ann Bungum** Thanks for your kind words

Jill Darrow Such a sweet story and tribute to the love of your life!

> **PeteandRuth Ann Bungum** Thanks Jill

Alexandra Bungum I love that you've shared this with all of us! Thank you ♡ We miss her ♡

> **PeteandRuth Ann Bungum** Thanks Alex and thanks for our time together after the funeral. I really needed that.
>
> **Alexandra Bungum** We had such a great time! We need to do it again ;)

Ken Winter In the end, all that ever matters is love. Well done, Ruth Ann and Pete.

> Peace I leave with you; my peace I give you. I do not give to you as the world gives. Do not let your hearts be troubled and do not be afraid.
> John 14:27

> **PeteandRuth Ann Bungum** Thanks Ken

Dorothy Bunting Montgomery This is so beautifully written! What a wonderful tribute to your life together! I'm sure you feel her presence each and every day! She was a wonderful lady!

PeteandRuth Ann Bungum Thanks Dorothy for your kind words

Cindy Meyer Norton Thank you for sharing this. I have enjoyed reading your story. So blessed to have had such a nice life together. So so sorry for your loss of your beloved Ruth Ann.

PeteandRuth Ann Bungum Cindy Meyer Norton Thanks Cindy—I appreciate them

Mark Holub Mr Bungum, I have really enjoyed reading this journey through your life together. I am going to miss opening Facebook and seeing your daily posts. So wonderful that you gathered the thoughts and shared them. You are a blessed man. All the best.

PeteandRuth Ann Bungum Thanks Mark. I really appreciate your words.

Steve Boyer Thank you for sharing this Pete. Carron had filled me in a bit on what was happening, and I want you to know my thoughts were with you every day. I am blessed to have your family in my life. ♡—Diane

PeteandRuth Ann Bungum Steve Boyer Thanks Diane. We were blessed to have you for our second daughter.

Rhonda Koppenhaver Mr. Bungum,
This has been such a beautiful story & tribute. What a fabulous life you had together. Thank you for sharing with us.

Karen Biere You have been truly blessed, Pete. What a beautiful story.

Jeffrey N Norton So very touching. Enjoyed your whole journal thoroughly. I remember and was part of the high school years with Brad mentioned. You had a great life.

Kimberly Bungum Sending you love ♡

Phyllis Michels Bless you and your bride! You shared an amazing 😊 life. I appreciated reading your journal. I have enjoyed your friendship over many of these years!

Pat Cooley Beautiful words

George Lah Losing your wife is a daunting situation. But your words Pete of starting each day with TYLFAD have helped me get through it. Thank you and God Bless.

> **PeteandRuth Ann Bungum** Thanks George. My memory isn't what it used to be—what is TYL?

> **George Lah** PeteandRuth Ann Bungum Thank You Lord For Another Day

Richard Stout You shared so warmly that I could understand all. Not just the moment to moment you wrote of, but all the unspoken moments as well.

Pete, you are a wonderful friend…and were a husband any woman would be proud to have. Ruth Ann was blessed to have you in her life…and you—her. Thanks again.

> **PeteandRuth Ann Bungum** Thanks Dick—your words are so appreciated. You are so thoughtful.

Bernie Paulson I'm glad you shared your journey with Ruth Ann. It gives people of our vintage a lot to think about and be grateful for.

> **PeteandRuth Ann Bungum** Thanks Bernie—your words are so appreciated.

Elsie Narveson So beautifully written. You could feel your passion. It is wonderful to have such beautiful memories

PeteandRuth Ann Bungum Thanks Elsie—much appreciated. Ruth Ann and I were blessed to have you and Jerry as our best friends since junior high. I'm doing okay—the nights are the worst but time will help. God Bless.

John Haigh You two had a wonderful life! God bless you.

Janice Blattie We'll never forget her...we had so many good times together. Thanks for sharing your life with her...love you!

PeteandRuth Ann Bungum We sure had some good times. As an in-law Ruth Ann always felt close to your Don. Thanks for your words. I'm doing okay. Writing our story of 59 years has helped a lot. I'm going to take a break and then start a new project.
Are you still using that thing to clean your carpet?

Elsie Narveson Hang in there

Michelle Andresen Toenjes Loved reading all your great memories! You two were the best! You were blessed to have such a great life together. Thank you for sharing. ♡

Dee Ihlenfeldt You're a great storyteller Pete. Thanks for sharing.

Pat McQuaid Schoon Pete, you and Ruth Ann were so blessed to have had so many wonderful memories together, and we appreciate so much that you shared them with all of us. Keep on writing! We look forward to your next project—maybe a book!!!

John Spilde Thank you for sharing about your life together Mr. Bungum! Sincerely, John Spilde

PeteandRuth Ann Bungum Thanks John. What grade were you in when you moved to Anamosa?

Alexandra Bungum *to* PeteandRuth Ann Bungum

Sending a little love your way today ♡

Granddaughter and Grandpa Pete enjoying a beer

You, Lene Rindom, David L. Eaton and 15 others

Comments

Brad Bungum Ahhhhhh…melts my heart…

Bret Lewison That's one awesome picture Alexandra Bungum with Bear Bungum.

Love the classic Old Gold & Black scarf PeteandRuth Ann Bungum.

> **PeteandRuth Ann Bungum** Bret Lewison Thanks Bret—that scarf was made for me by Inge in 1984. I love it too.

Bret Lewison PeteandRuth Ann Bungum I kind of like the pre-Hayden Old Gold stuff. I've never seen you in the Bear Bryant hat before. It's a good look for you. Just need to find one with black & gold check.

Brad Bungum Inge Bungum!!

PeteandRuth Ann Bungum My favorite photo of the two of us. Lots of good memories.

Mark Blattie Who knew my Uncle Pete was a hipster! Great picture.

> **PeteandRuth Ann Bungum** Thanks—I appreciate it

Janice Blattie Love the picture

Brad Bungum
June 18 at 10:06 PM

60 years ago today!!

Pete and Ruth Ann's wedding photo on wedding night. June 18, 1960

Lene Rindom, Suzy Waterschoot and 110 others

Comments

Eduardo Aguirre Happy Anniversary to your parents amigo.